The ABCs of
Microsoft Office
for Windows 95

The ABCs of
Microsoft® Office
for Windows® 95

Guy Hart-Davis

SYBEX®

San Francisco • Paris • Düsseldorf • Soest

Associate Publisher: Carrie Lavine
Acquisitions Manager: Kristine Plachy
Developmental Editors: Sherry Schmitt, Richard Mills, Neil Edde
Editor: Suzanne Rotondo
Technical Editor: Michele Petrovsky
Book Designer: Design Site
Desktop Publisher: GetSet! Prepress
Production Coordinator: Kim Wimpsett
Indexer: Ted Laux
Cover Designer: Design Site
Cover Photographer: David Bishop

Screen reproductions produced with Collage Complete.
Collage Complete is a trademark of Inner Media Inc.

Library of Congress Card Number: 96-67498
ISBN: 0-7821-1866-6

Manufactured in the United States of America
10 9 8 7 6 5 4 3 2 1

This book is dedicated to
Rhonda.

Acknowledgments

I'd like to thank the following people for their help and support with this book: Carrie Lavine for getting the project going; Richard Mills, Neil Edde, and Sherry Schmitt for helping develop the manuscript; Suzanne Rotondo for delicate and good-humored wielding of the editorial machete; Michele Petrovsky for the technical review of the manuscript; Dave Kamola at GetSet! Prepress for patient typesetting; Kim Wimpsett for coordinating the production of the book; and Ted "Fiat" Laux for creating the index.

Finally, thanks go to Van der Graaf Generator for *Godbluff* and *Still Life*.

Contents at a Glance

Table of Contents

Part 1: Microsoft Office

Part 2: Word

Chapter 5: Getting Started in Word 75

Chapter 6: Simple Formatting 91

Chapter 9: Columns, Tables, and Sorting 139

Chapter 10: Mail Merge 163

Chapter 11: Outlines and Advanced Features 183

✳ Part 3: Excel

Part 4: PowerPoint

Chapter 20: Bringing a Presentation to Life 337

Chapter 21: Giving the Presentation 351

Part 5: Schedule+

Introduction

Microsoft Office for Windows 95 comprises the latest versions of Microsoft's best-selling business-software applications: Word, the word processor; Excel, the spreadsheet application; PowerPoint, the presentations package; and Schedule+, the personal information manager. With these four applications, and the Office Binder mini-application that works with them, you can go a long way toward solving all your home or business computing needs.

This book is designed to get you quickly up to speed with Microsoft Office in as short a time as possible. It will show you the most useful features of Microsoft Office and teach you to use them productively and efficiently without burdening you with arcane and useless information.

What Will You Learn from This Book?

This book aims to teach you everything you need to know about Office to use it productively and swiftly in your home or in your office.

The Office applications offer so many features that it can take a while to work out what you really need to know about, as opposed to what is so specialized that you'll seldom even need to know it exists. This book discusses the features that you're likely to use the most. If you eventually need to learn to use the esoteric features that the Office applications offer, the knowledge you gain from this book will stand you in good stead for puzzling out what each command or feature does, or for rooting determinedly through the Help file for information.

What This Book Assumes

For concision, this book assumes that you know a few things about Windows 95:

- How to use Windows 95 and navigate its interface enough to start up an application, either with the keyboard or with your mouse.
- How to use Windows programs—how to start them and how to exit them; how to use the menus and dialog boxes to make choices; and how to get help whenever you need it by pressing the F1 key or clicking any convenient Help button.

> **NOTE** In this book, "mouse" is a generic term that refers to any mouse, trackball, touchpad, pointing stick, joystick, finger-ring mouse, 3-D motion sensor, infrared head-tracker, foot roller-pedals, or other pointing device you may be using.

- That you click toggle buttons (such as those for boldface and italic) to select them, and that they'll appear to be pushed in when they've been selected.
- That you *select* a check box for an item by clicking in it to place a check mark there, and that you *clear* a check box by clicking to remove the check mark from it.
- That you normally click the left (or primary) mouse button to choose an item or to perform an action on it, and that right-clicking (clicking with the right or non-primary mouse button) items in Windows 95 usually produces a shortcut menu (or *context* menu) of commands suited to that item.
- How to navigate through Windows 95's windows and dialog boxes, double-clicking items to drill down further through them, and clicking the Up One Level button (or pressing Backspace) to move back up through them.
- That Windows 95 applications let you open multiple documents at the same time, and that you can switch among them by using the Window menu.

How to Use This Book

The ABCs of Microsoft Office for Windows 95 is divided into five parts, and is set up so you can go straight to the topic you want and instantly learn what you need to know to get the current task done:

- Part 1 examines the common elements of Microsoft Office, from the basics of working with applications and files to how to e-mail files to your colleagues (and back).
- Part 2 discusses Word, where we'll look at subjects ranging from entering text to complex mail, creating macros, and customizing your work environment.
- Part 3 deals with Excel. You will learn how to create spreadsheet workbooks that use formulas and charts, and to customize Excel with macros and menus.
- Part 4 discusses how to create persuasive and convincing presentations with PowerPoint, how to deliver them, and even how to take them on the road.
- Part 5 tackles Schedule+. You will learn how to manage your appointments; how to track projects and tasks; and how to maintain an effective database of contacts.

With the five parts, chapters divide the material by topic; within each chapter, sections divide the material into easily accessible segments. For specific information, you should be able to dive right into a section and find exactly what you need to know to get the job done.

The Appendix looks at installing Office on your computer—both installing from scratch, and installing extra pieces that for whatever reason were not included in the original installation.

> **TIP** Notes, Tips, and Warnings, each identified clearly with this shading and a keyword, give you extra guidance with specific topics.

Conventions Used in This Book

This book uses a number of conventions to convey more information accurately in a few pages:

- ➤ designates choosing a command from a menu. For example, "choose File ➤ Open" means that you should pull down the File menu and choose the Open command from it.
- + signs indicate key combinations. For example, "press Ctrl+Shift+F9" means that you should hold down the Ctrl and Shift keys, then press the F9 key. Some of these key combinations are visually confusing (for example, "Ctrl++" means that you hold down Ctrl and press the + key—i.e., hold down Ctrl and Shift and press the = key), so you may need to read them carefully.
- ↑, ↓, ←, and → represent the arrow keys that should appear in some form on your keyboard. The important thing to note is that ← is *not* the Backspace key (which on many keyboards bears a similar arrow). The Backspace key is represented by "Backspace" or "the Backspace key."
- **Boldface** indicates items that you may want to type in letter for letter.
- *Italics* indicate either new terms being introduced or variable information (such as a drive letter that will vary from computer to computer and that you'll need to establish on your own).

Part 1

Microsoft Office

Chapter 1

GETTING STARTED

FEATURING

- **Introducing the applications in Microsoft Office**
- **Starting and exiting the Office applications**
- **Using the Office Shortcut bar**
- **Customizing the Office Shortcut bar**

In this chapter, we'll look at the applications contained in Microsoft Office—what they do, how to start them, and how to exit from them. We'll also look at the Office Shortcut bar, which provides quick access to the Office applications and the files you create in them.

The Applications in Microsoft Office

Microsoft Office comes in two versions: Standard and Professional. Office Standard contains four highly integrated applications; Office Professional contains five:

- Word, a powerful word processor capable of generating anything from a typewriter-style letter to a fully formatted book like this one. Word also offers WordMail, which lets you compose and edit e-mail messages within Word, then send them using Microsoft Exchange.
- Excel, a spreadsheet and charting application capable of performing horrendously complex mathematical and financial analysis
- PowerPoint, a presentation designer that will have you putting together slide shows in minutes, incorporating data from Word, Excel, and Schedule+ as needed
- Schedule+, a personal information manager and contact manager that will keep you on top of your to-do list and in touch with everyone you need to speak to
- Access (only in Office Professional), a relational database application capable of storing all the data your company produces and reassembling it in any style of report you care to design.

The applications in Microsoft Office are highly integrated with each other; not only can you share information among applications (for example, by inserting part of an Excel spreadsheet in a Word document or by using Schedule+ data to build a presentation in PowerPoint), but the applications also share tools, such as spelling dictionaries and AutoCorrect entries.

If you have questions about how the Office applications work, you will have no problem getting answers. Not only do the Office applications offer a comprehensive Help system built into their dialog boxes, but you can use the Answer Wizard to get answers to your questions from just about anywhere in the Office.

Microsoft Office also provides tools for integrating files from multiple Office applications into a special type of file called an Office binder. This can make coordinating a project far easier.

Rounding out Microsoft Office is the Office Shortcut bar, a utility that provides a shortcut to the Office applications and the files you create in them. We'll look at the Office Shortcut bar later in this chapter.

Starting and Exiting the Office Applications

You can start an Office application in several ways. The easiest way is to use the Windows 95 Start menu:

1. Click the Start button to display the Start menu.
2. Select the Programs item to display the Programs submenu.
3. Choose the Microsoft Office item to display the Office submenu.
4. Click the name of the application you want to start.

> **NOTE** Depending on how you installed Office, you may see the names of the applications on the Programs submenu rather than on an Office submenu.

If you've created a shortcut for an Office application on the Desktop, you can start the application by double-clicking the icon for the shortcut.

You can also start an Office application by opening a file associated with it or by starting a new file associated with it. We'll look at these operations in Chapter 2.

To exit an Office application, choose File ➢ Exit or click the Close button in the upper-right corner of the application's window. If any of the files open in the application contain unsaved changes, the application will prompt you to save them; we'll look at this in *Exiting the Application* in Chapter 2.

The Office Shortcut Bar

When you install Microsoft Office, the Microsoft Office Shortcut bar adds itself to the Startup group on your Start menu, so every time you start Windows 95, it automatically starts up. By default the Office Shortcut bar appears at the right-hand side of the top edge of your screen, but you can drag it elsewhere so it floats freely. By default, the Office Shortcut bar contains nine buttons for common Office operations, but you can customize the Office Shortcut bar to display the buttons you need, as we'll see in *Customizing the Office Shortcut Bar.*

Using the Office Shortcut Bar

The Office Shortcut bar provides quick access to the various Office applications, so you don't even have to decide which application you need to use for a task.

 The Start a New Document button displays the New dialog box (see Figure 1.1), from which you can start any type of file by choosing the template for it on one of the tabs (General, Binders, Presentation Designs, Letters & Faxes, Memos, Reports, Other Documents, Publications, Spreadsheet Solution, and Presentations) and clicking the OK button. If the Office application you need isn't already open, Office will open it for you.

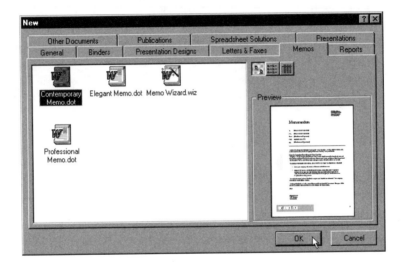

FIGURE 1.1:
In the New dialog box, choose the type of document you want to create.

 The Open a Document button displays the Open dialog box with all the Office files displayed—files with the extensions .doc (Word document), .xls (Excel spreadsheet), .ppt (PowerPoint presentation), .obd (Office binder), and .mdb (Access database)—as shown in Figure 1.2. To open a file, select it and click the Open button; if the Office application associated with that file isn't already open, Office will open it for you along with the file.

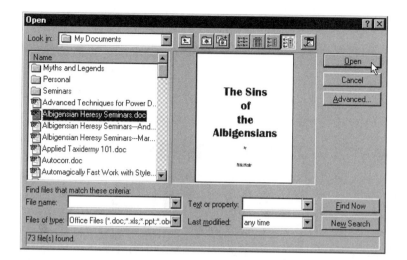

FIGURE 1.2:
In the Open dialog box, choose the file you want to open and click the Open button. Office will start the associated application if it isn't already running.

 The Send a Message button starts Exchange and opens WordMail as your e-mail editor. We'll look at sending messages via WordMail in Chapter 10.

 The Make an Appointment button starts Schedule+ (or activates it if it's already running) and opens the Appointment dialog box.

 The Add a Task button starts Schedule+ (or activates it if it's already running) and opens the Task dialog box.

 The Add a Contact button starts Schedule+ (or activates it if it's already running) and opens the Contact dialog box.

 The Getting Results button opens the Results Help file.

 The Office Compatible button starts up demos of Office-compatible products. Make sure that your Office CD-ROM is loaded before you click on this button.

 The Answer Wizard button opens the Answer Wizard dialog box, ready to answer any of your questions on Office. We'll look at the Answer Wizard in Chapter 3.

Customizing the Office Shortcut Bar

To customize the Office Shortcut bar:

1. Double-click in open space in the Shortcut bar to display the Customize dialog box (see Figure 1.3). Alternatively, click on the multicolored Office button and choose Customize from the shortcut menu.

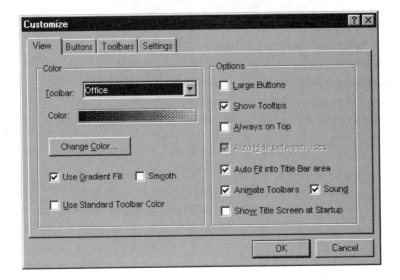

FIGURE 1.3:
The Customize dialog box for the Office Shortcut bar

2. On the View tab, specify how you would like the Office Shortcut bar to appear:
    *   In the Toolbar drop-down list, choose the toolbar you want to affect. (We'll look at displaying further toolbars in step 4.)
    *   Choose color options in the Color group box. Set a different color for the toolbar body by using the Change Color button, or select Use Standard Toolbar Color to use the standard toolbar gray.
    *   Choose display options in the Options group box. The most important options here are Always on Top, which ensures that the Office Shortcut bar will always be visible on screen, and Auto Fit into Title Bar Area, which fits the Office Shortcut bar into blank space at the right-hand end of the title bar of a maximized application. If you don't want the Office Shortcut bar permanently on screen, try Auto Hide between Uses, which will hide the Office Shortcut bar until you move the mouse pointer off the top edge of the screen.
3. On the Buttons tab, choose the buttons you want to have on the Office Shortcut bar:
    *   In the Show These Files as Buttons list box, select the check boxes for the buttons you want to see. For example, you could add Microsoft Word and Microsoft Excel to the Office Shortcut bar.

- To move a button to a different position on the Office Shortcut bar, select it in the Show These Files as Buttons list box and move it by using the up- and down-arrow buttons.

- To add a file or folder to the Show These Files as Buttons list, select the item in the list *above which* you want the new item to appear. Then click the Add File button or the Add Folder button to display the Add File dialog box or Add Folder dialog box. Select the file or folder, then click the Add button to close the dialog box and return to the Customize dialog box.

- To add a space to the list, select the item in the list *above which* you want the space to appear, then click the Add Space button.

- To remove an item (or a space) from the list, select it and click the Delete button.

4. On the Toolbars tab, choose the toolbars you want to display:

- In the Show These Folders as Toolbars list box, select the check boxes for the toolbars you want to display; clear the check boxes for those you don't want. Click a check box to toggle the check mark on (to select it) or off (to clear it).

- To create a new toolbar, click the Add Toolbar button to display the Add Toolbar dialog box (see Figure 1.4). To make a toolbar for a folder, select the Make Toolbar for this Folder option button and enter the name of the folder in the text box (if need be, click the Browse button to display the Browse dialog box, select the folder in the second Add Toolbar dialog box, and click the Add button). To create a blank toolbar, select the Create a New, Blank Toolbar Called option button and enter a name for the toolbar. Click the OK button to create the new toolbar.

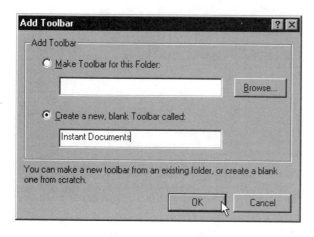

FIGURE 1.4:

In the Add Toolbar dialog box, choose whether to create a new toolbar from a folder or from scratch.

- To delete a toolbar, select it in the Show these Folders as Toolbars list box and click the Remove button.
- To reorder the toolbars in the list box, select a toolbar and move it up and down the list by clicking the up- and down-arrow buttons.

5. On the Settings tab, you can change the folder in which Office looks for user templates and workgroup templates: Select the item you want to change and click the Modify button to display the Modify Setting dialog box. Enter the new location in the Setting box, then click OK (if necessary, click the Browse button to display the User Templates Location dialog box or Workgroup Templates Location dialog box, choose the location, and click Add).

6. Click OK to close the Customize dialog box.

Displaying Multiple Office Toolbars

If you choose to display multiple Office toolbars (as described in step 4 of the previous section), Office will display the buttons for one of the toolbars and a panel for each of the other toolbars, as shown in Figure 1.5. To display the buttons for one of the other toolbars, click its button.

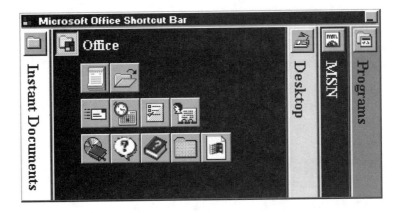

FIGURE 1.5:
To display the buttons for another toolbar, click its button.

Chapter 2

FILE OPERATIONS

- **Creating files**
- **Entering and editing text**
- **Saving files**
- **Opening files**
- **Exiting applications**

In this chapter, we'll run through the basics of working with Office applications—creating, saving, and manipulating files, be they Word documents, Excel spreadsheets, Office binders, or PowerPoint presentations.

This chapter assumes that you've got the relevant application running. If you haven't, start it from Windows 95 in the usual manner—click the Start button, choose Programs, and click the name of the application (Microsoft Binder, Microsoft Excel, Microsoft PowerPoint, Microsoft Schedule+, or Microsoft Word), or use any shortcut or keyboard shortcut you've arranged in Windows 95. If you haven't installed the Office applications, turn to the Appendix for instructions on installing them smoothly and swiftly.

> **NOTE**
>
> To save space and your effort, this book discusses the Office applications together in this chapter. Despite the impressive integration of the Office applications, you will notice some small differences in nomenclature. For example, when you choose File ➤ Open to open a file, Word and Excel display a dialog box named Open, whereas PowerPoint displays a dialog box called File Open. Beyond such slight differences, the applications work in highly similar ways.

Creating a New File

To create a new file based on the default template (NORMAL.DOT in Word, Workbook in Excel, and Blank Presentation.pot in PowerPoint), click the New button on the Formatting toolbar or press Ctrl+N. Word will open a new document named Document*x* (Document1, Document2, Document3, etc.), Excel a new spreadsheet named Book*x*, and PowerPoint a new presentation named Presentation*x*.

To create a new file based on a different template:

1. Choose File ➤ New to display the New dialog box for the application. Figure 2.1 shows the New Presentation dialog box that you will see in PowerPoint.

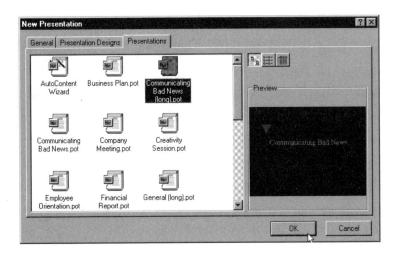

FIGURE 2.1:
To create a new file based on a different template, choose File ➤ New and select the template in the New dialog box (for PowerPoint, it's the New Presentations dialog box).

2.   In the New dialog box, choose the tab that contains the type of document you want to create. In PowerPoint, click the Presentations tab; in Excel, click the Spreadsheet Solutions tab; and in Word, choose from General, Letters & Faxes, Memos, Reports, Other Documents, or Publications.

- To see a preview of the templates in the tab you chose, click a template. The preview will appear in the box on the right side of the New dialog box.

NOTE   A *template* is a special type of file that you use as a basis for producing similar files. Take a look at the Preview box as you click some of the templates offered to get an idea of the different document designs that you can use.

- You can choose between three views of the templates available by clicking one of the three buttons above the Preview box. The leftmost button gives the Large Icons view; the second gives the List view; the third gives the Details view.

TIP   Details view offers the most information of the three views. In Details view, you can sort the templates by name, size, type, or date last modified by clicking the buttons at the top of the columns.

3.   To start a file based on the template you've chosen, double-click the icon or listing for the template, or click the icon or listing once and then click OK.

When you start Word or Excel, the application opens a new file for you based on the default template (PowerPoint displays the PowerPoint dialog box, which lets you choose whether to create a new presentation or open an existing one). If you want to create a new file based on another template or open another file, you don't need to close the file the application has just opened—the application will close it as soon as you start a file based on another template or open another file.

Saving a File

The first time you save a file, you assign it a name and choose the folder in which to save it. Thereafter, when you save the file, the application uses that name and folder and does not prompt you for changes—unless you decide to save the file under a different name. In that case, you need to use the File ➢ Save As command rather than File ➢ Save. We'll get into this in a moment.

Saving a File for the First Time

To save a file for the first time:

1. Choose File ➢ Save to display the Save As dialog box. (The dialog boxes in the different applications have slightly different names; Figure 2.2 shows the Save Binder As dialog box). Instead of choosing File ➢ Save, you can click the Save button on the Standard toolbar or press either Shift+F12 or Alt+Shift+F2.

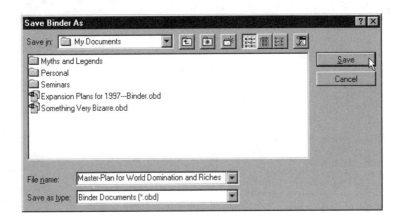

FIGURE 2.2:
In the Save Binder As dialog box (or the application's equivalent), choose the folder in which to save your file and then enter a name for the file.

2. In the Save In box at the top of the Save As dialog box, choose the folder in which to save the document.

    • Navigate the Save As dialog box in the same way that you would any common Windows 95 dialog box—click the Up One Level button (or press the Backspace key) to move up one level of folders or double-click the folders displayed in the main window to move down through them to the folder you want.

    • Use the Look in Favorites button to quickly display the list of Favorite folders.

3. In the File Name text box, enter a name for your file.
    • With Windows 95's long file names, you can enter a thorough and descriptive name—up to 255 characters, including the path to the file

(i.e., the name of the folder or folders in which to save the file).

- You can't use the following characters in file names (if you do try to use one of these, the application will advise you of the problem):

Colon   :
Semicolon   ;
Backslash   \
Forward slash   /
Greater-than sign   >
Less-than sign   <
Asterisk   *
Question mark   ?
Double quotation mark   "
Pipe symbol |

4.   Click OK to save the file.

5.   If the application displays a Properties dialog box for the document, enter any identifying information on the Summary tab.

NOTE   Whether or not the Properties dialog box appears depends on a setting in the Options dialog box (Tools ➤ Options). In Word, this setting is called Prompt for Document Properties and is on the Save tab; in Excel and PowerPoint, it's called Prompt for File Properties and is on the General tab. Select this check box to have the application prompt you for properties.

- In the Title box, Word and PowerPoint will display the first paragraph of the file if they deem it a likely candidate as a title (they won't display the first paragraph if it's a Joycean two-pager). You'll often want to change this. Excel doesn't usually suggest a title.
- In the Manager and Company boxes, the application displays the user name and company name from the User Info tab of the Options dialog box and the information with which you registered the application.
- Use the Subject box to describe the subject of the document and enter any keywords that will help you remember the document in the Keywords box.
- Fill in other boxes as necessary, then click OK to close the Properties dialog box and save the file.

Saving a File Again

To save a file that you've saved before, choose the Save command by using one of the methods given in the previous section:

- Click the Save button on the Standard toolbar.
- Choose File ➤ Save.
- Press Ctrl+S, Shift+F12, or Alt+Shift+F2.

The application will save the file without consulting you about the location or file name.

Saving a File under Another Name

> **TIP**
>
> One of the easiest ways to make a copy of an open file is to open it and save it under a different name. This technique can be particularly useful if you've made changes to the file and don't want to save it and replace the original file—for example, if you think you might need to revert to the original file and you've forgotten to make a backup before making your changes. The Save As command can also be useful for copying a file to a different folder or drive—for example, if you want to copy a document to a floppy drive or to a network drive.

To save a file under a different name or to a different folder:

1. Choose File ➤ Save As to display the Save As dialog box.
2. Enter a different name for the file in the File name box, or choose a different folder in the Save In area.
3. Click the OK button to save the file.

    If the folder you've chosen already contains a file with the same name, the application will ask whether you want to overwrite it. Choose Yes or No. If you choose No, the application will return you to the Save As dialog box so you can choose a different name or different folder.

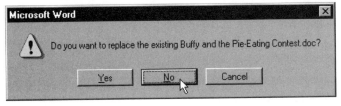

Opening a File

To open a file in the currently selected application:

1. Click the Open button on the Standard toolbar, choose File ➤ Open, or press Ctrl+O to display the Open dialog box. Figure 2.3 shows the Open dialog box for Word.

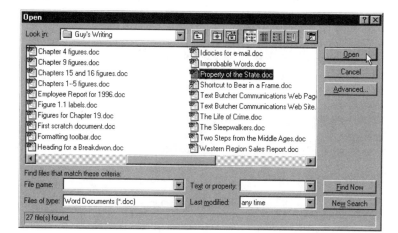

FIGURE 2.3:
In the Open dialog box, use the Look In box to navigate to the folder that contains the file you want to open, then highlight the file and click the Open button.

2. If you're already in the right folder, proceed to Step 3. If not, use the Look In box to navigate to the folder holding the file you want to open.
   - Move through the folders using standard Windows 95 navigation: Click the Up One Level button (or press the Backspace key) to move up one level of folders or double-click a folder to move down through it.

   - Click the Look in Favorites button (the left of the two buttons shown here) to display your list of favorite folders. Click the Add to Favorites button (the right button) to add a folder to that list.

3. Choose the file to open, then click the Open button. Use the List, Details,

Properties, and Preview buttons (shown here from left to right) to make sure you're picking the right file. The Properties button displays a panel containing the file's properties; the Preview button displays a small preview of the first page (you can scroll down to see more).

TIP

To open several files at once, click the first one in the Open dialog box to select it. Then, to select contiguous files, hold down Shift and click the last file in the sequence to select it and all the ones between it and the first file, and then click the Open button. To select noncontiguous files, hold down Ctrl and click each file you want to open, and then click the Open button.

Opening Files by Using Windows 95 Techniques

Windows 95 offers several ways to open a file quickly. If you've used the file recently, pop up the Start menu, choose Files, and choose the file from the list of the

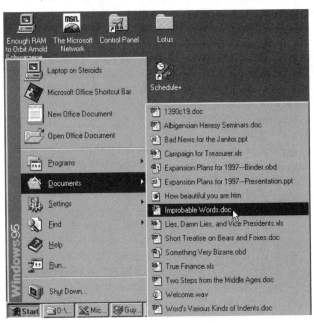

fifteen most recently used files (as shown here). If the application to which the file belongs is already open, Windows 95 will just open the file for you; if the application isn't open, Windows 95 will start it and open the file at the same time.

If you need to open a file frequently but can't be sure that it will always be among your fifteen most-recent files on the Start menu's File menu, create an icon for it on the Desktop. To do so, either right-click (click with the right mouse button) the Desktop and choose New ➢ Shortcut and then Browse for the file in the Create Shortcut dialog box; or, more simply, open an Explorer window or My Computer window, find the file you want to keep handy, and right-drag it to the Desktop. Windows 95 will invite you to create a shortcut to the file—go right ahead.

TIP

To quickly open one of the files you worked on most recently from inside an application, pull down the File menu and choose one of the most recently used files listed at the bottom of the menu. By default, Word and PowerPoint list four files, but you can change this by using Tools > Options, selecting the General tab, and changing the number under Entries in the Recently Used File List (from 1 to 9). Alternatively, you can turn off the display of recently used files by clearing the check mark from the Recently Used File List box; this works in Excel too, though in Excel you can't change the number of files on the Recently Used Files List.

Finding Files

The Open dialog box also lets you quickly search your computer for files that match a certain description. This can be useful when you need to find a file whose name or location you've forgotten but whose contents you can remember.

Finding a File from a Known Word

To find a file using a word you remember from the text of the file:

1. In the Open dialog box, navigate to the folder you think the file is in. (If you don't remember that, start with the drive you think the file is on.)
2. Make sure the File Name text box is blank. If it's not, click the New Search button to clear the details.
3. Make sure the Files of Type drop-down list shows the type of file you're looking for—e.g., *Word Documents (*.doc)* for Word documents or *Presentations (*.ppt)* for PowerPoint files.
4. In the Text or Property drop-down list box, enter the text to search for. Surround it with double quotation marks (e.g., **"surreal events"**).
5. Click the Find Now button to start the search. If the application finds the file, it will highlight it in the dialog box. (If the application finds several files containing the text, you'll need to decide which one you want.) Click the Open button to open the file.

Finding a File from Other Information

You can also search for a file using other known information, such as its contents, author, company, and so on. To do so:

1. Click the Advanced button to display the Advanced Find dialog box (see Figure 2.4).

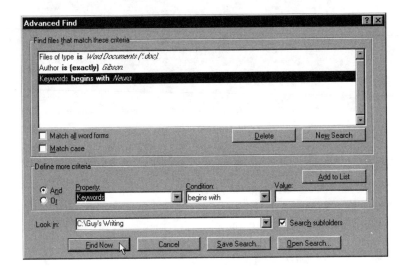

FIGURE 2.4:
The Advanced Find dialog box lets you find lost files swiftly.

2. In the Find File that Match These Criteria box, check that the application is showing only appropriate criteria, such as *Files of Type is Word Documents (*.doc)*. To remove inappropriate criteria, highlight them and click the Delete button.

3. In the Define More Criteria group box, leave the And option button selected and choose the item to search for in the Property drop-down list: Application Name, Author, Category, Client Company, and so on. You'll recognize some of these as properties from the Properties dialog box.

4. In the Condition drop-down list, choose from the options available for the Property you chose. For example, if you chose Author in the Property drop-down list, you could choose Is from the Condition drop-down list to search by author name.

5. In the Value box, enter the item you're searching by. For example, when searching for a file by author, specify the author's name here.

6. Click the Add to List button to add this criterion to the list.

7. Add more criteria if necessary by repeating steps 3 through 6.

8. In the Look In drop-down list, specify the folder in which to start the search for the missing file. If the folder has subfolders, check the Search Subfolders box to the right of the Look In drop-down list.

9. Click the Find Now button to have the application search for the files. If it finds them, it will display them in the Open dialog box, where you can open them as usual.

> **TIP** You can save search criteria by clicking the Save Search button in the Advanced Find dialog box, and you can open saved searches by clicking the Open Search button.

Opening a File Created in Another Application

Word, Excel, and PowerPoint can open files saved in a number of other formats: Word can open anything from plain-text ASCII files to spreadsheets (for example, Lotus 1-2-3) to calendar and address books; Excel can open various types of spreadsheets, including 1-2-3 and Quattro Pro formats; and PowerPoint can open various types of presentations, such as Harvard Graphics and Freelance Graphics.

> **NOTE** To open a file saved in another application's format, you need to have installed the appropriate converter so the Office application can read the file. Generally speaking, the easiest way to tell if you have the right converter installed for a particular file format is to try to open the file; if the application cannot open it, you probably need to install another converter. Run the application's Setup program again and choose to install the appropriate converter (see the Appendix for details on installation).

To open a file saved in another application's format:

1. Select File ➢ Open to display the Open dialog box.

2. Choose the folder containing the file you want to open.

3. Click the drop-down list button on the Files of Type list box at the bottom left-hand corner of the Open dialog box. From the list, select the type of file that you want to open.

> **TIP**
>
> If the application doesn't list the file that you want to open, choose All Files (*.*) from the drop-down list to display all the files in the folder.

4. Choose the folder in the main window of the Open dialog box, then click the Open button or press Enter to open the file.

Saving a File in a Different Format

Not content with just letting you open files saved in different formats, Word, Excel, and PowerPoint also let you save files in formats other than their own. Again, this procedure depends on your having the right converters installed. If you don't, you'll need to install them. To install another converter, run the Setup program again (as described in the Appendix) and choose to install the appropriate converter.

To save an existing file in a different format:

1. Choose File ➤ Save As to display the Save As dialog box.
2. Scroll down the Save as Type drop-down list and choose the file type you want to save the current file as.
3. If you want, enter a different file name for the file. (You don't have to, because the file will get the new extension you chose in step 2 and therefore will not overwrite the existing file.)
4. Click the Save button or press Enter.

> **NOTE**
>
> If you haven't saved the file before, you can choose File ➤ Save instead of File ➤ Save As to open the Save As dialog box. You'll also need to specify a name for the file (unless you want to accept the default name that Word, Excel, or PowerPoint suggests for it).

Closing a File

To close the current file, choose File ➤ Close, press Ctrl+F4, or click the Close button on the file window. If the file contains unsaved changes, the application will prompt you

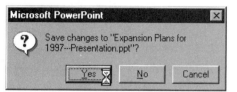

to save them and will close the file when you're finished.

If the file has been saved before and if there are no new changes, the application will simply close the file.

> **TIP** To close all open files at once in Word or Excel, hold down either Shift key on your keyboard and then use the mouse to choose File ➤ Close All.

Exiting the Application

When you've finished working in the application, exit it to get back to the Windows 95 Desktop and remove from the hard disk any temporary files that the application created while it was doing your bidding.

Choose File ➤ Exit or click the Close button at the top-right corner of the application's window. If you have unsaved files, the application will prompt you to save them; save them as described earlier in this chapter in *Saving a File*. If you have open files you've saved but subsequently changed without saving, the application will prompt you to save those changes.

Managing Your Files with the Office Applications

Like other Windows 95 applications, the Office applications provide file-management capabilities in their common dialog boxes, such as the Open dialog box and the Save dialog box.

Renaming a File

To rename a file or folder in a common dialog box, right-click it and choose Rename from the shortcut menu. (Alternatively, click the file or folder once to select it, wait a sec-

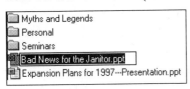

ond, then click again.) Type the new name for the file or folder in the resulting expanded box (drag through a word or part of a word to select it if you don't want to change the whole name). Then press Enter or click elsewhere in the dialog box to apply the new name.

Copying a File

To copy a file or folder quickly in a common dialog box, right-click it and choose Copy from the shortcut menu. Then navigate to the folder into which you want to place the file or folder, right-click in it (or on its icon) and choose Paste from the shortcut menu to paste the file into the new location.

NOTE You can also paste a copy of a file back into the same folder. The copy will be identified as *Copy of* plus the original file name. You can then rename the copy as described in the previous section.

Deleting a File

To delete a file in a common dialog box, right-click it, hold down Shift, and choose Delete from the shortcut menu. The application will ask you to confirm the deletion; click Yes.

To send a file to the Recycle Bin from a common dialog box, right-click it and choose Delete from the shortcut menu. The application will ask you to confirm the deletion; click Yes.

TIP If you send a file to the Recycle Bin, it will remain there awaiting dele-tion until either you empty the Recycle Bin or the Recycle Bin gets full and is emptied automatically. If you discover you've accidentally sent something still valuable to the Recycle Bin, retrieve it immediately.

Creating a Shortcut to a File

To create a shortcut to a file, right-click it and choose Create Shortcut from the shortcut menu. The application will create a shortcut to the file in the same folder and will name it *Shortcut to* plus the file's original name (unless the combination will be more than 255 characters including the path, in which case the application will truncate the name accordingly). You can then move the shortcut to wherever you need it.

> **TIP**
>
> **To create a shortcut on the Desktop to a file, open an Explorer or My Computer window, right-click the file and right-drag it to the Desktop, then choose Create Shortcut Here from the shortcut menu that appears.**

Checking a File's Properties

To check a file's properties from a common dialog box, right-click it and choose Properties from the shortcut menu to display the Properties dialog box. Click OK to close the Properties dialog box when you're finished.

Searching for a File

Windows 95 and Office provide several ways of searching for files that you know exist but can't quite locate. In *Finding Files* earlier in this chapter, you saw how to locate a file by building as elaborate a list of its details as you can, but here is the simplest way of assembling a list of files that match certain criteria.

First, choose Start ➢ Find ➢ Files or Folders to display the Windows 95 Find dialog box (see Figure 2.5).

On the Name & Location tab, enter the closest approximation of the name of the file you're looking for in the Named box—for example, enter ***.doc** if you're looking for Word documents with any name, or **My*.ppt** if you're looking for PowerPoint presentations that have names starting with *My*. In the Look In drop-down list, choose the drive on which to search for the file; to specify a folder on the drive, click the Browse button, choose the folder in the Browse for Folder dialog box, and then click OK.

On the Date Modified tab, choose either to find All Files or to Find All Files Created or Modified within a certain time range. Specify the time range for the second option in the boxes underneath the option.

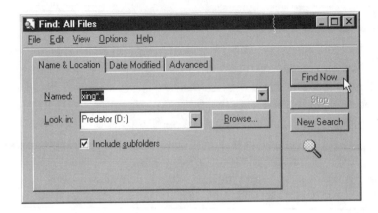

FIGURE 2.5:
Use the Windows 95 Find dialog box to quickly find files matching certain criteria.

On the Advanced tab, choose advanced options as necessary:

- In the Of Type drop-down list, choose the type of file you're looking for—for example, 1-2-3 Worksheet or DeScribe Word Processor 5.
- In the Containing Text text box, enter the text you know the file contains in double quotations marks.
- In the Size Is drop-down list, choose At Least or At Most, then specify the minimum or maximum file size in kilobytes in the KB box. For example, you could specify At Least 2048KB to find files larger than 2MB.

Click the Find Now button to find the files with the criteria you've specified. Windows 95 will display the found files in the Find window. To open one, double-click it.

Chapter

3

USING SHARED TOOLS

- **Using the menu bars and key combinations**
- **Displaying and customizing toolbars**
- **Using Undo and Redo**
- **Using the Spelling checker and AutoCorrect**
- **Understanding shared Office tools**

In this chapter, we'll look at the screen items (such as menu bars, key combinations, and toolbars) and the tools common between the various Office applications. By examining them as a common unit rather than as a feature of each application in turn, we can save a great deal of time (and a large number of pages in the book).

Menu Bars

You'll see that Word, Excel, and PowerPoint share most of their menus: File, Edit, View, Insert, Format, Tools, Window, and Help, with each application having a different menu between Tools and Window. Schedule+ has fewer commands and so has only File, Edit, View, Insert, Tools, and Help menus. This commonality of menus makes it easy to find the commands you need when working in the Microsoft Office applications.

Key Combinations

As well as the shared menus with their common access keys (Alt+F for the File menu, Alt+E for the Edit menu, etc.), the Office applications have common key combinations for operations such as Cut (Ctrl+X), Copy (Ctrl+C), Paste (Ctrl+V), and Undo (Ctrl+Z). Other shared keyboard combinations include Ctrl+P for Print and Ctrl+S for Save (not to mention Shift+F12 and Alt+Shift+F2, also for Save).

Cut, Copy, and Paste

The Cut, Copy, and Paste commands work smoothly between the various Office applications: You can copy, say, a telephone number from a spreadsheet or e-mail message and paste it into Schedule+, or you can cut a number of paragraphs from a Word document and paste them into a PowerPoint slide.

Cut, Copy, and Paste use the Clipboard, which is an area of reserved memory in Windows 95. The Clipboard can hold only one item at a time, so every time you cut or copy something new, that item replaces the previous contents of the Clipboard. When you paste an item, you paste in a copy of the newest item from the Clipboard; the item remains on the Clipboard until supplanted by another item, so you can paste it more than once if you wish.

You can access the Cut, Copy, and Paste commands in a number of ways:

- By clicking the Cut, Copy, and Paste toolbar buttons (shown here in that order, from left to right).
- By choosing Edit ➢ Cut, Edit ➢ Copy, or Edit ➢ Paste.
- By using the Cut (Ctrl+X), Copy (Ctrl+C), and Paste (Ctrl+V) keyboard shortcuts.
- By right-clicking in the item to cut or copy, or in the location to which to paste the item, and choosing Cut, Copy, or Paste from the shortcut menu.

Drag-and-Drop Editing

Word, Excel, and PowerPoint support *drag-and-drop*, a feature that allows you to select an item in one application and drag it to another application to move it there. For example, you can select a table in Word, drag it to an Excel window, and drop it there, and Excel will take in the information as cells.

Drag-and-drop works best with plain text or with items that work in similar ways in the different applications (such as the Word table and the Excel cells mentioned in the previous paragraph), but you can also use drag-and-drop to move such items as graphics between Word documents and PowerPoint slides.

TIP If you hold down Ctrl when dragging, you'll copy the item rather than move it.

Toolbars

All the Office applications use toolbars to present some of the most useful commands for frequent use; Word, Excel, and PowerPoint have multiple toolbars, while Schedule+ has only one (because it has fewer commands than the other applications). By default, Word, Excel, and PowerPoint display the most widely useful toolbars, but you can easily choose to display other toolbars when you need them. Alternatively, you can hide all the toolbars to give yourself more room on screen to work in. You can also customize the toolbars so they contain the commands you need most.

The following sections illustrate the general steps for working with toolbars. The specifics vary a little from application to application, so we'll look at a variety of examples here.

Displaying Toolbars

TIP To quickly display or hide one toolbar, click with the right mouse button anywhere in a displayed toolbar. The application will display a list of toolbars with check marks next to those currently displayed. Click next to a displayed toolbar to hide it or next to a hidden toolbar to display it.

To display and hide toolbars in Word, Excel, or PowerPoint:

1. Choose View ➤ Toolbars to display the Toolbars dialog box. The checked boxes in the Toolbars list box indicate which toolbars are displayed. Figure 3.1 shows the Toolbars dialog box for Word.

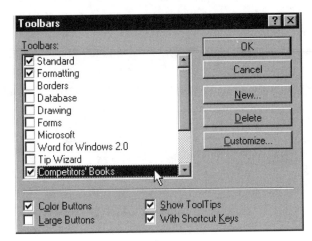

FIGURE 3.1:
In the Toolbars dialog box, select the check boxes next to the toolbars you want displayed. This is the Toolbars dialog box for Word.

2. Select the check box next to each toolbar you want to display. To hide a toolbar, clear the check box next to it.

WARNING **Don't display too many toolbars at once if you're using a low screen resolution such as 640x480—you won't have much of the screen left for working in.**

3. At the bottom of the dialog box, choose the view options for the toolbars: Color Buttons, Large Buttons, Show ToolTips (the name of the button appears when you drag the mouse pointer over it), and With Shortcut Keys (any shortcut for the button appears next to the ToolTip; Word only). Again, select the options you want.

4. Click the OK button to close the Toolbars dialog box and return to your document. The application will display the toolbars you selected and will hide the other toolbars.

NOTE **To toggle the display of the Schedule+ toolbar on and off, choose View ➤ Toolbar.**

Moving and Reshaping Toolbars

Word, Excel, and PowerPoint can display their toolbars as either *docked* panels attached to one side of the screen or as free-floating panels that you can drag anywhere on your screen (see Figure 3.2).

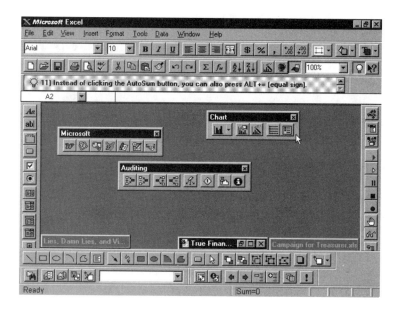

FIGURE 3.2:
You can display your toolbars at any extremity of the screen or place them plumb in the middle.

To move a toolbar from its current position, click in an open space inside the toolbar (i.e., not on a button) and drag it to where you want it—either to one of the edges, in which case it will snap into position, or to the middle of the screen.

TIP You can also undock a docked toolbar by double-clicking in an open space inside it. Dock a floating toolbar by double-clicking its title bar or by double-clicking in open space inside it.

To reshape a floating toolbar, move the mouse pointer over one of its borders until the pointer turns into a double-ended arrow, then click and drag to resize the toolbar. Because of the shape of their buttons, toolbars resize in jumps rather than smoothly like windows.

Customizing Toolbars

You can customize the toolbars in Word, PowerPoint, and Excel: You can create new toolbars that contain the macros or commands most important to you, modify your own toolbars or the existing ones, and (if push comes to shove) delete your own toolbars.

> **NOTE** Word has even greater abilities with toolbars than do Excel and PowerPoint; we'll examine these in detail in the chapters on Word.

Creating a New Toolbar

To create a new toolbar:

1. Choose View ➤ Toolbars to display the Toolbars dialog box.
   You can also display the Toolbars dialog box by right-clicking in any displayed toolbar and choosing Toolbars from the shortcut menu.

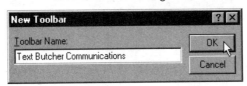

2. Click the New button to display the New Toolbar dialog box. In Excel, enter a name in the Toolbar Name text box (below the Toolbars list box) and then click New. Skip to step 4.

3. Enter a name for the new toolbar in the Toolbar Name text box.

> **TIP** In Word, if you want to make the toolbar available only to the current template, choose the template's name in the Make Toolbar Available To drop-down list. Otherwise, make sure All Documents (Normal.dot) has been chosen in the Make Toolbar Available To drop-down list.

4. Click the OK button to create the toolbar. The application will display the new toolbar (with space for just one button, and most of its name truncated) and the Customize dialog box.
   - In Word, the Customize dialog box has three tabs; the Toolbars tab will be displayed, as shown in Figure 3.3.
   - In PowerPoint, the Customize Toolbars dialog box will appear.

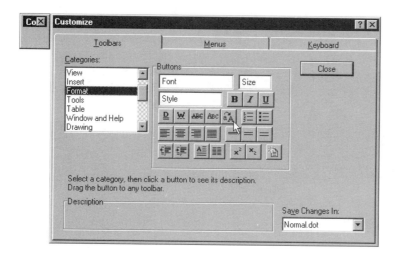

FIGURE 3.3:
Drag buttons from the Customize dialog box to the new toolbar.

5.   Add the buttons you want to the new toolbar:

• From the Categories list, select the type of command you're looking for. The categories vary with the application, but include most of the regular menus (File, Edit, etc.); Word includes Macros, Fonts, AutoText, and Styles as well.

• The available buttons for most categories appear in the Buttons group box; simply click the button for the command you want (a description of the command will appear in the Description box in the lower-left corner of the Customize dialog box) and drag the button to the toolbar to add it.

• Choosing All Commands in Word or PowerPoint (or Macros, Fonts, AutoText, or Styles in Word) displays a list box of commands (or macros, fonts, AutoText entries, and styles). Choose an item from the list box and drag it to the toolbar to add it. If a button is assigned to the item, Word or PowerPoint will use it; if no button is yet assigned, Word or PowerPoint will display the Custom Button dialog box (see Figure 3.4). Choose one of the suggested buttons or leave the Text Button selected and type in a suitable name in the Text Button Name text box. Then click the Assign button to assign the button to the macro (or command) and return to the Customize dialog box.

TIP

To customize a graphical button, choose one from the Custom Button dialog box and click the Edit button. In the Button Editor dialog box, draw a button—the drawing tools are virtually intuitive, so I won't go into details—in the Picture box. When you've finished, choose OK to close the Button Editor dialog box and then click Assign in the Custom Button dialog box to assign the button to the command chosen.

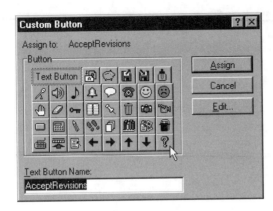

FIGURE 3.4:
Choose a button
to assign to the
macro in the
Custom Button
dialog box.

- To rearrange the buttons on the new toolbar, drag and drop them while the Customize dialog box is open. To remove a button from the toolbar, drag it off and drop it somewhere in the document.

6. Click the Close button in the Customize dialog box when you've finished creating your toolbar.

7. In Word, choose File ➤ Save All to save the changes to the template.

Modifying a Toolbar

To modify a toolbar:

1. Display it on screen by choosing View ➤ Toolbars, selecting the check box next to it in the Toolbars dialog box, and clicking OK. Alternatively, right-click in a displayed toolbar and choose the toolbar you want to display from the shortcut menu.

2. Add, move, copy, or remove buttons as appropriate:
   - To remove a button from the toolbar, hold down Alt and drag the button off the toolbar and into an open space in a document. Drop it there and it'll disappear.

WARNING
In Word or PowerPoint, if you remove a custom button (one that you've created) from a toolbar this way, the application will delete the details of the button so you'll have to re-create it if you want to use it again. If you want to store your custom buttons safely, create a toolbar as described in the previous section and keep it for safely storing buttons for future use.

- To move a button from one toolbar to another, hold down Alt and drag the button from one toolbar to the other. You can also rearrange the buttons on a toolbar (and add spaces between them) by holding down Alt and dragging the buttons.

- To copy a button from one toolbar to another, hold down Ctrl and Alt, then drag the button from one toolbar to the other.
- To add buttons to a toolbar, choose View ➢ Toolbars, select the toolbar, and click the Customize button to display the Customize dialog box (or the Customize Toolbar dialog box in PowerPoint). Add the buttons to the toolbar as described in the previous section. Close the Customize dialog box when you've finished.

3. In Word, choose File ➢ Save All to save the changes to the template.

Deleting a Toolbar

To delete a toolbar you've created, choose View ➢ Toolbars to display the Toolbars dialog box. Highlight the toolbar to delete and then click the Delete button. Word and Excel will display a message box asking if you want to delete the toolbar; choose Yes in Word and OK in Excel. (PowerPoint will simply delete the toolbar and change the Delete button to Undelete in case you change your mind.) Click Close to exit the Toolbars dialog box.

NOTE   **Word, Excel, and PowerPoint won't let you delete any of their own toolbars—you can delete only ones you've created.**

Renaming a Toolbar

Word and PowerPoint let you rename a toolbar you've created:

1. Display the Rename dialog box:
    - In Word, choose File ➢ Templates and click the Organizer button in the Templates and Add-ins dialog box to display the Organizer dialog box. Choose the Toolbars tab and select the toolbar to rename in the left-hand or right-hand box, then click the Rename button.
    - In PowerPoint, choose View ➢ Toolbars to display the Toolbars dialog box, then click the toolbar you want to rename and click the Rename button.

2. Specify the new name for the toolbar in the Rename dialog box.
3. Click OK to rename the toolbar.

4. Close the Organizer dialog box or the Toolbars dialog box.

Displaying and Hiding the Status Bar and Scroll Bars

The status bar at the bottom of the screen provides details about the Office application you're working in, and the scroll bars let you quickly access other parts of your document, spreadsheet, or presentation; however, they also take up valuable space on screen. To toggle the display of the status bar in Word, Excel, and PowerPoint, and the display of the scroll bars in Word and Excel:

1. Choose Tools ➤ Options to display the Options dialog box.
2. If the View tab is not displayed at the front of the dialog box, click it to display it there.
3. Select the Status Bar, Horizontal Scroll Bar, and Vertical Scroll Bar check boxes to display them; clear the check boxes to hide them. In Excel, you can also choose to display or hide the Formula bar.
4. Click OK to close the Options dialog box and apply your choices.

NOTE In Schedule+, choose View ➤ Status bar to toggle the display of the status bar on and off (or right-click in the toolbar and click Status Bar in the shortcut menu).

Undo and Redo

All the Office applications have Undo and Redo capabilities for undoing an action you've just performed and for redoing an action you've just undone: Excel and Schedule+ can undo and redo only one action, whereas Word and PowerPoint can undo and redo a number of actions.

Undo

To undo the last action, click the Undo button, press Ctrl+Z, or choose Edit ➤ Undo. To undo another action in PowerPoint, click the Undo button again (or press Ctrl+Z or choose Edit ➤ Undo again).

To undo more than one action in Word, click the arrow to the right of the Undo button and choose the number of actions to undo from the drop-down list.

Redo

To redo an action in Excel, PowerPoint, or Word, click the Redo button. To redo more than one action in PowerPoint, click the Redo button again. To redo more than one action in Word, click the arrow to the right of the Redo button and choose the number of actions to redo from the drop-down list.

To redo an action in Schedule+, click the Undo button again (to undo the undo, so to speak).

> **TIP**
>
> You can set the number of items you can undo in PowerPoint by specifying a number (from 3 to 150) in the Maximum Number of Undos box on the Advanced tab of the Options dialog box (Tools ➤ Options). With higher numbers of undos enabled, you may find PowerPoint runs more slowly on your computer.

Spell Checking

The Office Spelling checker can be a great tool for making sure your documents, spreadsheets, and presentations contain no embarrassing typos. However, the Spelling checker is limited in its goal—it simply tries to match words you type against the lists in its dictionary files, flagging any words it does not recognize, and suggesting replacements that seem to be close in spelling. It does not consider the word in context beyond making sure a word does not match the word immediately before it (i.e., it questions the second instance of a repeated word).

The Spelling checker used to belong to Word; it now works in Excel and PowerPoint as well, but Word still has the edge in new and flashy spell-checking features. Before the latest generation of word processors (of which Word for Windows 95 is one), spell-checking was mostly carried out after you'd finished entering text. But now Word (and its rivals such as Lotus' Word Pro and Novell's WordPerfect) offer on-the-fly spell-checking and can flag any offending word just microseconds after you type it. Excel and PowerPoint don't support this, but we'll look at both types of spell-checking in this section.

The Office AutoCorrect feature offers another form of spell-checking. We'll look at AutoCorrect in the next section of this chapter.

NOTE

Before you ask, Word has not only the Spelling checker but also a Grammar checker and a Thesaurus (both on the Tools menu). I'll leave you to explore the Grammar checker and Thesaurus on your own. In my honest opinion, while the Thesaurus can be a great help for finding synonyms and antonyms, the Grammar checker is borderline useless because the richness and complexity of the English language makes it almost impossible to assess mechanically.

Regular Spell-Checking

To run the Spelling checker:

1. Choose Tools ➤ Spelling to start the Spelling checker.
   - If you have selected any text (or a picture) in Word, or a range of cells in Excel, the Spelling checker assumes that you want to spell-check the selection. After the Spelling checker has finished checking the selection, in Word it displays a message box asking if you want to spell-check the rest of the document; in Excel it displays a message box saying that it has finished checking the range of cells. If you have not selected anything, the Spelling checker will automatically start spell-checking from the insertion point.
   - If the Spelling checker does not find any words that it does not recognize, it will display a message box telling you that the spelling-check is complete.
2. As soon as the Spelling checker encounters a word that does not match an entry in its dictionary, it displays the Spelling dialog box. Figure 3.5 shows the Spelling dialog box you'll see in Word; you will see slightly different Spelling dialog boxes in Excel and PowerPoint, but they work in almost exactly the same way.
   - The Not in Dictionary box shows the offending word.
   - The Change To box shows Word's best guess at the word you intended.
   - The Suggestions box contains other words that Word considers close to what you typed.
3. You now have several choices:
   - If the word is correct and is the only instance in the document, click the Ignore button to skip it.
   - Click the Ignore All button to have the Spelling checker skip all instances of this word. Use this for names, technical terms, or foreign words that will appear in only one document and which you don't want to add to your custom dictionaries.

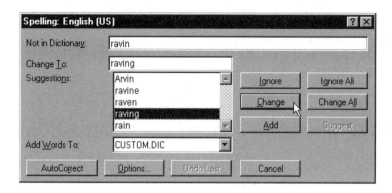

FIGURE 3.5:
The Spelling
dialog box

- Click the Change button to change this instance of the word in the Not in Dictionary box to the word in the Change To box (or one of the suggested words—highlight it before clicking Change).
- Accept the word in the Change To box (or choose another of the suggested words) and click the Change All button to change all instances of the word in the Not in Dictionary box to the word you've chosen.
- Click the Add button to add the word in the Not in Dictionary box to the custom dictionary currently selected in the Add Words To drop-down list box (see *Creating a Custom Dictionary* later in the chapter). Once you've added the word to the dictionary, the Spelling checker will not flag it again. (To select another dictionary, choose one from the Add Words To drop-down list.)
- If the Spelling checker has found a typo you feel you're likely to repeat, click the AutoCorrect button to add the Not in Dictionary word and the chosen suggestion to the list of AutoCorrect entries.
- Click the Undo Last button to undo the last spell-checking change you made.
- Click the Suggest button to have the Spelling checker suggest words in the Suggestions box. (This option is only available if you have turned off the Always Suggest option on the Spelling tab of the Option dialog box in Word; in PowerPoint, the Always Suggest check box is in the Spelling box on the Edit tab of the Options dialog box in PowerPoint, and in Excel it's in the Spelling dialog box itself.)
- Click the Cancel button to stop the spell check.

On-the-Fly Spell-Checking in Word

On-the-fly spell-checking is new in Word for Windows 95 and offers you the chance to correct each spelling error the moment you make it or to highlight all the spelling errors in a document and deal with them one by one. This is one of those partially great features that isn't right for everybody. It can be intrusive and distracting when you're typing like a maniac trying to finish a project on time; nonetheless, try enabling it and see how you do.

To enable Word's on-the-fly spell-checking:

1. In Word, choose Tools ≻ Options to display the Options dialog box.
2. Click the Spelling tab to bring it to the front.
3. Select the Automatic Spell Checking check box in the Automatic Spell Checking group box.
4. Click OK to close the Options dialog box.

Word will now put a squiggly red line under any word that doesn't match an entry in its dictionary. To spell-check one of these words quickly, right-click in it. Word will display a spelling menu with suggestions for spelling the word (or what it thinks the word is) along with three options:

Ignore All ignores all instances of this word.

Add adds the word to the spelling dictionary currently selected (we'll get to this in a minute).

Spelling fires up a full-fledged spell check (as described in the previous section).

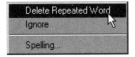

Once you have chosen Add or Ignore All for one instance of a word that the Spelling checker has flagged, Word removes the squiggly red underline from all other instances of that word. (If you have chosen another spelling for a flagged word, Word doesn't change all instances of that word.)

If you type the same word twice in immediate succession, Word will flag that, too, and offer you a different menu—Delete Repeated Word, Ignore, and Spelling—when you right-click in it.

Working with Dictionaries

The Office Spelling checker comes with a built-in dictionary of words that it uses for spell-checking. You can't change this dictionary—to save you from yourself, perhaps—but you can create and use custom dictionaries to supplement the main dictionary. You can open and close these as needed for the particular documents you're working on; however, the more dictionaries you have open, the slower spell-checking will be.

The Default Custom Dictionary

Office starts you off with a default custom dictionary named CUSTOM.DIC, located in the \WINDOWS\MSAPPS\PROOF\ folder. Whenever you run the Spelling checker, it adds any words that you select to the CUSTOM.DIC dictionary using the Add command—unless you tell it otherwise by selecting another dictionary from the Add Words To drop-down list in the Spelling dialog box (see Figure 3.6).

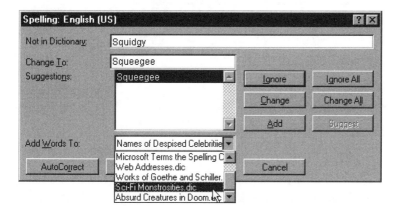

FIGURE 3.6:
To add words to a dictionary other than CUSTOM.DIC, choose the dictionary from the Add Words To drop-down list in the Spelling dialog box, and then click the Add button.

TIP

When adding words to your custom dictionary, use lowercase letters unless the words require special capitalization. If you enter a word in lowercase, the Spelling checker will recognize it when you type it in uppercase or with an initial capital letter, but if you enter a word with an initial capital letter, the Spelling checker will not recognize it if you type it using all lowercase letters.

Creating a Custom Dictionary

To create a new custom dictionary—for example, for foreign words you use in your English documents, spreadsheets, or presentations (as opposed to foreign words you use in your foreign-language documents, spreadsheets, or presentations), or for technical terms that you don't want to keep in CUSTOM.DIC—here's what to do:

1. In Word, choose Tools ➢ Options to display the Options dialog box, and then click the Spelling tab. Alternatively, click the Options button in the Spelling dialog box in Word if you're in the middle of spell-checking.

2. Click the Custom Dictionaries button to display the Custom Dictionaries dialog box.
3. Click the New button to open the Create Custom Dictionary dialog box (see Figure 3.7).

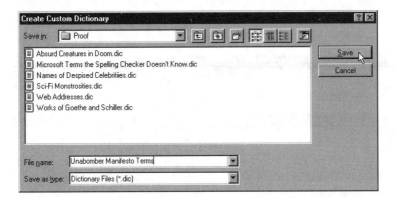

FIGURE 3.7:
In the Create
Custom Dictionary
dialog box, enter
the name of the
dictionary you
want to create,
and then click
the Save button.

4. Enter a name for the dictionary in the File Name text box and then click the Save button. Word will return you to the Custom Dictionaries dialog box, where you will see the new dictionary in the Custom Dictionaries list box.
5. Make sure that a check mark appears next to the name of the new dictionary to indicate that it has been selected, then click the OK button to close the Custom Dictionaries dialog box.
6. Click the OK button in the Options dialog box to close it.

Adding Custom Dictionaries from Other Folders

If you have custom dictionaries stored in folders other than the \PROOF\ folder (for example, you might share dictionaries with colleagues via a network), you need to tell the Spelling checker where they are:

1. In Word, choose Tools ➢ Options to display the Options dialog box, then click the Spelling tab. Alternatively, click the Options button in the Spelling dialog box in Word if you are in the middle of spell-checking.
2. Click the Custom Dictionaries button to display the Custom Dictionaries dialog box.
3. Click the Add button to display the Add Custom Dictionary dialog box, which you'll recognize as a variant of the Open dialog box.
4. Navigate to the folder containing the custom dictionary you want to add using standard Windows 95 navigation techniques.

5.   Select the dictionary to add then click the OK button. Word will add the dictio-
     nary to the list of custom dictionaries and then return you to the Custom
     Dictionaries dialog box.

6.   Make sure a check mark appears next to the new dictionary in the Custom
     Dictionaries list box, then click the OK button to close the Custom Dictionaries
     dialog box.

7.   Click the OK button in the Options dialog box to close it and return to your
     document or to the Spelling checker.

NOTE   To remove a custom dictionary from the Custom Dictionaries list in
            the Custom Dictionaries dialog box, select the dictionary you want to
            remove and then click the Remove button. (This option just removes
            the dictionary from the list—it does not delete the dictionary file.)

Editing a Custom Dictionary

One way of adding the words you need to your custom dictionaries is by clicking the
Add button whenever you run into one of those words during a spell check. However, you
can also open and edit your custom dictionaries in Word. This is particularly useful when
you have added a misspelled a word to a dictionary, and the Spelling checker is now mer-
rily accepting a mistake in every document you write.

To edit a custom dictionary:

1.   Choose Tools ➢ Options to display the Options dialog box, then click the
     Spelling tab.

2.   Click the Custom Dictionaries button to display the Custom Dictionaries
     dialog box.

3.   In the Custom Dictionaries list box, choose the dictionary you want to edit
     and click the Edit button. Word will display a warning telling you that it is
     about to turn automatic spell-checking off, and then it will open the dictionary
     as a Word file.

4.   Edit the dictionary as you would any other document, making sure you have
     only one word per line.

5.   Choose File ➢ Save to save the dictionary.

6.   Choose File ➢ Close to close the dictionary and return to your document.

7.   Choose Tools ➢ Options to display the Options dialog box, and turn automatic
     spell-checking back on by checking the Automatic Spell Checking check box
     on the Spelling tab of the Options dialog box. Click OK to close the Options
     dialog box.

AutoCorrect

AutoCorrect offers a number of features that help you quickly enter your text in the right format. AutoCorrect works in a similar way to Word's on-the-fly Spelling checker that we looked at in the previous section, but AutoCorrect has far greater potential for improving your working life—and it works in Excel and PowerPoint as well. Every time you finish typing a word and press the spacebar, press Tab, press Enter, or type any form of punctuation (comma, period, semicolon, colon, quotation marks, exclamation point, question mark, or even a % sign), AutoCorrect checks it for a multitude of sins and, if it finds it guilty, takes action immediately.

> **NOTE** In Excel, pressing ←, →, ↑, or ↓ to move to another cell activates AutoCorrect as well.

The first four of AutoCorrect's features are straightforward; the fifth is a little more complex:

Correct TWo INitial CApitals stops you from typing an extra capital at the beginning of a word. If you need to type technical terms that need two initial capitals, clear the check box to turn this option off.

Capitalize First Letter of Sentences does just that (in Word only). If you and Word disagree about what constitutes a sentence (if you start a new paragraph without ending the one before it with a period, Word will not capitalize the first word), turn this option off by clearing the check box.

Capitalize Names of Days does just that.

Correct accidental usage of cAPS lOCK key is a neat feature (in Word only) that works most of the time. If Word thinks you've got the Caps Lock key down and you don't know it, it will turn Caps Lock off and change the offending text from upper- to lowercase and vice versa. Word usually decides that Caps Lock is stuck when you start a new sentence with a lowercase letter and continue with uppercase letters; however, the end of the previous sentence may remain miscased.

Replace Text as You Type is the best of the AutoCorrect features. We'll look at it in detail in the next section.

Replace Text as You Type

AutoCorrect's Replace Text as You Type feature keeps a list of AutoCorrect entries. Each time you finish typing a word, AutoCorrect scans this list for that word. If the word is on the list, AutoCorrect substitutes the replacement text for the word.

Replace Text as You Type is a great way of fixing typos you make regularly, and in fact Office 95 ships with a decent list of AutoCorrect entries already configured—if you type *awya* instead of *away* or *disatisfied* instead of *dissatisfied*, AutoCorrect will automatically fix the typo for you. But AutoCorrect is even more useful for setting up abbreviations for words, phrases, titles, or even names that you use frequently in your day-to-day work, saving you not only time and keystrokes but also the effort of memorizing complex spellings or details.

You can add AutoCorrect entries to the list in two ways—automatically while running a spelling check, or manually at any time.

Adding AutoCorrect Entries While Spell-Checking

Adding AutoCorrect entries while spell-checking a document is a great way to teach AutoCorrect the typos you make regularly. When the Spelling checker finds a word it doesn't like, make sure the appropriate replacement word is highlighted in the Change To box; if the word in the Change To box isn't the appropriate one, type in the right word. Then click the AutoCorrect button in the Spelling dialog box. AutoCorrect will add the word from the Not in Dictionary box to the Replace list in AutoCorrect and the word from the Change To box to the With list in AutoCorrect. This way you can build an AutoCorrect list tailored precisely to your typing idiosyncrasies.

Adding AutoCorrect Entries Manually

Adding AutoCorrect entries while spell-checking is great for building a list of your personal typos but of little use for setting up AutoCorrect with abbreviations that will increase your typing speed dramatically. For that, you need to add AutoCorrect entries manually.

To add AutoCorrect entries manually:

1. If the replacement text for the AutoCorrect entry is in the current document, spreadsheet, or presentation, select it.

TIP   Word supports AutoCorrect entries that contain formatting, such as bold, italic, or paragraph formatting; Excel and PowerPoint do not support formatting in AutoCorrect entries. To create an AutoCorrect entry that contains formatting, select the formatted text in a Word document before opening the AutoCorrect dialog box.

2. Choose Tools ➤ AutoCorrect to display the AutoCorrect dialog box. Figure 3.8 shows the AutoCorrect dialog box for Word; the AutoCorrect dialog boxes for Excel and PowerPoint are the same in all but a couple of details.

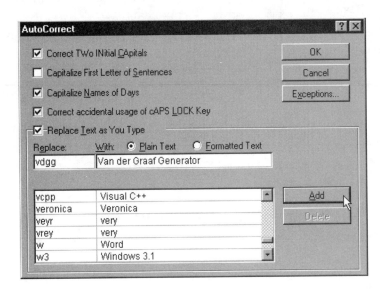

FIGURE 3.8: Choose settings in the AutoCorrect dialog box to save yourself time and typos. This is the AutoCorrect dialog box for Word and has a couple more options than those for Excel and PowerPoint.

3. Make sure that the Replace Text as You Type check box has been selected.

4. Enter the typo or abbreviation to replace in the Replace box.

> **TIP**
>
> When choosing the Replace text for an abbreviated AutoCorrect entry, avoid using a regular word that you might type and not want to have replaced. Try reducing the word or phrase to an abbreviation that you'll remember—for example, omit all the vowels and include only the salient consonants. If you doubt you will remember the right abbreviation, set up several AutoCorrect entries for the same Replace text—for example, set up *thr*, *thru*, *throgh*, and *thrugh* for *through* and you will barely be able to go wrong.

5. Enter the replacement text in the With box.
   - If you selected text before opening the AutoCorrect dialog box, that text will appear in the With box.

- In Word, if the text needs to retain its formatting, make sure the Formatted Text option button has been selected. (The Formatted Text option button also needs to be selected if your selection contains a paragraph mark or tab—that counts as formatting.)

6. Click the Add button or press Enter to add the AutoCorrect entry to the list. If there already is an AutoCorrect entry stored for that Replace text, the Add button will be replaced with a Replace button. When you press Enter or click this button, Word (or Office) will display a confirmation dialog box to make sure that you want to replace the current AutoCorrect entry.

7. To add another AutoCorrect entry, repeat steps 3 to 6.

8. To close the AutoCorrect dialog box, click the Close button.

TIP

You can include graphics, frames, borders, and so on in AutoCorrect entries for Word. For example, you can easily include your company's logo in an AutoCorrect entry for the company address for letterhead. Be imaginative—AutoCorrect can save you plenty of time. One other thing—unless you create truly massive numbers of AutoCorrect entries (say, several thousand), you shouldn't need to worry about AutoCorrect slowing your computer down.

Deleting AutoCorrect Entries

To delete an AutoCorrect entry, open the AutoCorrect dialog box (by choosing Tools ➢ AutoCorrect) and select the entry from the scroll list at the bottom of the dialog box. (You can also type the first few letters of an entry's Replace designation in the Replace box to scroll to it quickly.) Then click the Delete button.

WARNING

Remember that the Office applications share the AutoCorrect entries, so if you delete an entry while in Excel, it will no longer be available in Word or PowerPoint either. The only exception is that Excel and PowerPoint can have AutoCorrect entries that have the same Replace designations as formatted AutoCorrect entries in Word. If you're going to try this, be very careful when creating and deleting AutoCorrect entries.

You can then delete additional AutoCorrect entries at the same time or click the OK button to close the AutoCorrect dialog box.

Find and Replace

Word, Excel, and PowerPoint all have Find and Replace features, and Schedule+ includes a Find feature. Find and Replace let you search for any *string* of text (a letter, several letters, a word, or a phrase) and replace chosen instances or all instances of that string with another string—for example, you could replace all instances of "dangerous" with "unwise," or you could replace selected instances of "this fearful lunatic" with "the Vice President of Communications." You can also use Find independent of Replace to locate strategic parts of your files quickly.

To find and replace text:

1. Choose Edit ➢ Replace to display the Replace dialog box (or, from the Find dialog box, click on the Replace button). Figure 3.9 shows the Replace dialog box for PowerPoint.

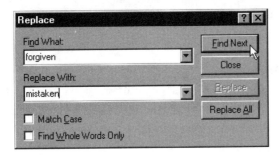

FIGURE 3.9:
The Replace dialog box for PowerPoint. The Replace dialog boxes for Word and Excel are similar but contain other features as well.

2. In the Find What box, enter the text to find.
   To find text you've searched for before in the current session, click the arrow at the right-hand end of the Find What box and choose the text from the drop-down list.

3. In the Replace With box, enter the text you want to replace the found text with.
   To reuse replacement text from the current session, click the arrow at the right-hand end of the Replace With box and choose the text from the drop-down list.

4. If applicable, choose a search direction from the Search drop-down list: Word offers Down, Up, or All; Excel offers By Rows or By Columns; and Schedule+ offers to search in Appointments, To Do List, Contact List, or Events.

5. Choose Replace options as appropriate:
    - Match Case makes Find pay attention to the capitalization of the word in the Find What box. For example, with Match Case selected and **indolence** entered in the Find What box, Find will ignore instances of *Indolence* in the document and find only *indolence*.
    - Find Whole Words Only makes Find look only for the exact word entered in the Find What box and not for the word when it is part of another word. For example, by checking Find Whole Words Only, you could find *and* without finding *land*, *random*, *mandible*, and so on. In Word, Find Whole Words Only is not available if you type a space in the Find What box.

NOTE   Excel has a feature similar to Find Whole Words Only called Find Entire Cells Only. Word has much more powerful Find and Replace features than the other Office applications. We'll look at these features in Chapter 11.

6. Start the Replace operation by clicking the Find Next button, the Replace button, or the Replace All button:
    - The Find Next button and Replace button will find the next instance of the text in the Find What box. Once you've found it, click the Find Next button to skip to the next occurrence of the text without replacing it with the contents of the Replace With box. Otherwise, click the Replace button to replace the text with the contents of the Replace With box and then find the next instance of the Find What text.
    - The Replace All button will replace all instances of the text in the Find What box with the text in the Replace With box.

7. When you've finished your Replace operation, click the Close button to close the Replace dialog box.

Macros

Word and Excel include macro languages that you can use to write macros that can range from the very simple (but useful) to the extremely complex and powerful. *Macros* are sequences of commands that can save you time and keystrokes. Word's macro language is called WordBasic; Excel's is called Visual Basic for Applications (VBA for short), which is a close relation of the full Visual Basic language that you can install and run separately to build custom applications in Windows.

We'll look at macros in the chapters on Word (Part 2) and Excel (Part 3).

Templates and Wizards

Word, Excel, PowerPoint, and the Office Binder application all come with *templates*, special files on which you can base different types of documents, spreadsheets, or presentations. For example, Word has templates for faxes, reports, memos, and more; Excel has templates for invoices, car loans, budgets, etc.; PowerPoint has templates for business plans, financial reports, company meetings, and so on; and Office Binder has templates for reports, client billing, meetings, and marketing plans.

Word also has Wizards, which are powerful macros that help you choose templates, enter information in them in the appropriate places, make formatting decisions, and generally produce convincing documents in a short amount of time. For example, when you run the Newsletter Wizard, Word will shepherd you through the creation of a newsletter in either a classic style or a modern style, with your choice of columns (from one to four) and contents.

Help and the Answer Wizard

The Office applications also come with a sophisticated Help system designed to solve all your problems (or at least the Office-related ones) swiftly and smoothly. You can get help in several ways:

- Choose Help ➤ Help Topics (e.g., Help ➤ Microsoft Binder Help Topics) to display the Index tab of the Help Topics dialog box (see Figure 3.10). Enter the first few letters of the relevant word in the first text box, then choose the index entry in the list box and click the Display button to display it.
- Choose Help ➤ Answer Wizard to display the Answer Wizard tab of the Help Topics dialog box. Type your question into the text box, then click the Search button. Topics of possible interest will appear in the list box, divided into the categories How Do I, Tell Me About, and (if there's anything relevant) Programming and Language Reference. Choose the most appealing of the possible topics and click the Display button to display it. (If nothing appeals, rephrase your question and try again.)

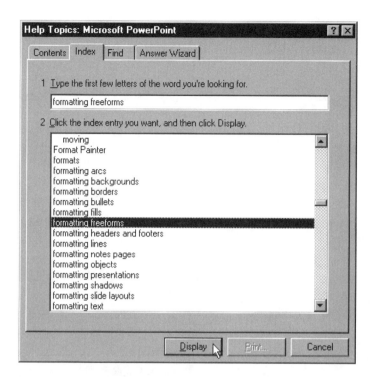

FIGURE 3.10:
On the Index tab
of the Help Topics
dialog box, enter
the first few letters
of the word you're
looking for, then
choose the index
entry and click
Display.

NOTE   If you enter something really off the wall (such as *Death in Venice*),
Help will display a message box saying "Sorry, but I don't know what
you mean. Please rephrase your question." If you change this to *Who
wrote Death in Venice?*, Help will obligingly find some topics (though
nothing relevant—just general things involving writing). Be civil.

- Display the Help Topics dialog box, click the Contents tab for an overview of the Help topics available, then move down through the topics that interest you until you find the information that you want.
- Display the Help Topics dialog box and click the Find tab. Enter the word you're looking for in the first box; select matching words from the second box to narrow the search, then choose a topic in the third box and click the Display button.
- To get help in a dialog box, click the Help button (the button bearing the question mark in the upper-right corner of the dialog box) so the mouse pointer grows a question mark. Click this on the part of the dialog box that puzzles you and the application will display an explanation of that item.

Chapter 4

OLE, OFFICE BINDERS, AND E-MAIL

FEATURING

- **Linking and embedding objects**
- **Creating Office binders**
- **Working with binders**
- **Sending files via e-mail**

As we'll see in the coming chapters, the Office applications provide enough features for just about any type of document, from plain text to complex tables to slides to a spreadsheet. Sooner or later, you'll find yourself needing to include data created in one application in a different application: For example, you might want to include in a Word document or PowerPoint slide part of a spreadsheet created in Excel; or you might want to use a Word table or an Excel chart in a PowerPoint presentation. Beyond that, you may find you need to group several heterogenous Office files—say, some slides, a couple of Word documents, and an Excel spreadsheet or two— together to form a complex document.

In this chapter, we'll look at how you can use Microsoft Office's Object Linking and Embedding feature (OLE for short) to enhance your Office files. When such integrated files fall short of your needs, you can use Office binders to pull together disparate elements into a superdocument. Finally, we'll discuss how Word, Excel, and PowerPoint integrate with the Microsoft Exchange client software contained in Windows 95 to let you send files to colleagues or friends and have the files return automatically to you.

If you're reading through this book in order and these topics seem arcane or intimidating, leave this chapter for the time being and come back when you're familiar with the Office applications.

Object Linking and Embedding

Object Linking and Embedding (OLE) gives you two ways to include an *object* (information) created in one application in files created in other applications. By *linking* an object from, say, an Excel spreadsheet to a Word document, you can have the object automatically updated whenever you open or print the document (or indeed any time you choose to update the object manually). By *embedding* the Excel object in the Word document, you can make that object part of the document, so you can change that object even when you don't have access to Excel—for example, you can include data from an Excel spreadsheet in a Word document, transfer the document to your laptop, and then hit the road.

> **NOTE** *Object* is one of those great computer terms whose meaning people can never quite agree on. For the moment, think of an object as being a chunk of information (data) that knows which application it was created in—for example, a group of spreadsheet cells that knows it was created in Excel.

Linking

Linking connects an object from one application (the *source* application) to a file created in another application (the *destination* application). The object appears in the destination application but stays connected to its source application, so if you change the object in the source application, you can have the destination application automatically update the object as well. For example, by linking the sales figures in an Excel spreadsheet to a Word document, you can make sure the document always has the latest sales figures in it.

For example, here's how to link information from another application to a Word document:

1. Start the source application for the object you want to link to a Word document.
2. Open the file containing the object.

> **TIP**
>
> **Linking objects to your documents enlarges them only a little—not nearly as much as embedding. To keep your documents as small as possible, choose linking over embedding when you have the choice.**

3. Select the object to insert. For example, if you're inserting a group of cells from a spreadsheet, select those cells (as shown here).

4. Choose Edit ➤ Copy (or click the Copy button in that application or choose Ctrl +C) to copy the object to the Clipboard.

5. Switch back to Word (or start Word if it isn't already running) by clicking the Microsoft Word icon on the Taskbar or by pressing Alt+Tab until the Word icon is selected in the task-switching list.

6. Position the insertion point where you want the linked item to appear.
7. Choose Edit ➤ Paste Special to display the Paste Special dialog box (see Figure 4.1).
8. Select the Paste Link option on the left side of the dialog box.
9. In the As list box, choose the option that describes the item you're linking as "Object." (Here it's Microsoft Excel Worksheet Object because Excel is the source application; with other source applications, you'll see different descriptions.)
10. To have the item display as an icon rather than at its full size, select the Display as Icon check box. To change the icon, click the Change Icon button and select a different icon in the Change Icon dialog box; then click OK. (The Change Icon button appears when you select the Display as Icon check box.)
11. Click OK to insert the object in your document (see Figure 4.2).

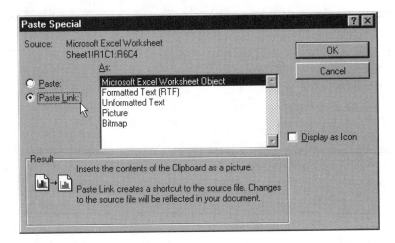

FIGURE 4.1:
To link information, select the Paste Link option in the Paste Special dialog box and choose the option from the As list box that describes the item as "Object"—here it's Microsoft Excel Worksheet Object.

FIGURE 4.2:
The cells from the Excel spreadsheet inserted in the document

You can now format the linked object, for example, by adding borders and shading (which we'll discuss in Chapter 7) or by placing it in a frame (Chapter 5).

TIP   To open the source file for the linked object in the application that created it, double-click the linked object (or the icon for it) in your document.

Updating Links

You can update links either manually or automatically so that a link is updated every time you open the document that contains it or every time the source file is updated (when the document containing the link is open). You can also lock a link so that it cannot be updated.

To set updating for links:

1. Open the document containing the links. Here we'll look at updating a PowerPoint slide that contains data from Excel and from Word.

2. Choose Edit ➢ Links to display the Links dialog box (see Figure 4.3).

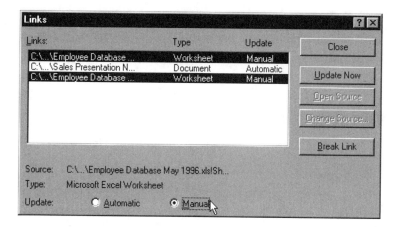

FIGURE 4.3:
Choose how to update your links in the Links dialog box.

3. In the list box, select the link or links on which to work. (Use Shift+click to select several adjacent links or Ctrl+click to select nonadjacent links.)

4. Choose how the link or links should be updated by selecting the Automatic option button or the Manual option button.
    *   To update a link manually, click the Update Now button.
    *   To lock the link or links in Word, click the Locked check box. Word will then dim the Automatic option button and the Manual option button to indicate the choices are not available. To unlock a link, select it in the list box and clear the Locked check box.

5. Click OK to close the Links dialog box.

Breaking Links

If you no longer need to be able to update a link or if you're planning to share a document with someone who won't have the linked information available, you can break the link in Word or PowerPoint. This essentially turns the linked information into embedded information.

To break a link:

1. Choose Edit ➢ Links to display the Links dialog box.

2. Select the link or links in the list box.

3. Click the Break Link button. Word will display a message box to make sure that you want to break the link; PowerPoint will not.
4. Click the Yes button to break the link.
5. Click OK or Close to close the Links dialog box.

WARNING Once you've broken a link, you cannot restore it (except by reinserting the linked information, thus creating the link again).

Deleting Linked Objects

To delete a linked object, click it to select it, then press the Delete key or choose Edit ➢ Clear.

Embedding

To embed an object in a document, you follow a similar procedure to linking, but the result is completely different: Instead of creating a connection from the object in the destination file to its source file in the source application, the destination application saves in the file all the information needed to edit the object in place. Because the object is not connected to the source file, you cannot update the object in the destination file, but you can edit the object in the destination file to your heart's content without worrying about changing the source file.

TIP The advantage of embedding over linking is that you can edit the embedded information even if you don't have the application that created the information on your computer. The disadvantage is that embedding objects makes the destination files much larger than linking objects does because all the information needed to edit the object is stored in the destination file (instead of just the information pointing to the source file and source application).

Embedding an Existing Object

To embed an existing object in a document:

1. Start the source application for the object you want to embed.
2. Open the file containing the object.
3. Select the object to embed. Here, we'll select a Word table to include in a PowerPoint slide.

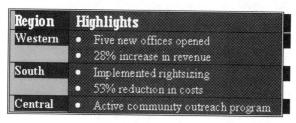

4. Choose Edit ➤ Copy (or click the Copy button in that application or choose Ctrl+C) to copy the object to the Clipboard.
5. Switch to the destination application (in this case, PowerPoint) by using the Taskbar or by pressing Alt+Tab. (Start the destination application if it isn't yet running.)
6. Position the insertion point where you want to embed the object.
7. Choose Edit ➤ Paste Special to display the Paste Special dialog box (see Figure 4.4).

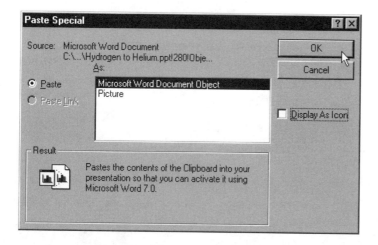

FIGURE 4.4:
To embed information, select the Paste option in the Paste Special dialog box and choose the option in the As list box that describes the item as "Object"— here it's Microsoft Word Document Object.

8. Select the Paste option button.
9. In the As list box, choose the option that describes the item you're embedding as "Object." (Here it's Microsoft Word Document Object because Word is the source application; with other source applications, you'll see different descriptions.)

10. To have the item display as an icon rather than at its full size, check the Display as Icon box. To change the icon, click the Change Icon button (which will materialize when you select the Display as Icon check box) and select a different icon in the Change Icon dialog box; click OK to return to the Object dialog box.

11. Click OK to insert the object in your document.

So far this all seems singularly similar to linking. But you'll notice the difference when you double-click the embedded object—it displays a border from its source application (in this case, Word) and the toolbars and menus change to those of the source application, so you can edit the object within PowerPoint as if you were working in the source application, Word (see Figure 4.5).

NOTE When you activate an embedded object from another source application, the current application's menu bar will change to the source application's.

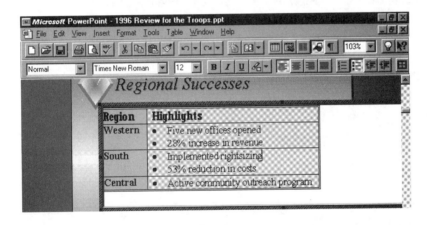

FIGURE 4.5: Double-click an embedded object to edit it in place. The destination application will display the menus and toolbars from the source application.

TIP To edit a sound clip or video clip, right-click the object and choose the Edit options (e.g., Edit Wave Sound) from the shortcut menu. Double-click an embedded sound or video clip to run it.

Embedding a New Object

You can also create a new object and embed it at the same time. For example, you could insert a sound clip in your document like this:

1. Choose Insert ➤ Object to display the Object dialog box (see Figure 4.6).

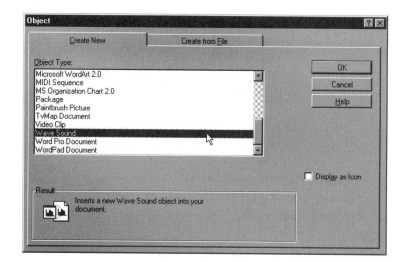

FIGURE 4.6:
On the Create New tab in the Object dialog box, choose the type of object to create, then click OK.

2. In Word or Excel, click the Create New tab to bring it to the front of the dialog box (unless it's already there). In PowerPoint, make sure the Create New option button is selected.

3. From the Object Type list, choose the type of object you want to insert. (Here I've chosen Wave Sound.)

4. Check the Display as Icon box if you want the object to display as an icon in the document. To change the icon for the object, click the Change Icon button (which will appear when you select the Display as Icon check box) and select a different icon in the Change Icon dialog box; click OK to return to the Object dialog box.

5. Click OK. The destination application will start the source application you chose.

6. Create the object as usual in that application.

7. Choose File ➤ Exit and Return to *Document Name* to close the source application and return to the destination application. The destination application will insert the object, which you can then position and format as necessary.

Deleting an Embedded Object

To delete an embedded object, select it by clicking it, then press the Delete key or choose Edit ➤ Clear.

Office Binders

Office binders are a way of putting together projects that contain files created in the different applications that constitute Microsoft Office—Word, Excel, PowerPoint, and (if you have Office Professional) Access.

A binder contains sections, each of which can contain either a complete Office file (Word document, PowerPoint slide presentation, Excel spreadsheet, and so on) or part of one.

Creating a Binder

To create a binder, choose Start ➢ Programs ➢ Microsoft Binder to open a Microsoft Office Binder window with a fresh binder in it.

To start a binder from the templates that come with Office (Client Billing, Meeting Organizer, Proposal and Marketing Plan, and Report), from Windows 95 choose Start ➢ New Office Document to display the New dialog box for Office documents, then click the Binders tab (see Figure 4.7). After selecting the template for the new binder, click OK.

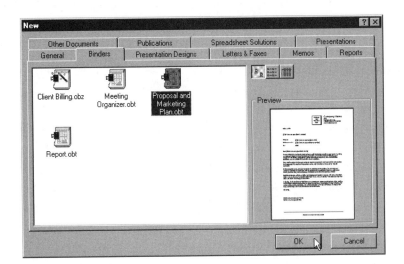

FIGURE 4.7:
To start a new binder based on a template, choose the template on the Binders tab of the New dialog box for Office documents.

Adding Items to a Binder

The easiest way to add files to the binder is to open an Explorer window (or My Computer window) and drag the files from it to the left pane of the binder window. When you drop the first file in the left pane, the Office Binder copies the information to the binder and activates the application in which the file was created, displaying the application's menus and toolbars along with the information in the file. In Figure 4.8, I've just dragged the file *Expansion Plans for 1997—Presentation.ppt* from the My Computer window to the Binder window. The Office Binder has displayed the first slide in the presentation, together with the PowerPoint menus and toolbars.

You can also add files by choosing Section ➤ Add from File to display the Add from File dialog box. Select the file, and click the OK button.

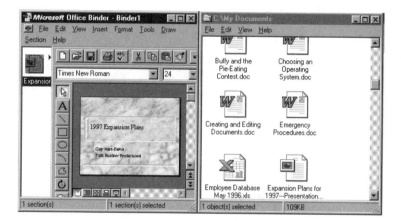

FIGURE 4.8: To add a file to a binder, drag it from My Computer window or an Explorer window and drop it in the left pane of the Binder window.

Adding Sections to a Binder

To bridge the transitions between the different files you place in the binder, you can add blank sections to the binder and then enter material in them.

To add a section to a binder, right-click anywhere in the left pane of the Office Binder window and choose Add from the shortcut menu to display the Add Section dialog box.

In the Add Section dialog box, choose the type of section you want to add—Excel Chart, Excel Worksheet, PowerPoint Presentation, or Word Document—from the As a Blank Section group box and click the OK button.

Once Office Binder has inserted the new section, you are to all extents and purposes working in an Excel chart or worksheet, a PowerPoint presentation, or a Word document. To give yourself a little more room to maneuver, you can hide the left pane of the Office Binder window by clicking the Pane button; click it again to display the pane again.

Moving Items around in the Binder

To move an item up or down the binder, you can simply click and drag the icon for the item in the left pane of the Office Binder window. If you're rearranging more items, you may find it easier to choose Section , Rearrange and work in the Rearrange Sections dialog box (see Figure 4.9). Highlight the section to move in the Reorder Sections box, then click the Move Up or Move Down button to move it to its new location (each click moves it up or down one file). Repeat as needed for other sections, then click the OK button to close the Rearrange Sections dialog box.

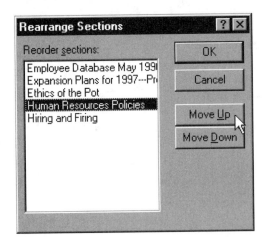

FIGURE 4.9:
In the Rearrange Sections dialog box, select the section you want to move in the Reorder Sections box, then click the Move Up or Move Down button to put it in its new place.

Removing Items from a Binder

To remove an item from the binder, right-click it in the left pane of the Office Binder window and choose Delete from the shortcut menu. Word will display a confirmation message box to make sure you want to remove the item; click OK to remove it.

Editing in the Binder

You can create and edit your documents in the binder if necessary, but generally you'll do better to create a binder from already existing documents. If you then need to modify those documents, open them in their source applications and edit them there rather than editing them in the binder, then put the edited version back in the binder (replacing the previous version).

When working in a binder, you'll find that a few features of particular applications don't work or are not available. For example, you cannot use Excel's AutoCalculate feature in a binder because the binder's status bar replaces Excel's status bar (which contains the AutoCalculate feature). Likewise, you cannot use Print Preview in a binder.

> **TIP**   If you need to use toolbars, macros, or AutoText entries stored in the template to which a Word document that you put in a binder is attached, drag the template to the binder as well.

Printing a Binder

To print a binder, open it and choose File ➢ Print Binder to display the Print Binder dialog box. Choose options for printing the binder, then click the OK button to print the binder.

Sending Files via E-mail

Word, Excel, and PowerPoint work together with the Microsoft Exchange features built into Windows 95, so that you can easily send files via e-mail:

1. Start Word, Excel, or PowerPoint and open the document, spreadsheet, or presentation you want to send.
2. Choose File ➢ Add Routing Slip to display the Routing Slip dialog box. Figure 4.10 shows the Routing Slip dialog box for Word. Word's Routing Slip dialog box offers one more feature than the Routing Slip dialog box in Excel and the Add Routing Slip dialog box in PowerPoint, but is otherwise identical.
3. First, choose the recipients. Click the Address button to display the Address Book dialog box.
4. Select the names of the recipients and click the To button to add them to the list.

- You can Shift-click to select a range of recipients or Ctrl-click to select a group of recipients one by one.
- If need be, choose another address book from the Show Names drop-down list.

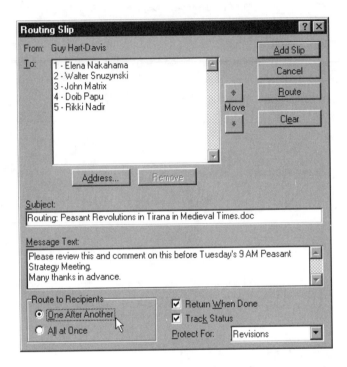

FIGURE 4.10:
Choose recipients for the open document, specify a subject, enter message text, and decide how to route the message in the Routing Slip dialog box or Add Routing Slip dialog box.

5. Click OK when you've finished selecting your recipients. The application will return you to the Routing Slip dialog box.

6. Check the Subject line that the application has automatically entered from the Subject of the file set in File ➤ Properties. Change it if necessary.

7. Enter any message text in the Message Text box.

8. Choose how to route the message to recipients: One After Another, or All at Once. If you choose One After Another, the application will send out only one copy of the file, and it will be passed on from one recipient to the next (we'll look at how they pass the file on in a moment). Each will see their predecessor's changes and comments, so you may want to arrange the To list carefully. (Highlight a name and use the Move buttons to move it up or down the To list).

9. Choose from among the options in the lower-right corner of the Routing Slip dialog box.

- Leave Return When Done selected if you want the file to come back to you after its routing experience.
- Check the Track Status box if you want to have an electronic message sent to you each time one of the recipients in a One After Another routing sends the message and file on to the next recipient.
- In Word, choose how to protect the document in the Protect For drop-down list: (none), Revisions, Annotations, or Forms.

10.   To route the file now, click the Route button. To save your recipient list, subject, and message before routing it so you can return to the document to do more work, choose Add Slip. You can then choose File ➢ Edit Routing Slip to display the Routing Slip dialog box again with the information you already entered in it.

Receiving and Reviewing Files

When you receive a mailed file, open it in the appropriate Office application and review or revise it as appropriate.

> **NOTE**   If the file is a Word document, it may be protected for revisions, for annotations, or as a form. If it's protected for revision marks, the revision marks will appear automatically whenever you alter the document; if it's protected for annotations, you'll only be able to insert annotations; and if it's a form, you will only be able to fill in the form fields.

Returning Files via E-mail

When you're finished, choose File ➢ Send to send the document either on to the next recipient or back to the sender; Exchange will automatically choose which action to perform, based on the originator's instructions.

Part 2

Word

Chapter 5

GETTING STARTED IN WORD

- **Setting up the Word screen**
- **Entering text, graphics, and frames**
- **Moving the insertion point**
- **Selecting items**
- **Using Word's different views**

In this chapter, we'll race through the basics of creating documents with Word—setting up the screen so you have on it what you need, entering the text of your document (and illustrations), moving the insertion point and selecting items, and using the different views that Word provides for working with your documents.

Setting Up Your Screen

First, let's quickly look at how Word appears on the screen (see Figure 5.1).

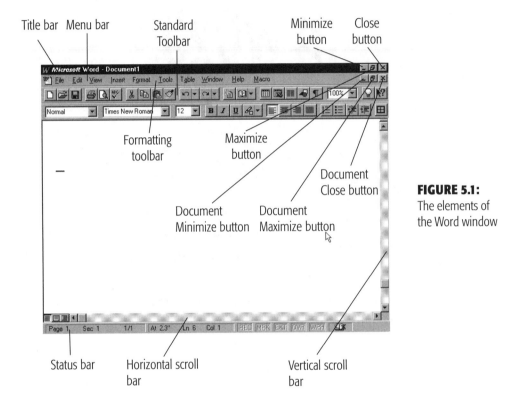

Title bar Menu bar   Standard
                        Toolbar

Minimize Close
button   button

Formatting   Maximize
toolbar   button

Document
Close button

Document   Document
Minimize button Maximize button

FIGURE 5.1:
The elements of
the Word window

Status bar   Horizontal scroll
              bar

Vertical scroll
bar

Before you start work in Word, you may want to customize your screen. At a minimum, consider maximizing the Word window by clicking the Maximize button on the title bar and then the document you're working on within the Word window by clicking the Document Maximize button.

You may also want to use Zoom to enlarge or shrink the display. If so, skip ahead to *Viewing the Document* later in this chapter.

Displaying and Hiding the Rulers

To help you position your text optimally on the page, Word offers a horizontal ruler in Normal view and both horizontal and vertical rulers in Page Layout view and Print Preview.

When you don't need the ruler or rulers, you can hide them by choosing View ➤ Ruler. To display the ruler or rulers again, choose View ➤ Ruler once more.

Working with Text, Graphics, and Frames

As with most word-processing applications, the basic unit Word thinks in is the paragraph. These aren't paragraphs as people generally understand them: A paragraph in Word consists of a paragraph mark (made by pressing Enter) and any text between it and the previous paragraph mark (or the beginning of the document). In other words, a paragraph consists of anything (text, space, or even nothing at all) that appears between two paragraph marks, up to and including the second paragraph mark. This seems a strange way to describe it, but a paragraph mark with no text between it and the previous paragraph mark is still considered a full paragraph. You can treat each paragraph as a unit for formatting with styles (which we'll look at in Chapter 7) or for moving and copying.

> **TIP**
>
> If you're not seeing paragraph marks on your screen, click the ¶ button on the Formatting toolbar. This is the Show/Hide ¶ button, and it toggles the display of spaces, tabs, paragraph marks, and the like. Some people find it easier to work with these marks displayed; others find them distracting. You can also display and hide these marks by pressing Ctrl+Shift+ 8.

Entering Text

To enter text in your document, simply position the insertion point where you want the text to appear and type it in. Word will automatically wrap text as it reaches the end of a line. Press Enter to start a new paragraph.

If you want to move to a new line without starting a new paragraph—for example, so there is space between paragraphs—press Shift+Enter to start a new line within the same paragraph.

As you reach the end of a page, Word will automatically break text onto the next page. If you want, you can start a new page at any point by inserting a page break. To do so, press Ctrl+Enter.

Insert and Overtype Modes

Word offers two modes for adding text to your documents: *Insert mode* and *Overtype mode*. In Insert mode (the default mode), characters you type are inserted into the text to the left of the insertion point, pushing any characters to the right of the insertion point farther to the right. If you want to replace existing text in Insert mode, select the text using either the mouse or the keyboard and type in the text you want to insert in its place (see the next section for instructions on selecting text).

In Overtype mode, any character you type replaces the character (if any) to the immediate right of the insertion point. When Word is in Overtype mode, the OVR indicator on the status bar is darkened.

To toggle between Insert mode and Overtype mode, double-click the OVR indicator on the status bar or press the Insert key.

Inserting and Sizing Pictures

You can easily insert pictures of various types into Word documents. Once you've inserted them, you can resize them and crop them as necessary.

Inserting a Picture

To insert a picture at the insertion point:

1. Choose Insert ➤ Picture to display the Insert Picture dialog box (see Figure 5.2).

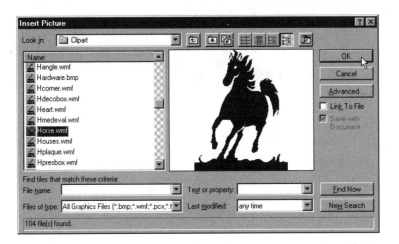

FIGURE 5.2:
In the Insert Picture dialog box, choose the picture to insert and click OK.

2. Navigate to the folder containing the picture you want using standard Windows 95 techniques. To display different types of graphics files, use the Files of Type drop-down list.

3. Choose the picture file to insert in the Name list box. Use the Preview box to make sure you've got the right file.

4. Click the OK button to insert the picture in your document.

Resizing and Cropping Pictures

To resize a picture quickly, click it to display an outline around it with eight handles: one at each corner and one in the middle of each side. Drag a corner handle to resize the image proportionally; drag a side handle to resize the image only in that dimension (horizontally or vertically).

To crop a picture quickly (cutting off part of it), click the picture and then move the mouse pointer over one of the picture's handles. Hold down the Shift key, and the mouse pointer will change from a two-headed arrow to a cropping marker: Hold down Shift as you click and then drag inwards or outwards to crop the picture.

To resize or crop a picture precisely:

1. Click the picture to display the outline and handles around it.

2. Choose Format ➢ Picture to display the Picture dialog box (see Figure 5.3).

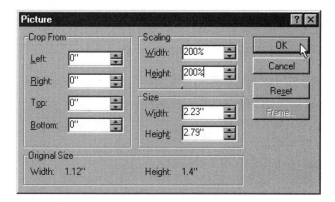

FIGURE 5.3:
The Picture dialog box lets you resize and crop pictures precisely.

3. To crop the picture, enter how much to crop in the Left, Right, Top, and Bottom boxes in the Crop From group box.

4. To resize the picture, either set Width and Height percentages in the Scaling group box or enter the desired width and height in the Width and Height boxes in the Size group box.

5. Click OK to close the Picture dialog box and apply your changes.

Inserting, Positioning, and Formatting Frames

To position a picture precisely in a document, use a frame. A *frame* is a container that Word uses to position items (pictures, text, etc.) exactly on the page. You can position a frame relative to a paragraph (so it moves with the text) or relative to the margin or page (so it remains in place even if the text moves). The advantage of positioning a frame relative to the page, rather than relative to one or the other margin, is that you can adjust the margins without the frame moving. Frames are held in place by *anchors* and display a shaded border when they're selected, as we'll see in a moment. (You can also add borders and shading to frames.)

Inserting a Frame

To insert a frame around a picture:

1. Click the picture to select it.
2. Choose View ➤ Page Layout to switch to Page Layout view. (We'll look at the different views Word offers in *Viewing the Document* later in this chapter.)
3. Choose Insert ➤ Frame to insert a frame around the picture. The frame will appear as a shaded border around the outline of the picture, as shown here.

NOTE You can also insert a frame without selecting an object. In this case, the mouse pointer changes to a small + sign, with which you click and drag to place and size the frame.

Positioning a Frame

To position a frame quickly:

1. Click inside the frame to display the frame border.
2. Move the mouse pointer into the frame so the pointer grows a four-headed compass arrow.
3. Click and drag the frame to wherever you want to place it on the page.

To position a frame exactly:

1. Right-click in the frame and choose Format Frame from the shortcut menu to display the Frame dialog box (see Figure 5.4). Alternatively, click in the frame and choose Format ➤ Frame.

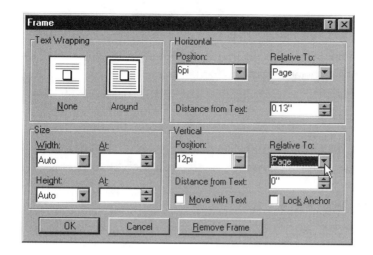

FIGURE 5.4:
Choose the frame's position on the page in the Frame dialog box.

2. In the Horizontal group box, specify the horizontal positioning for the frame:
   - Choose Left, Right, Center, Inside, or Outside from the Position drop-down list, or enter a specific measurement in the Position box. For example, in Figure 5.4 the frame will have a horizontal position of 6 picas from the left edge of the page and a vertical position of 12 picas from the top of the page.
   - Choose Margin, Page, or Column in the Relative To drop-down list.
   - Enter a measurement in the Distance from Text box.
3. In the Vertical group box, specify the vertical positioning for the frame:
   - Choose Top, Bottom, or Center from the Position drop-down list, or enter a specific measurement in the Position box.
   - Choose Paragraph, Page, or Margin in the Relative To drop-down list.
   - Enter a measurement in the Distance from Text box.
4. To allow a frame to move when the text it is attached to moves, select the Move with Text check box.
5. To lock the frame to the paragraph it is with (so you can't move it by accident to another paragraph), click to place a check mark in the Lock Anchor box.
6. Click OK to close the Frame dialog box and apply the settings to the frame.

Sizing a Frame

To resize a frame quickly, click in the frame to display the border and then drag one of the handles to the size you want.

To resize a frame precisely:

1. Right-click in the frame and choose Format Frame to display the Frame dialog box.
2. In the Size group box, specify the size of the frame:
   - In the Width drop-down list, choose Auto or Exactly. If you choose Exactly, enter the exact measurement in the At box.

- In the Height drop-down list, choose Auto, At Least, or Exactly. If you choose At Least or Exactly, enter the measurement in the At box.
3. In the Text Wrapping box, choose Around so the text wraps around the frame or None so it does not wrap around the frame.
4. Click OK to close the Frame dialog box and apply the settings to the frame.

Removing a Frame

To remove a frame, right-click anywhere inside it and choose Format Frame from the shortcut menu to display the Frame dialog box, then click the Remove Frame button.

Moving the Insertion Point

In Word, you move the insertion point using either the mouse or the keyboard.

Using the Mouse

To position the insertion point using the mouse, simply move the insertion point to where you want it and click.

Use the vertical scroll bar to move up and down through your document (as you drag the box in the scroll bar in a multipage document, Word will display a small box by it showing you which page you're at). Use the horizontal scroll bar to move from side to side as necessary.

> **TIP**
>
> If you're continually scrolling horizontally in Normal view to see the full width of your documents, turn on the Wrap to Window option, which makes the text fit into the current window size, regardless of the window's width. To turn on Wrap to Window, choose Tools ➤ Options, click the View tab, and select the Wrap to Window check box. Click OK to close the Options dialog box. (One word of warning—Wrap to Window isn't available in Page Layout view.)

Using Keyboard Shortcuts

Word offers a number of key combinations to move the insertion point swiftly through the document. Besides ← to move left one character, → to move right one character, ↑ to move up one line, and ↓ to move down one line, you can use the keystrokes in following table.

Keystroke	Action
Ctrl+→	One word to the right
Ctrl+←	One word to the left
Ctrl+↑	To the beginning of the current paragraph or (if the insertion point is at the beginning of a paragraph) to the beginning of the previous paragraph
Ctrl+↓	To the beginning of the next paragraph
End	To the end of the current line
Ctrl+End	To the end of the document
Home	To the start of the current line
Ctrl+Home	To the start of the document
PageUp	Up one screen's worth of text
PageDown	Down one screen's worth of text
Ctrl+PageUp	To the first character on the current screen
Ctrl+PageDown	To the last character on the current screen

TIP You can quickly move to the last three places you edited in a document by pressing Shift+F5 (Go Back once, twice, or thrice).

Selecting Text

Word offers a number of different ways of selecting text: using the keyboard, the mouse, or the two in combination. You'll find that some ways of selecting text work better than others with certain equipment; experiment to find which are the fastest and most comfortable methods for you.

Selecting Text with the Mouse

The simplest way to select text with the mouse is to position the insertion point at the beginning or end of the block you want to select, click, and drag to the end or beginning of the block.

> **TIP**
>
> Word offers an Automatic Word Selection option in the Options dialog box to help you select whole words more quickly with the mouse. When Automatic Word Selection is on, as soon as you drag from one word to the next, Word will select the whole of the first word and the whole of the second; when the mouse pointer reaches the third, it selects that too. To temporarily override Automatic Word Selection, hold down the Alt key before you click and drag. To turn off Automatic Word Selection, choose Tools ➢ Options to display the Options dialog box. Click the Edit tab to bring it to the front of the dialog box, and clear Automatic Word Selection to turn it off, then click OK. To turn it on, check the Automatic Word Selection box.

You can also select text with multiple clicks:

- Double-click in a word to select it.
- Triple-click in a paragraph to select it.
- Ctrl-click in a sentence to select it.

In the selection bar on the left side of the screen (where the insertion point turns from an I-beam to an arrow pointing up and to the right), you can click to select the following text:

- Click to select the line the arrow is pointing at.
- Double-click to select the paragraph the arrow is pointing at.
- Triple-click (or Ctrl-click) to select the entire document.

Selecting Text with the Keyboard

To select text with the keyboard, hold down the Shift key and move the insertion point by using the keyboard shortcuts given in *Using Keyboard Shortcuts* earlier in the chapter.

Selecting Text with the Mouse and Keyboard

Word also offers ways of selecting text using the mouse and keyboard together. These techniques are well worth trying out, as you can quickly select awkward blocks of text—for example, you can select a few sentences from a paragraph or several columns of characters.

To select a block of text using the mouse and the keyboard, position the insertion point at the start (or end) of a block and click. Then move the insertion point to the end (or start) of the block—scroll if necessary, but don't use the keyboard—hold down the Shift key, and then click again.

To select columns of characters, hold down the Alt key and click and drag from one end of the block to the other (see Figure 5.5). This technique can be very useful for getting rid of extra spaces or tabs that your colleagues have used to align text.

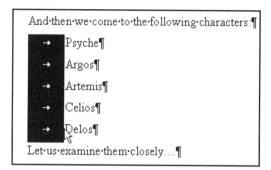

FIGURE 5.5:
To select columns of characters without selecting whole lines, hold down the Alt key and drag through the block.

Deleting Text

Word lets you delete text swiftly and easily:

- To delete the character to the left of the insertion point, press Backspace.
- To delete the character to the right of the insertion point, press Delete.
- To delete a block of text, select it and press the Delete key.
- To delete the word to the right of the insertion point, press Ctrl+Delete. (This deletes from the insertion point to the beginning of the next word—or the end of the line, if the current word is the last one in the line—so if the insertion point is in a word when you press Ctrl+Delete, you will delete only the remainder of the word.)
- To delete the word to the left of the insertion point, press Ctrl+Backspace. (Again, if the insertion point isn't at the end of the word, only the part of the word to the left of the insertion point will be deleted.)

Viewing the Document

Word offers five different ways of viewing your documents, each of which has its strengths and its weaknesses:

- Normal view
- Page Layout view
- Draft Font view
- Print Preview
- Outline view

In Page Layout view and in Print Preview, the vertical scroll bar includes Previous Page and Next Page buttons at its south end. In all views, the horizontal toolbar contains buttons on the far left for switching between Normal view, Page Layout view, and Outline view.

Normal View

Normal view provides the easiest view of the text and other elements on screen and is probably the Word view you'll spend most of your time using. In Normal view, Word approximates the fonts and other formatting that you'll see when you print your document, but adapts the document so you can see as much of it as possible on your screen. In Normal view you don't see the margins of the paper, or the headers and footers, or the footnotes and annotations. Word can wrap the text horizontally to the size of the window so no text disappears off the side of the screen.

To switch the document to Normal view, choose View ➤ Normal.

NOTE Another Word option that's almost a separate view is Draft Font view, a relic of the Draft View of Word versions 2.0x and earlier. Draft Font view, located in the Show box on the Options Dialog box's View tab, is now an option that you choose for Normal or Outline view. Draft font view uses standard fonts (with underline to indicate any form of emphasis, such as bold or italic) in order to speed up the display of text; for most purposes, it's hardly worth using in this version of Word.

Page Layout View

Page Layout view is useful for getting a rough idea of how your documents will look when you print them. In Page Layout view, Word shows you the margins of the sheet or sheets of paper you're working on, any headers or footers, and any footnotes or annotations. Word doesn't wrap text to the size of the window because doing so would change the page from its printable format.

To switch to Page Layout view, choose View ➤ Page Layout. You'll see an approximation of the layout of your document, complete with margins (see Figure 5.6). If necessary, zoom to a more appropriate zoom percentage (see *Zooming the View*, a couple of blocks south of here).

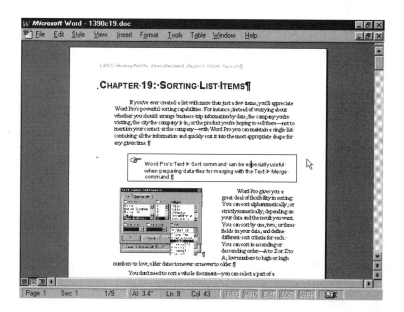

FIGURE 5.6:
Page Layout view shows you where each element in your document will really appear.

Print Preview

Word's *Print Preview* provides a way for you to scan your documents on screen for formatting howlers before you actually immortalize them on dead trees. Print Preview shows you, as closely as Word knows how, the effect you'll get when you print your document on the currently selected printer. We'll look at Print Preview in detail in Chapter 8.

Outline View

Word's *Outline view* lets you collapse your documents to a specified number of heading levels—for example, you could choose to view only the first-level heads in your documents or the first three levels of heads. Outline view is very useful for structuring long documents and is somewhat more complex than the other views. We'll examine it in detail in Chapter 11.

Zooming the View

In any of Word's views, you can use the Zoom feature to increase or decrease the size of the display to make it easily visible. Word lets you set any zoom percentage between 10 percent and 200 percent of full size.

You can use either the Zoom box on the Standard toolbar or the Zoom dialog box to set the zoom percentage.

Zooming with the Zoom Box on the Standard Toolbar

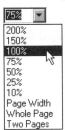

To zoom the view with the Zoom box on the Standard toolbar:

1. Display the Standard toolbar if it isn't visible.
2. Click the button to the right of the Zoom box to display a drop-down list of zoom percentages.
3. Choose a zoom percentage from the drop-down list or type in a different percentage (between 10% and 200%).

Zooming with the Zoom Dialog Box

To zoom the view with the Zoom dialog box:

1. Choose View ➤ Zoom to display the Zoom dialog box.
2. In the Zoom To box, choose the zoom percentage you want:
    *   To zoom to 200%, 100%, 75%, Page Width, or Whole Page (which is available only in Page Layout view and Print Preview), click the appropriate option button in the Zoom To box.
    *   To display more than one page at a time (only in Page Layout view and Print Preview), click the monitor next to the Many Pages option button and drag it through the grid that appears to indicate the configuration of pages you want to view: 2x2 pages, 2x3 pages, and so on.
    *   To display the page or pages at a precise zoom percentage of your choosing, adjust the setting in the Percent box.
3. Click the OK button to apply the zoom percentage you've selected.

Split-Screen View

Word also offers split-screen view, in which the screen is divided into two panes. You can use a different view in each pane and can zoom each pane to a different zoom percentage.

To split the screen, choose Window ➢ Split. The mouse pointer will change to a double-headed arrow pointing up and down and dragging a thick gray line. Move the line up or down the screen to where you want to split it and then click to place the line. Figure 5.7 shows a split window.

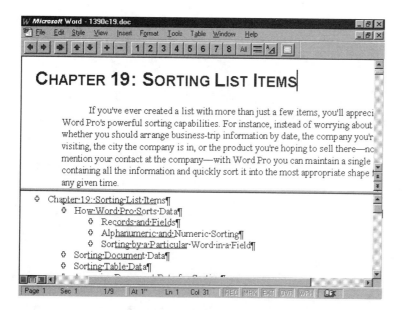

FIGURE 5.7:
Choose Window ➢ Split to split the screen into two panes. You can then work in a different view or at a different zoom percentage in each pane.

To remove the split screen, choose Window ➢ Remove Split.

TIP   To split the window in half quickly, double-click the *split bar*, the tiny horizontal bar at the top of the vertical scroll bar. Double-click the split bar again to remove the split screen.

Chapter 6

SIMPLE FORMATTING

- **Formatting characters and words**
- **Formatting paragraphs**
- **Setting indents and line spacing**
- **Setting and using tabs**

Word supplies you with enough formatting options to typeset a long work of moderate complexity. The basic types of formatting options start with character formatting—how the individual letters look—and move through paragraph formatting—how paragraphs appear on the page—to style formatting (which combines character and paragraph formatting, among other formatting) and finally page setup. In this chapter, we'll look at character and paragraph formatting; in the next chapter, we'll look at the more advanced types of formatting.

Character Formatting

Character formatting is formatting that you can apply to one or more characters in a document. Character formatting consists of

- character attributes, such as **bold**, *italic*, <u>underline</u>, and ~~strikethrough~~ (among others).
- fonts (different styles for text characters; also known as *typefaces*), such as Courier New, Times New Roman, and Arial.
- a font size—the size of the font (measured in points).
- character spacing, such as superscripts and subscripts (vertical spacing), and kerning (horizontal spacing).

You can apply character formatting in several ways—using the Font dialog box, using keyboard shortcuts, or by using the Formatting toolbar. Each of these has advantages and disadvantages depending on what you're doing when you decide to start applying formatting and how much of it you need to apply. Let's look at each of them in turn.

Character Formatting Using the Font Dialog Box

The Font dialog box offers you the most control over font formatting, providing all the character-formatting options together in one handy location.

To set character formatting using the Font dialog box:

1. Select the text whose formatting you want to change. If you want to change the formatting of just one word, place the insertion point inside it.

2. Choose Format ➤ Font to display the Font dialog box (see Figure 6.1). If the Font tab isn't displayed, click it to bring it to the front of the dialog box.

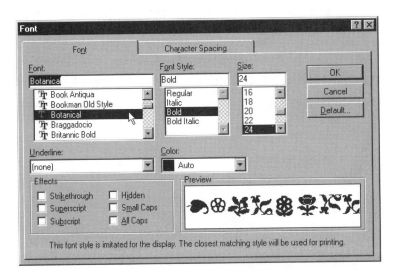

FIGURE 6.1:
The Font dialog box gives you quick access to all the character-formatting options Word offers.

3. Choose the formatting options you want from the Font tab:
    - In the Font list box, choose the font (or typeface) for the text.
    - In the Font Style list box, choose the font style: Regular, Italic, Bold, or Bold Italic.

TIP   Watch the Preview box at the bottom right corner of the dialog box to see approximately how your text will look.

- In the Size box, choose the font size you want. To choose a font size between two of the sizes Word offers, type it into the top Size box—for example, enter 13 to produce 13-point text. (Word offers 12-point and 14-point options in the list box.)
- In the Underline box, choose the underlining style you want: None, Single, Words Only (single underline underneath words, no underline underneath spaces), Double, or Dotted.
- Select any special effects you want in the Effects group box by clicking the check boxes for Strikethrough, Superscript, Subscript, Hidden, Small Caps, or All Caps. (Hidden text is invisible under normal viewing conditions and does not print unless you choose to include it.)
- Finally, choose a color for your text from the Color drop-down list. This will affect the text on screen—and on printouts if you have a color printer.

4. For special effects, try adjusting the settings on the Character Spacing tab of the Font dialog box.
    - The Spacing option controls the horizontal placement of letters relative to each other—closer to each other, or further apart. From the Spacing drop-down list, you can choose Expanded or Condensed, then use the up and down spinner arrows in the By box to adjust the degree of expansion or condensation. (Alternatively, simply click the spinner arrows and let Word worry about making the Spacing drop-list match your choice.) Again, watch the Preview box for a simulation of the effect your current choices will have.
    - The Position option controls the vertical placement of letters relative to the baseline they're theoretically resting on. From the Position list, you can choose Normal, Raised, or Lowered, then use the spinner arrows in the By box to raise or lower the letters—or simply click the spinner arrows and let Word determine whether the text is Normal, Raised, or Lowered.

- To turn on automatic kerning for fonts above a certain size, select the Kerning for Fonts check box and adjust the point size in the Points and Above box if necessary.

> **NOTE**
>
> *Kerning* is adjusting the space between letters so no letter appears too far from its neighbor. For example, if you type WAVE in a large font size without kerning, Word will leave enough space between the W and the A, and the A and the V, for you to slalom a small truck through. With kerning, you'll only be able to get a motorcycle through the gap.

5. When you've finished making your choices in the Font dialog box, click the OK button to close the dialog box and apply your changes to the selected text or current word.

Setting a New Default Font

To set a new default font for all documents based on the current template, make all your choices on the Font and Character Spacing tabs of the Font dialog box, then click the Default button (on either tab). Word will display a message box to confirm that you want to change the default font. Click Yes to make the change.

Character Formatting Using the Formatting Toolbar

The Formatting toolbar offers a quick way to apply some of the most used character formatting options: font, font size, bold, italic, underline, and highlighting (see Figure 6.2).

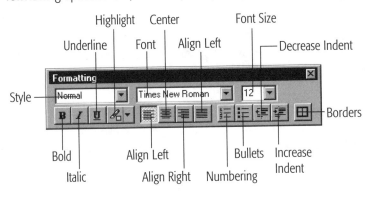

FIGURE 6.2: The Formatting toolbar provides a quick way to apply formatting to your documents.

To change font with the Formatting toolbar, select the text you want to affect, then click the drop-down list button on the Font box and select the new font from the list that appears.

- The fonts you've used most recently will be listed at the top of the list, with an alphabetical listing of all the fonts underneath that.
- To move quickly down the list of fonts to the one you want, type the first letter of the font's name.

To change the font size, select the text to change, then click the drop-down list button on the Font Size box and select the font size from the list that appears.

> **TIP**
>
> **To change the font or font size of just one word, you don't need to select it—just placing the insertion point within the word is enough.**

To apply bold, italic, or underline, select the text you want to emphasize, then click the Bold, Italic, or Underline button on the Formatting toolbar. When you've applied one of these attributes, the relevant button will appear to be pushed in.

> **NOTE**
>
> **To remove bold, italic, or underline, select the emphasized text, then click the Bold, Italic, or Underline button to remove the formatting.**

To apply highlighting to one instance of text, select the text and click the Highlight button.

To apply highlighting to several instances of text easily, click the Highlight button before selecting any text. Your mouse pointer will grow a little highlighter pen. Drag this over text to highlight it.

To turn the highlighting off, click the Highlight button again or press the Esc key.

To change the color of the highlighting, click the drop-down list arrow next to the Highlight button and choose another color from the list. (The default color for highlighting is the classic fluorescent yellow—Enhanced French Headlamp, as it's known in the trade—beloved of anyone who's ever had a highlighter pen break in their shirt pocket.)

To remove highlighting, drag the highlighter pen over the highlighted text again.

Character Formatting Using Keyboard Shortcuts

Word offers the following keyboard shortcuts for formatting text with the keyboard. For all of them, select the text you want to affect first, unless you want to affect only the word in which the insertion point is currently resting.

Action	Shortcut
Increase font size (in steps)	Ctrl+Shift+>
Decrease font size (in steps)	Ctrl+Shift+<
Increase font size by 1 point	Ctrl+]
Decrease font size by 1 point	Ctrl+[
Change case (cycle)	Shift+F3
All capitals	Ctrl+Shift+A
Small capitals	Ctrl+Shift+K
Bold	Ctrl+B
Underline	Ctrl+U
Underline (single words)	Ctrl+Shift+W
Double-underline	Ctrl+Shift+D
Hidden text	Ctrl+Shift+H
Italic	Ctrl+I
Subscript	Ctrl+=
Superscript	Ctrl+Shift+= (i.e., Ctrl++)
Remove formatting	Ctrl+Shift+Z
Change to Symbol font	Ctrl+Shift+Q

Paragraph Formatting

With paragraph formatting, you can set a number of parameters that influence how your paragraphs in Word look: alignment, indentation, line spacing, text flow, and tabs. The following sections discuss each of these paragraph-formatting options in turn.

Setting Alignment

Word offers you several ways to set paragraph alignment: You can use the alignment buttons on the Formatting toolbar, or the keyboard shortcuts, or the options in the Paragraph dialog box. Using the buttons on the Formatting toolbar is the easiest way, and the one you'll probably find yourself using most often, so we'll look at that first.

Setting Alignment Using the Formatting Toolbar

To set alignment using the Formatting toolbar:

1. Place the insertion point in the paragraph that you want to align. To align two or more paragraphs, select them.

2. Click the Align Left, Center, Align Right, or Justify button on the Formatting toolbar (see Figure 6.3).

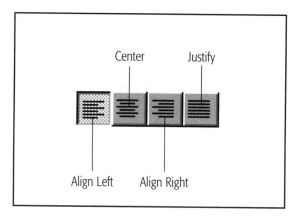

FIGURE 6.3:
To align the current paragraph or selected text quickly, click the appropriate button on the Formatting toolbar.

Setting Alignment Using Keyboard Shortcuts

When you're typing, the quickest way to set the alignment of paragraphs is by using these keyboard shortcuts:

Shortcut	Effect
Ctrl+L	Align left
Ctrl+E	Center
Ctrl+R	Align right
Ctrl+J	Justify

Setting Alignment Using the Paragraph Dialog Box

The third way of setting alignment—and usually the slowest—is to use the Paragraph dialog box. Why discuss this? Because you're very likely to be making other formatting changes in the Paragraph dialog box, so sometimes you may find it useful to set alignment there too.

To set alignment using the Paragraph dialog box:

1. Place the insertion point in the paragraph you want to align. To align two or more paragraphs, select them.
2. Choose Format ➤ Paragraph to display the Paragraph dialog box (see Figure 6.4).

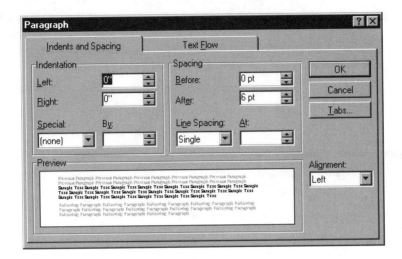

FIGURE 6.4:
In the Paragraph dialog box, you can set many paragraph-formatting options, including alignment.

3. Choose the alignment you want from the Alignment drop-down list.
4. Click the OK button to close the Paragraph dialog box.

Setting Indents

As with setting alignment, you can set indents in more than one way. Again, the quickest way is with the ruler, but you can also use the Paragraph dialog box and some obscure keyboard shortcuts.

Setting Indents with the Ruler

To set indents using the ruler, click and drag the indent markers on the ruler (see Figure 6.5).

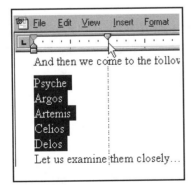

FIGURE 6.5:
Click and drag the indent markers on the ruler to change the indentation of the current paragraph or selected paragraphs.

- The first-line indent marker specifies the indentation of the first line of the paragraph (including a hanging indent, if any).
- The left-margin marker specifies the position of the left margin.

NOTE To move the left-margin marker and first-line indent marker together, drag the left margin marker by the square box at its base rather than by the upward-pointing mark, which will move the left-margin marker but leave the first-line indent marker where it was.

- The right-margin marker specifies the position of the right margin.

Setting Indents with the Paragraph Dialog Box

Depending on whether you have a graphical or literal mindset, you may find setting indents in the Paragraph dialog box easier than setting them with the ruler.

To set paragraph indents with the Paragraph dialog box:

1. Place the insertion point in the paragraph for which you want to set indents. To set indents for two or more paragraphs, select them.
2. Choose Format ➤ Paragraph to display the Paragraph dialog box.
3. Make sure the Indents and Spacing tab is selected (if it's not visible, click it to bring it in front of the Text Flow tab).
4. In the Left box, enter the distance to indent the paragraph from the left margin.
5. In the Right box, enter the distance to indent the paragraph from the right margin.
6. In the Special box, choose from (none), First Line, and Hanging:
   - (none) formats the paragraph as a regular paragraph, with indents controlled solely by the Left and Right settings.
   - First Line adds an indent to the first line of the paragraph. This indent is in addition to the Left setting. For example, if you choose a Left setting of 0.5″ and a First Line setting of 0.5″, the first line of the paragraph will be indented one inch.

TIP Use a first-line indent instead of a tab to start off your paragraphs.

   - Hanging makes the first line of the paragraph hang out to the left of the rest of the paragraph. (Excessively logical people call this an *outdent*.) Hanging indents are great for bulleted or numbered paragraphs—the bullet or number hangs way out to the left of the paragraph, and the wrapped lines of the paragraph align neatly with the first line.

- Figure 6.6 illustrates the different types of indentation Word provides for paragraphs.

- **Hanging indents** are most useful for bulleted lists and the like, so that the bullet stands clear of the text.

    First-line indents save you from using tabs at the start of each paragraph and can make your documents appear more professional to the viewer. The second and subsequent lines are flush left.

    This paragraph is **not indented at all** and looks suitably dense as a result. If you're going to use no indentation, set extra space between paragraphs so that the reader can see where any paragraph ends and the next starts.

    > To set off a quotation, you may want to **indent it from both margins**. That way, the reader's eye can swiftly jump to it and isolate it on the page. Common practice is to run shorter quotations into the paragraph in which you quote them (using quotation marks), but to have longer quotations self-standing like this. You might also want to use a smaller font size.

FIGURE 6.6: Word provides these different types of indentation for formatting paragraphs.

---

7. If you chose a Special setting of First Line or Hanging, enter a measurement in the By box.

8. Click the OK button to close the Paragraph dialog box.

NOTE When setting indents, you can use negative values for Left and Right indents to make the text protrude beyond the margin. Negative indents can be useful for special effects, but if you find yourself using them all the time, you probably need to adjust your margins. One other thing—for obvious reasons, you can't set a negative hanging indent, no matter how hard you try.

Setting Indents Using Keyboard Shortcuts

Here are the keyboard shortcuts for setting indents:

Action	Shortcut
Indent from the left	Ctrl+M
Remove indent from the left	Ctrl+Shift+M
Create (or increase) a hanging indent	Ctrl+T
Reduce (or remove) a hanging indent	Ctrl+Shift+T
Remove paragraph formatting	Ctrl+Q

Choosing Measurement Units

You may have noticed that the measurement units (inches, centimeters, etc.) in the Paragraph dialog box on your computer are different from those in the screens shown here—for example, you might be seeing measurements in centimeters or picas rather than in inches.

If so, don't worry. Word lets you work in any of four measurements: inches, centimeters, points, and picas. Points and picas – $1/72$ of an inch and $1/6$ of an inch, respectively— are most useful for page layout and typesetting, but if you're not doing those, you might want to switch between inches and centimeters.

To change your measurement units:

1. Choose Tools ➤ Options to display the Options dialog box.
2. Click the General tab to bring it to the front.
3. Click the Measurement Units drop-down list to drop the list down.
4. Choose Inches, Centimeters, Points, or Picas as your measurement unit.
5. Click the OK button to close the Options dialog box.

Setting Line Spacing

You can change the line spacing of your documents by using either the Paragraph dialog box or keyboard shortcuts:

1. Select the paragraphs whose line spacing you want to change.

NOTE To select the whole document quickly, choose Edit ➤ Select All, or hold down the Ctrl key and click once in the selection bar at the left edge of the Word window. Alternatively, press Ctrl+5 (that's the 5 on the numeric keypad, not the 5 in the row above the letters R and T).

2. Choose Format ➤ Paragraph to display the Paragraph dialog box (shown in Figure 6.4 earlier).

3. If the Indents and Spacing tab isn't at the front of the Paragraph dialog box, click it to bring it to the front.

4. Use the Line Spacing drop-down list to choose the line spacing you want:

Line Spacing	Effect
Single	Single spacing, based on the point size of the font.
1.5 lines	Line-and-a-half spacing, based on the point size of the font.
Double	Double spacing based on the point size of the font.
At least	Sets a minimum spacing for the lines, measured in points. This can be useful for including fonts of different sizes in a paragraph, or for including in-line graphics.
Exactly	Sets the exact spacing for the lines, measured in points.
Multiple	Multiple line spacing, set by the number in the At box to the right of the Line Spacing drop-down list. For example, to use triple line spacing, enter 3 in the At box; to use quadruple line spacing, enter 4.

5. If you chose At Least, Exactly, or Multiple in the Line Spacing drop-down list, adjust the setting in the At box if necessary.

6. Click the OK button to apply the line spacing setting to the chosen text.

TIP

To set line spacing with the keyboard, press Ctrl+1 to single-space the selected paragraphs, Ctrl+5 to set 1.5-line spacing, and Ctrl+2 to double-space paragraphs.

Setting Spacing Before and After Paragraphs

As well as setting the line spacing within any paragraph, you can adjust the amount of space before and after any paragraph to position it more effectively on the page. So instead of using two blank lines (i.e., two extra paragraphs with no text) before a heading and one blank line afterwards, you can adjust the paragraph spacing to give the heading plenty of space without using any blank lines at all.

TIP The easiest way to set consistent spacing before and after paragraphs of a particular type is to use Word's *styles*, which we'll discuss in the next chapter.

To set the spacing before and after a paragraph:

1. Place the insertion point in the paragraph whose spacing you want to adjust, or select several paragraphs to adjust their spacing all at once.
2. Choose Format ➤ Paragraph to display the Paragraph dialog box (shown in Figure 6.4).
3. Make sure the Indents and Spacing tab is foremost. If it isn't, click it to bring it to the front.
4. In the Spacing box, choose a Before setting to specify the number of points of space before the selected paragraph. Watch the Preview box for the approximate effect this change will have.
5. Choose an After setting to specify the number of points of space after the current paragraph. Again, watch the Preview box.

NOTE The Before setting for a paragraph adds to the After setting for the paragraph before it; it does not change it. For example, if the previous paragraph has an After setting of 12 points, and you specify a Before setting of 12 points for the current paragraph, you'll end up with 24 points of space between the two paragraphs (on top of the line spacing you've set).

6. Click the OK button to close the Paragraph dialog box and apply the changes.

TIP Word also has a feature for quickly adding or removing one line's worth of space before a paragraph: Press Ctrl+0 (Ctrl+zero).

Using the Text Flow Options

Word offers six options for controlling how your text flows from page to page in the document. To use them, click in the paragraph you want to apply them to, or select a number of paragraphs. Then choose Format ➤ Paragraph to display the Paragraph dialog box, click the Text Flow tab to bring it to the front of the dialog box (unless it's already at the front), and select the options you want to use:

- Widow/Orphan Control tells Word to rearrange your documents to avoid widows and orphans. A *widow* (in typesetting parlance) is when the last line of a paragraph appears on its own at the top of a page; an *orphan* is when the first line of a paragraph appears by itself at the foot of a page.
- Keep Lines Together tells Word to prevent the paragraph from breaking over a page. If the whole paragraph will not fit on the current page, Word moves it to the next page.

WARNING If you write long paragraphs, choosing the Keep Lines Together option can produce painfully short pages.

- Keep with Next tells Word to prevent a page break from occurring between this paragraph and the next. Use this option to make sure that a heading appears on the same page as the paragraph of text following it, or that an illustration appears together with its caption, but be careful not to use it for body text paragraphs.
- Page Break Before tells Word to force a page break before the current paragraph. This is useful for making sure that, for example, each section of a report starts on a new page.
- Suppress Line Numbers tells Word to turn off line numbers for the current paragraph. This applies only if you are using line numbering in your document.
- Don't Hyphenate tells Word to skip the current paragraph for automatic hyphenation.

When you've chosen the options you want, click the OK button to apply them to the paragraph or paragraphs.

Setting Tabs

To align the text in your documents, Word offers five kinds of tabs: left-aligned (the conventional kind), centered, right-aligned, decimal-aligned (right-aligned on the decimal point), and bar (|).

Setting Tabs Using the Ruler

The quickest way to set tabs for the current paragraph, or for a few paragraphs, is to use the ruler (choose View ➤ Ruler to display the ruler if it isn't visible).

Adding a Tab

L — LEFT TAB
⊥ — CENTER TAB
⅃ — RIGHT TAB
⅃. DECIMAL TAB.

To add a tab, display the ruler if necessary, then:

1. Select the paragraph or paragraphs to which you want to add the tab.
2. Choose the type of tab you want by clicking the tab selector button at the left end of the ruler to cycle through left tab, center tab, right tab, and decimal tab.

3. Click in the ruler where you want to add the tab. The tab mark will appear in the ruler.

> **TIP**
>
> When adding a tab, you can click with either the left or the right mouse button. For moving or removing a tab, only the left button works. Don't ask.

Moving a Tab

To move a tab, display the ruler if necessary, then click the tab marker and drag it to where you want it.

Removing a Tab

To remove a tab, display the ruler if it's not visible, then click the marker for the tab you want to remove and drag it into the document. The tab marker will disappear from the ruler.

Setting Tabs Using the Tabs Dialog Box

When you need to check exactly where the tabs are in a paragraph, or if you set too many tabs in the ruler and get confused, turn to the Tabs dialog box to clear everything up.

First, select the paragraphs whose tabs you want to change, then choose Format ➤ Tabs to display the Tabs dialog box (see Figure 6.7) and follow the procedures described in the next sections.

> **NOTE**
>
> To quickly display the Tabs dialog box, double-click in the bottom half of the ruler. (Make sure the mouse pointer is in the bottom half of the ruler—otherwise, Word will display the Page Setup dialog box.). The only problem with this, at least in the early releases of Word for Windows 95, is that the first click places a tab even though you don't want it to . . . . You can also get to the Tabs dialog box quickly by clicking the Tabs button on either panel of the Paragraph dialog box.

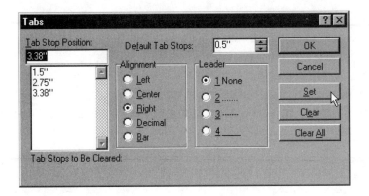

FIGURE 6.7:
The Tabs dialog box gives you fine control over the placement and types of tabs in your document.

Setting Default Tabs

To set a different spacing for default tabs, adjust the setting in the Default Tab Stops box at the top of the Tabs dialog box. For example, a setting of 1" will produce tabs at 1", 2", 3", and so on.

Setting Tabs

To set tabs:

1. Enter a position in the Tab Stop Position box.
    -   If you're using the default unit of measurement set in the copy of Word you're using, you don't need to specify the units.
    -   If you want to use another unit of measurement, specify it: 2.3", 11 cm, 22 pi, 128 pt.
2. Specify the tab alignment in the Alignment box: Left, Center, Right, Decimal, or Bar. (Bar inserts a vertical bar—|—before the text for specialized purposes.)
3. In the Leader box, specify a tab leader if you want one: periods, hyphens, or underlines leading up to the tabbed text. (Periods are often used as tab leaders for tables of contents, between the heading and the page number.)
4. Click the Set button.
5. Repeat steps 1 through 4 to specify more tabs if necessary.
6. Click the OK button to close the Tabs dialog box and apply the tabs you set.

Clearing Tabs

To clear a tab, select it in the Tab Stop Position list and click the Clear button. Word will list the tab you chose in the Tab Stops to Be Cleared area at the bottom of the Tabs dialog box. Choose other tabs to clear if necessary, then click the OK button.

To clear all tabs, simply click the Clear All button, then click the OK button.

Moving Tabs

To move tabs using the Tabs dialog box, you need to clear them from their current position and then set them elsewhere—you can't move them as such. (To move tabs easily, use the ruler method described earlier in this chapter.)

Chapter 7

PAGE LAYOUT AND STYLES

- **Using language formatting**
- **Applying borders and shading**
- **Creating and using styles**
- **Setting up the page**
- **Using Word's AutoFormat options**
- **Creating headers and footers**

In this chapter, we'll look at the more advanced formatting features that Word offers. You can format text as being in one language or another (which is useful for spelling checks and Find operations); you can add borders and shading to paragraphs or other elements; you can use styles to apply complex formatting quickly to different paragraphs; and you can set up Word to use various different sizes of paper.

Language Formatting

You can format text as being written in a language other than English. Not only can you then spell-check the text written in other languages, but you can use the Find feature to search for text formatted in those languages for quick reference. (Chapter 3 discusses spell checking, while Chapter 11 discusses advanced use of Find.)

To format selected text written in another language:

1. Choose Tools ➤ Language to display the Language dialog box.
2. In the Mark Selected Text As list box, choose the language in which to format the text.
3. Click OK to apply the language formatting to the selected text.

Borders and Shading

If a picture or a part of your text needs more emphasis, select it and add borders and shading:

1. Choose Format ➤ Borders and Shading to display one of the Borders and Shading dialog boxes.

NOTE Just which Borders and Shading dialog box Word will display depends on what you have selected: Text will produce the Paragraph Borders and Shading dialog box; a picture will produce the Picture Borders dialog box (no shading, because you shouldn't need to shade a picture); a table will produce the Table Borders and Shading dialog box, and so on. Figure 7.1 shows the Paragraph Borders and Shading dialog box.

2. On the Borders tab, choose the type of border you want to add from the options displayed:
   - In the Presets box, choose None, Box, or Shadow (for tables and cells, you'll get Grid instead of Shadow). Watch the effect in the Border demonstration box.
   - In the Line group box, choose the type of line you want from the Style list, and choose a color from the Color drop-down list if you want. To change all

the lines shown in the Border demonstration box at once, choose a type of line from the Style list. To change one of the lines, click the line in the Border demonstration box to select it (and remove it), and then choose the type of line you want from the Style list and click again where the line was in the Border demonstration box to place the new line.

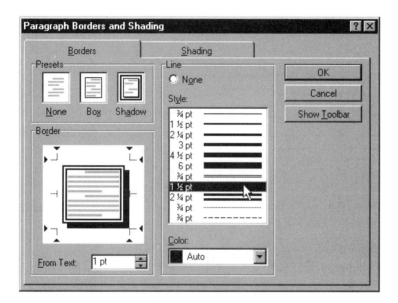

FIGURE 7.1:
The Paragraph Borders and Shading dialog box is one of the many Borders and Shading dialog boxes that Word produces for different elements.

- For paragraphs, specify a From Text setting to adjust the distance between the border and the text. (This option is not available in tables.)

3.   On the Shading tab, choose the type of shading to add:

- Click in the Shading list box to activate the Custom option button and choose the intensity of shading: Clear, Solid (100%), one of the options from 5% through 90%, or one of the striped or gridded options further down the list. Watch the Preview box for the effect this will have.

WARNING   Any shading over 20 percent will completely mask text on most black-and-white print-outs (even if it looks wonderfully artistic on screen).

- Adjust the colors in the Foreground and Background drop-down lists if necessary to fine-tune the visual effect.

4.   Click OK to close the Borders and Shading dialog box and apply your changes to the selection.

TIP

To remove borders and shading, select the item, then choose Format ➤ Borders and Shading to display the Borders and Shading dialog box. To remove a border, choose None in the Presets box on the Borders tab; to remove shading, choose None in the Fill group box on the Shading tab. Click OK to close the Borders and Shading dialog box.

Style Formatting

Word's paragraph styles bring together all the formatting elements discussed in the previous chapter and the early part of this chapter—character formatting, paragraph formatting (including alignment), tabs, language formatting, and even borders and shading. Each style contains complete formatting information that you can apply with one click of the mouse or one keystroke.

NOTE

Word also offers character styles, which are similar to paragraph styles but contain only character formatting. Character styles are suitable for picking out elements in a paragraph formatted with paragraph styles.

Using styles not only gives your documents a consistent look—every Heading 1 paragraph will appear in the same font and font size, with the same amount of space before and after it, etc.—but also saves you a great deal of time in formatting your documents.

You can either use Word's built-in styles—which are different in Word's various predefined templates—or create your own styles. Every paragraph in Word uses a style; Word starts you off in the Normal style unless the template you're using dictates otherwise.

Applying Styles

To apply a style, place the insertion point in the paragraph or choose a number of paragraphs, then click the Style drop-down list button on the Formatting toolbar and choose the style you want from the list, as shown here.

TIP **Some of the most popular styles have keyboard shortcuts: Ctrl+Shift+N for Normal style; Ctrl+Alt+1 for Heading 1, Ctrl+Alt+2 for Heading 2, Ctrl+Alt+3 for Heading 3; and Ctrl+Shift+L for List style.**

You can also apply a style by choosing Format ➢ Style to display the Style dialog box (see Figure 7.2), then choosing the style in the Styles list box and clicking the Apply button.

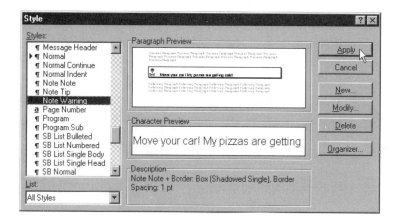

FIGURE 7.2:
To apply a style, choose it in the Styles list box in the Style dialog box (Format ➢ Style) and click the Apply button.

The style name of the current paragraph appears in the Style box on the Formatting toolbar. To see at a glance which style multiple paragraphs are in, you can display the style area, a vertical bar at the left side of the Word window that displays the style name for each paragraph as shown here. To display the style area, choose Tools ➢ Options to display the Options dialog box

and click the View tab to bring it to the front. Enter a measurement in the Style Area Width box in the Window group box and then click OK.

NOTE **You cannot display the style area in Page Layout view or Print Preview.**

Creating a New Style

As you can see in the Styles list box shown in Figure 7.3, Word's templates come with a number of built-in styles. If they're not enough for you, you can create your own styles.

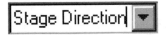

The easiest way to create a style is to set up a paragraph of text with the exact formatting you want for the style—character formatting, paragraph formatting, borders and shading, bullets or numbers, and so on. Then click in the Style list text box, type the name for the new style into the box, and press Enter.

The more complex way of creating a style is as follows:

1. Choose Format ➤ Style to display the Style dialog box (shown in Figure 7.2).
2. Click the New button. Word will display the New Style dialog box (see Figure 7.3).

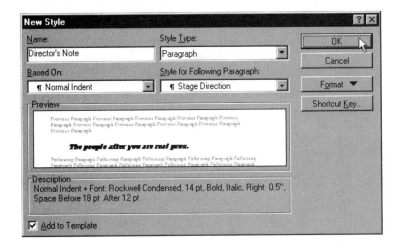

FIGURE 7.3:
Creating a new style in the New Style dialog box

3. Set the information for your new style:
    *   In the Name box, enter a name for the style. Style names can be a decent length—Word will accept over 100 characters—but you'll do better to keep them short enough to fit in the Style box on the Formatting toolbar. If your style name is over 20 characters long, you should probably rethink your naming conventions.
    *   In the Based On drop-down list box, choose the style on which you want to base the new style. Bear in mind that if you change the other style later, the new style will change too. The Preview box will show what the Based On style looks like.
    *   In the Style Type box, choose whether you want a paragraph style or a character style.

- In the Style for Following Paragraph box, choose the style that you want Word to apply to the paragraph immediately after this style. For example, after the Heading 1 style, you might want Body Text, or after Figure, you might want Caption. But for many styles you'll want to continue with the style itself.

4. To adjust the formatting of the style, click the Format button and choose Font, Paragraph, Tabs, Border, Language, Frame, or Numbering from the drop-down list. This will display the dialog box for that type of formatting. When you've finished, click the OK button to return to the New Style dialog box.

5. Repeat step 4 as necessary, selecting other formatting characteristics for the style.

6. Select the Add to Template check box to add the new style to the template.

7. To set up a shortcut key for the style, click the Shortcut Key button. Word will display the Customize dialog box. With the insertion point in the Press New Shortcut Key box, press the shortcut key combination you'd like to set, click the Assign button, then click the Close button.

> **WARNING**
>
> Watch the Currently Assigned To area of the Customize dialog box when selecting your shortcut key combination. If Word already has assigned that key combination to a command, macro, or style, it will display its name there. If you choose to assign the key combination to the new style, the old combination will be deactivated.

8. In the New Style dialog box, click the OK button to return to the Style dialog box.

9. To create another new style, repeat steps 2 through 8.

10. To close the Style dialog box, click the Apply button to apply the new style to the current paragraph or current selection, or click the Close button to save the new style without applying it.

Modifying a Style

Modifying a Word style is similar to creating a new style, except that you work in the Modify Style dialog box, which offers one fewer option than the New Style dialog box does—you don't get to choose whether the style is a paragraph style or a character style because Word already knows which it is.

Open the Style dialog box by choosing Format ➤ Style, then choose the style you want to work on from the Styles list. (If you can't see the style you're looking for, make sure the

List box at the bottom-left corner of the Style dialog box is showing All Styles rather than Styles in Use or User-Defined Styles.)

Click the Modify button. Word will display the Modify Style dialog box. From there, follow steps 3 to 8 in the previous section to modify the style and step 10 to leave the Style dialog box.

Removing a Style

Removing a style is much faster than creating one. Simply open the Style dialog box by choosing Format ➤ Style, select the style to delete in the Styles list, and click the Delete button. Word will display a message box confirming that you want to delete the style; click the Yes button.

You can then delete another style the same way or click the Close button to leave the Style dialog box.

Using the Style Gallery

Word provides the Style Gallery to give you a quick overview of its many templates and the myriad styles they contain. To open the Style Gallery, choose Format ➤ Style Gallery. Word will display the Style Gallery dialog box (see Figure 7.4).

To preview a template in the Preview Of box, select it in the Template list box. Then choose the preview you want in the Preview box:

- Document shows you how your current document looks with the template's styles applied.

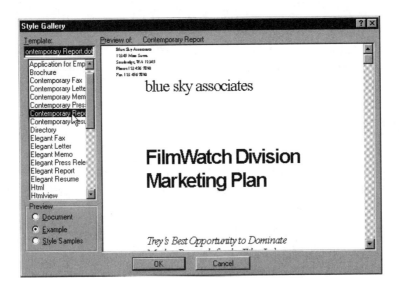

FIGURE 7.4:
The Style Gallery dialog box gives you a quick view of the styles in Word's templates.

- Example shows you a sample document that uses the template's styles.
- Style Samples shows each of the styles in the document.

To apply the template you've chosen to your document, click the OK button. Alternatively, click the Cancel button to close the Style Gallery.

Page Setup

NOTE | The best time to set paper size is at the beginning of a project. While you can change it at any time during a project without trouble, having the right size (and orientation) of paper from the start will help you lay out your material.

If you're ever going to print a document, you need to tell Word how it should appear on the page. You can change the margins, the paper size, the layout of the paper, and even which printer tray it comes from (which we'll look at in Chapter 8).

To alter the page setup, choose File ➤ Page Setup to display the Page Setup dialog box, then follow the instructions for setting margins, paper size, and paper orientation in the next sections. (If you want to change the page setup for only one section of a document, place the insertion point in the section you want to change before displaying the Page Setup dialog box. Alternatively, you can choose This Point Forward from the Apply To drop-down list on any tab of the Page Setup dialog box to change the page setup for the rest of the document.

TIP | To quickly display the Page Setup dialog box, double-click in the top half of the ruler. (Double-clicking in the bottom half of the ruler displays the Tabs dialog box, so be precise.)

Setting Margins

To set the margins for your document, click the Margins tab in the Page Setup dialog box (see Figure 7.5). In the boxes for Top, Bottom, Left, and Right margins, use the spinner arrows to enter the measurement you want for each margin; alternatively, type in a measurement.

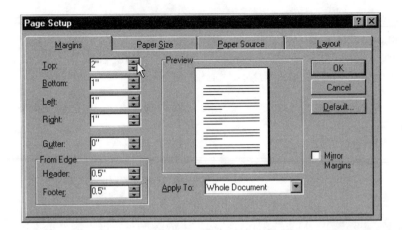

FIGURE 7.5:
The Margins tab of
the Page Setup
dialog box

NOTE

The unit of measurement is controlled by the Measurement Units setting on the General tab of the Options dialog box. You can choose inches, points ($1/72$ of an inch), centimeters, or picas (six points, or $1/6$ of an inch).

If you're typesetting documents (rather than simply using the word processor to put them together), you may want to check the Mirror Margins check box. This makes the two inner-margin measurements the same as each other; the two outer-margin measurements the same as each other; and changes the Left and Right settings in the column under Margins in the Page Setup dialog box to Inside and Outside, respectively.

The Gutter measurement is the space that your document will have on the inside of each facing page. For example, if you're working with facing pages, you could choose to have a Gutter measurement of 1" and Inside and Outside margins of 1.25 inches. That way, your documents would appear with a 1.25" left margin on left-hand pages, a 1.25" inch right margin on right-hand pages, and a 2.25" margin on the inside of each page (the gutter plus the margin setting).

TIP

Use gutters for documents you're planning to bind. That way, you won't end up with text bound unreadably into the spine of the book.

Use the Preview box in the Page Setup dialog box to give you an idea of how your document will look when you print it.

Setting Paper Size

Word can print on paper of various sizes, offering a Custom option to allow you to set a peculiar paper size of your own, in addition to various standard paper and envelope sizes.

To change the size of the paper you're printing on, click the Paper Size tab of the Page Setup dialog box. In the Paper Size drop-down list box, choose the size of paper you'll be working with (for example, Letter 8.5x11 in). If you can't find the width and height of paper you want, use the Width and Height boxes to set the width and height of the paper you're using; Word will automatically set Custom Size in the Paper Size box.

Setting Paper Orientation

To change the orientation of the page you're working on, click the Paper Size tab of the Page Setup dialog box and choose Portrait or Landscape in the Orientation group box. (Portrait is taller than it is wide; Landscape is wider than it is tall.)

Section Formatting

Often you'll want to create documents that use different page layouts, or even different sizes of paper, for different pages. Word handles this by letting you divide documents into *sections*, each of which can have different formatting characteristics. For example, you could use sections to set up a document to contain both a letter and an envelope, or to have one-column text and then multi-column text, and so on.

Creating a Section

To create a section:

1. Place the insertion point where you want the new section to start.
2. Choose Insert ➤ Break. Word will display the Break dialog box.
3. Choose the type of section break to insert by clicking an option button in the Section Breaks group box:
   - Next Page starts the section on a new page. Use this when you have a drastic change in formatting between sections—for example, an envelope on one page and a letter on the next.
   - Continuous starts the section on the same page as the preceding paragraph. This is useful for creating layouts with differing numbers of columns on the same page.

- Even Page starts the section on a new even page.
- Odd Page starts the section on a new odd page. This is useful for chapters or sections that should start on a right-hand page for consistency.

4. Click the OK button to insert the section break. It will appear in Normal view and Outline view as a double dotted line across the page containing the words End of Section:

··End of Section··

The Sec indicator on the status bar will indicate which section you're in:

Page 28   Sec 12   28/89

TIP

You can change the type of section break on the Layout tab of the Page Setup dialog box (File ➢ Page Setup): Place the insertion point in the relevant section, then choose the type of section you want from the Section Start drop-down list and click the OK button.

Deleting a Section

To delete a section break, place the insertion point at its beginning (or select it) and press the Delete key.

WARNING

When you delete a section break, the section before the break will take on the formatting characteristics of the section after the break.

Using AutoFormat

To automate the formatting of documents, Word offers automatic formatting with its AutoFormat features: AutoFormat regular, which applies styles when you choose the Format ➢ AutoFormat command, and AutoFormat As You Type, which applies automatic formatting to paragraphs as you finish them.

To set AutoFormat options:

1. Choose Tools ➤ Options and click the AutoFormat tab of the Options dialog box to bring it to the front.
2. Choose the option button for AutoFormat or AutoFormat As You Type.
3. In the Apply or Apply As You Type box, check the boxes next to the auto-formatting options you want to use: for AutoFormat choose from Headings, Lists, Automatic Bulleted Lists, and Other Paragraphs, and for AutoFormat As You Type, choose from Headings, Borders, Automatic Bulleted Lists, and Automatic Numbered Lists.

Headings	Word applies Heading 1 style when you press Enter, type a short paragraph starting with a capital letter and press Enter twice; Word applies Heading 2 when that paragraph starts with a tab.
Automatic Numbered Lists	Word creates a numbered list when you type a number followed by a punctuation mark (such as a period, hyphen, or closing parenthesis), and then type a space or tab and some text.
Automatic Bulleted Lists	Word creates a bulleted list when you type a bullet-type character (e.g., a bullet, an asterisk, a hyphen, or a dash) and then a space or tab followed by text.
Borders	Word adds a border to a paragraph that follows a paragraph containing three or more dashes, under-scores, or equal signs: Dashes produce a thin line of dashes, underscores produce a thick line, and equal signs produce a double line.
Other Paragraph	Word applies styles based on what it judges your text to be.

4. Choose Replace As You Type options as necessary.
5. Click the OK button to close the Options dialog box.

TIP You can stop an automatic numbered or bulleted list by pressing Enter twice.

AutoFormat As You Type options will now spring into effect as you create your documents. If you decide to use the regular AutoFormat feature instead of AutoFormat As You Type, create your document and then choose Format ➤ AutoFormat. Word will display an AutoFormat dialog box, which lets you access the Options dialog box to refine your predefined AutoFormat settings if necessary.

Click the OK button to start autoformatting. When it's finished, Word will display another AutoFormat dialog box offering you the chance to review the changes, accept them, reject them, or visit the Style Gallery to choose a different look for your document.

Headers and Footers

Headers and footers give you an easy way to repeat identifying information on each page of your document. For example, in a header (across the top of each page), you might include the title of a document and the author, while in a footer (across the bottom of each page) you might include the file name, the date, and the page number out of the total number of pages in the document (e.g., *Page 1 of 9*).

You can repeat headers and footers throughout all the pages of your document or you can vary them from page to page. For example, if a proposal has two different authors, you might want to identify in the header which author wrote a particular part of the proposal. If you want to identify the different part titles in the header, you can easily display that, too. You can also arrange for odd pages to have different headers and footers from those on even pages, or for the first page in a document to have a different header and footer than subsequent pages.

Setting Headers and Footers

To include a header in your document:

1. Choose View ➤ Header and Footer. Word will display the page in Page Layout view and will display the Header and Footer toolbar (see Figure 7.6). Time

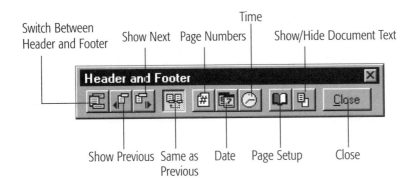

Switch Between
Header and Footer   Show Next   Page Numbers   Time   Show/Hide Document Text

Show Previous   Same as   Date   Page Setup   Close
                 Previous

FIGURE 7.6:

The Header and Footer toolbar offers nine buttons that help you produce headers and footers quickly and easily—and a Close button to get you out of the header or footer.

NOTE
Unlike some previous versions of Word that used a separate pane for headers and footers in Normal view, in Word 6 and Word for Windows 95, you can work with headers and footers only in Page Layout view and Print Preview. If you choose View ➤ Header and Footer from Normal view or Outline view, Word will switch you to Page Layout view. When you leave the header or footer area, Word will return you to the view you were in before.

2. Enter the text (and graphics, if you like) for the header in the Header area at the top of the page. Use the buttons on the Header and Footer toolbar to speed your work:

Switch Between Header and Footer moves the insertion point between header and footer. Alternatively, you can use the up and down arrow keys to move between the two.

Show Previous moves the insertion point to the header or footer in the previous section (if there is one; we'll get into this in a minute) or page (if you're using different headers and footers on the first page).

Show Next moves the insertion point to the header or footer in the next section (if there is one) or page (if you're using a different header and footer on the first page).

Same as Previous makes the current header or footer the same as the header or footer in the previous section (if there is one) or page (if you're using different a header and footer on the first page).

Page Numbers inserts a code for the current page number at the insertion point.

Date inserts a code for the current date in the document.

Time inserts a code for the current time in the document.

Page Setup displays the Page Setup dialog box with the Layout tab at the front.

Show/Hide Document Text displays and hides the document text. Its purpose is a little esoteric: You probably won't want to hide your document's text unless you're trying to place a header or footer behind the text. For example, you might want to add a watermark behind the text on a business letter or a brochure.

WARNING Unwittingly clicking the Show/Hide Document Text button can lead you to think you've lost all the text in your document. If your text suddenly disappears under suspicious circumstances, check to see if the Show/Hide Document Text button is highlighted. If it is, restore the display of the document text by clicking the Show/Hide Document Text button again. If the Show/Hide Document Text button isn't the culprit and your text has really vanished, try undoing actions (by choosing Edit ➢ Undo or pressing Ctrl+Z), or closing the document without saving changes.

3. To return to your document, either double-click anywhere in the main document or choose View ➢ Header and Footer again to leave the header or footer area.

TIP You can also use ↑ and ↓ to move between the header and footer areas.

Formatting Headers and Footers

Despite their special position on the page, headers and footers contain regular Word elements (text, graphics, frames, and so on) and you work with them as described in the previous chapters.

By default, Word starts you off with the Header style in the header area and the Footer style in the Footer area. You can modify these styles (as described earlier in this chapter), choose other styles (including Header First, Header Even, and Header Odd, which Word provides in some templates) from the Styles drop-down list on the Formatting toolbar (or by choosing Format ➢ Style and using the Styles dialog box), or apply extra formatting.

TIP Headers and footers aren't restricted to the header and footer areas that appear on your screen—you can also use headers and footers to place repeating text anywhere on your page. While in the header or footer area, you can insert a frame at a suitable location on the page, then insert text, graphics, and so on inside the frame (as described in Chapter 5).

Producing Different Headers and Footers

Often you'll want different headers and footers on different pages of your documents. Word gives you three options to choose from:

- A different header and footer on the first page of a document
- Different headers and footers on odd and even pages (combined, if you like, with a different header and footer on the first page)
- Different headers and footers in different sections (combined, if you like, with the previous two options for those sections).

Different First-Page Headers and Footers

To produce different headers and footers on the first page of a document:

1. Choose File ➤ Page Setup to display the Page Setup dialog box, then click the Layout tab to bring it to the front.

2. In the Headers and Footers box, select Different First Page.

3. Click the OK button to close the Page Setup dialog box.

After setting up your header and footer for the first page of the document, move to the second page and set up the header and footer for it and subsequent pages.

Different Headers and Footers on Odd and Even Pages

To create different headers and footers on odd and even pages, select the Different Odd and Even check box in the Headers and Footers box on the Layout tab of the Page Setup dialog box (File ➤ Page Setup). Move the insertion point to an odd page and set its header and footer, then move to an even page and set its header and footer.

Different Headers and Footers in Sections

To set different headers and footers in the different sections of a document, create the document, then divide it into sections as described in *Section Formatting* earlier in this chapter. To adjust the header or footer for any section, click in that section, then choose View ➤ Header and Footer to display the Header area of the document.

By default, Word sets the header and footer for each section after the first to be the same as the header and footer in the previous section; so the Same as Previous button on the Header and Footer toolbar will appear pushed in, and the legend Same as Previous will appear at the top-right corner of the header or footer area. To change this, click the Same as Previous button on the Header and Footer toolbar, and then enter the new header or footer in the header or footer area.

 To move through the headers or footers in the sections of your document, click the Show Previous and Show Next buttons on the Header and Footer toolbar.

Chapter 8

PRINTING A DOCUMENT

- **Using Print Preview**
- **Printing documents**
- **Printing envelopes**
- **Printing labels**

Once you've written, set up, and formatted your documents, you'll probably want to print them. As with its other features, Word offers a wealth of printing options. Printing can be as simple as clicking one button to print a whole document, or as complicated as choosing which parts of your document to print, what to print them on, how many copies to print, and even what order to print them in.

In this chapter, we'll first look at how to use Word's Print Preview mode to nail down any glaring deficiencies in your text before you print it. After that we'll tackle straightforward printing, and then move on to the tricky stuff.

Using Print Preview

Before you print any document, use Word's Print Preview mode to establish that the document looks the way you want it to look. Choose File ➤ Print Preview to display the current document in Print Preview mode (see Figure 8.1).

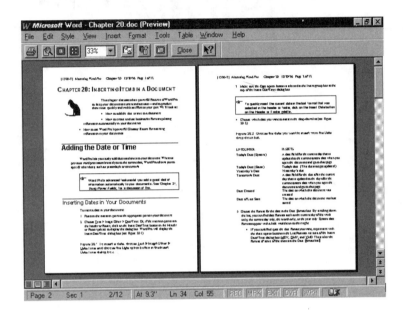

FIGURE 8.1:
In Print Preview mode, Word displays your document as it will appear when you print it—to the best of Word's ability.

In Print Preview mode, Word displays the Print Preview toolbar (see Figure 8.2), which offers the following buttons:

Print prints the current document using the default print settings.

Magnifier switches between Magnifier mode and Editing mode. In Magnifier mode, the mouse pointer appears as a magnifying glass containing a plus sign (when the view is zoomed out) or a minus sign (when the view is zoomed in). In Editing mode, the mouse pointer appears at the insertion point—you can use it to edit as usual.

One Page zooms the view to one full page.

Multiple Pages zooms the view to multiple pages. When you click the Multiple Pages button, Word displays a small grid showing the display combinations possible—one full page; two pages side by side; three pages side by side; two pages, one on top of the other; four pages, two on top, two below, etc. Click the arrangement of pages you want.

Zoom Control lets you choose the zoom percentage that suits you.

View Ruler toggles the display of the horizontal and vertical rulers on and off.

Shrink to Fit attempts to make your document fit on one fewer page (by changing the font size, line spacing, and margins). This is useful when your crucial fax strays a line or two on to a second or third page and you'd like to shrink it down.

Full Screen removes the menus, status bar, scroll bars, etc., from the display. This is useful for clearing more screen real estate to see exactly how your document looks before you print it.

Close closes Print Preview, returning you to whichever view you were in before.

Help displays Word Help.

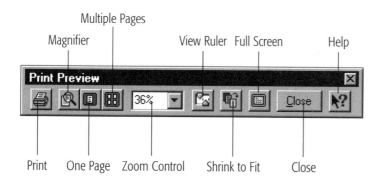

FIGURE 8.2:
The Print Preview toolbar offers quick access to the Print Preview features.

I'll let you explore Print Preview on your own, but here's one thing to try: Display the rulers (by choosing View ➤ Ruler), then click and drag the gray margin borders in the rulers to quickly adjust the page setup of the document.

TIP

Print Preview will show you how the document will look on the current printer. If you're using Print Preview to check that your documents look okay before you print them, make sure that you've already selected the printer you're going to use for the document.

To exit Print Preview, click the Close button on the Print Preview toolbar to return to the view you were in before Print Preview, or choose File ➤ Print Preview again.

Printing a Document

Once you've checked a document in Print Preview and made any necessary adjustments, you're ready to print it. Next, you need to decide whether you want to print the whole document at once or just part of it.

Printing All of a Document

The easiest way to print a document in Word is simply to click the Print button on the Standard toolbar. This prints the current document without offering you any options—to be more precise, it prints one copy of the entire document in page-number order (1, 2, 3) to the currently selected printer.

Printing Part of a Document

If you want to print only part of a document, don't click the Print button. Instead, choose File ➤ Print to display the Print dialog box (see Figure 8.3).

> **TIP**
>
> The keyboard shortcuts for the Print command are Ctrl+P and Ctrl+Shift+F12. I'd recommend using Ctrl+P for simplicity.

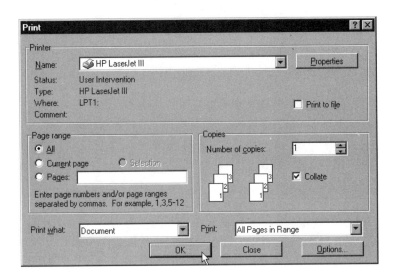

FIGURE 8.3:
In the Print dialog box, choose the printer you want to use, which pages you want to print, and the number of copies you want. Then click the OK button to print.

1. First, make sure the printer named in the Name drop-down list of the Printer group box is the one you want to use. If it's not, use the drop-down list to select the right printer.

2. Next, choose which pages to print in the Page Range group box by clicking one of the option buttons:

   All prints the whole document.

   Current Page prints the page where the insertion point is currently.

   Selection prints only the selected text in your document. If you haven't selected any text, this option button will be dimmed.

   Pages lets you print individual pages by number or a range (or ranges) of pages. Use commas to separate the page numbers (e.g., 1, 11, 21) and a hyphen to separate page ranges (e.g., 31-41). You can combine the two: 1, 11, 21-31, 41-51, 61.

> **TIP**
> To print from a particular page to the end of the document, you don't need to know the number for the last page of the document—simply enter the page number followed by a hyphen (e.g., 11-).

3. If you want to print only odd pages or even pages, use the Print drop-down list at the bottom-right corner of the Print dialog box to specify Odd Pages or Even Pages.

4. Choose how many copies of the document you want to print by using the Number of Copies box in the Copies section.
   You can also choose whether to collate the pages or not—if you collate them, Word prints the first set of pages in order (1, 2, 3, 4, 5) and then prints the next set and subsequent sets; if you don't collate them, Word prints all the copies of page 1, then all the copies of page 2, and so on.

5. When you've made your choices in the Print dialog box, click the OK button to send the document to the printer.

Printing on Different Paper

So far we've looked only at printing on your default-sized paper (for example, 8½x11" paper). Sooner or later you're going to need to print on a different size of paper, be it to produce a manual, an application to some bureaucracy, or a birthday card. This section discusses how to proceed.

Not only can you use various sizes of paper with Word, but also you can use different sizes of paper for different sections of the same document, as discussed in Chapter 7.

The first thing to do when you want to print on paper of a different size is to set up your document suitably—paper size, margins, and orientation. (Look back to the *Page Setup* section of Chapter 7 for more details on this if you need to.)

Next, choose the paper source for each section of your document.

Choosing a Paper Source

If you're writing a letter or a report, you may want to put the first page on special paper. For example, the first page of a letter might be on company paper that contains the company's logo, name, and address, while subsequent pages might be on paper that contains only the company's name and logo.

To choose the paper source for printing the current section of the current document:

1. Choose File ➤ Page Setup. In the Page Setup dialog box, click the Paper Source tab.
2. In the First Page list box, choose the printer tray that contains the paper for the first page. (If your printer has only one tray, choose Manual Feed.)
3. In the Other Pages list box, choose the printer tray that contains the paper you want to use for the remaining pages of the document. Usually, you'll want to choose the Default Tray here, but on occasion you may want to use another tray or Manual Feed for special effects.
4. In the Apply To drop-down list box, choose the section of the document that you want to print on the paper you're choosing. (The default is Whole Document unless the document contains sections, in which case the default is This Section. You can also choose This Point Forward to print the rest of the document on the paper you're choosing.)
5. Click the OK button to close the Page Setup dialog box; it will automatically save your changes.

> **NOTE** To set the paper source for other sections of the document, click in a section and repeat these steps.

Setting a Default Paper Source

If you always print from a different paper tray than your copy of Word is set up to use, you'd do well to change it. This might happen if you were always needing to use letterhead on a networked printer that had a number of paper trays, and your colleagues kept filling the default paper tray with unflavored white bond.

To set your default paper source:

1. Choose File ➤ Page Setup to display the Page Setup dialog box.
2. Make your selections in the First Page list box and Other Pages list box.
3. Choose an option from the Whole Document drop-down list if necessary.
4. Click the Default button. Word will display a message box asking for confirmation of your choice.
5. Click Yes. Word will close the Page Setup dialog box and make the change.

Printing Envelopes

Printing envelopes has long been the bane of the computerized office. Envelopes have been confusing to set up in word processing applications and—worse—they tend to jam in laser printers (and that's not even mentioning what dot-matrix printers think of envelopes). There have been four traditional ways of dealing with these problems: handwrite the labels, use a typewriter, use window envelopes, or use sheets of labels. If these methods don't appeal to you, read on.

To print an envelope:

1. Choose Tools ➤ Envelopes and Labels. Word will display the Envelopes and Labels dialog box (see Figure 8.4). If Word finds what it identifies as an address in the current document, it will display it in the Delivery Address box. If you don't think Word will find the address hidden in the document—for example, if the document contains more than one address—highlight the address before choosing Tools ➤ Envelopes and Labels.
2. If Word hasn't found an address in the document, you'll need to choose it yourself.

- To include a recently used address, click the Insert Address drop-down list button in the Envelopes and Labels dialog box and choose the name from the drop-down list.
- To include an address from an address book, click the Insert Address button and choose the address book from the *Show Names from the* drop-down list in the Select Name dialog box. Then choose the name, either by typing the first characters of the name into the Type Name or Select from List text box, or by selecting it from the list box. Click the OK button to insert the name in the Delivery Address box of the Envelopes and Labels dialog box.

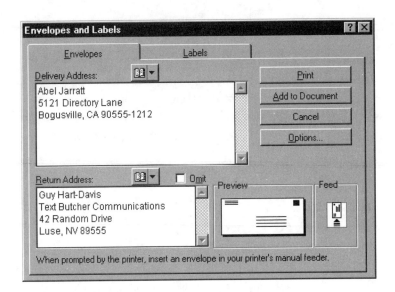

FIGURE 8.4:
Word displays any address it finds—or the address you selected—in the Delivery Address box of the Envelopes and Labels dialog box.

- Alternatively, type the name and address into the Address box.

3. Verify the return address that Word has inserted in the Return Address box. Word automatically picks this information out of the User Info tab of the Options dialog box. If the information is incorrect, you can correct it in the Return Address box, but you'd do better to correct it in the Options dialog box if you regularly work with the computer you're now using. (Choose Tools ➤ Options, then click the User Info tab.)

    - You can also use the Insert Address button's drop-down list to insert a recently used address or click the Insert Address button and choose a name in the Select Name dialog box.

    - Alternatively, you can omit a return address by checking the Omit check box.

4. Next, check the Preview box to see how the envelope will look and the Feed box to see how Word expects you to feed it into the printer. If either of these is not to your liking, click the Options button (or click the Preview icon or the Feed icon) to display the Envelope Options dialog box (see Figure 8.5).

5. On the Envelope Options tab of the Envelope Options dialog box (yes, this gets weird), use the Envelope Size drop-down list to choose the size of envelope you're using. (Check the envelope box for the size before you get out your ruler to measure the envelopes.)

6. If you want to customize the look of the addresses, use the options in the Delivery Address box and Return Address box. The Font button in these boxes opens a version of the Font dialog box, which you'll recognize from Chapter 6. Choose the font and effects you want, then click the OK button. Use the From

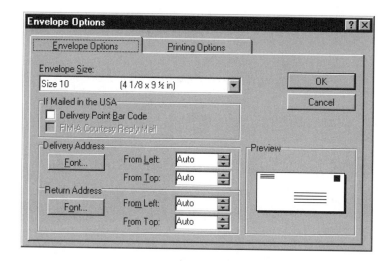

FIGURE 8.5:
In the Envelope Options dialog box, use the Envelope Options tab to set the size of the envelope and the fonts for the delivery address and return address. Use the Printing Options tab to set the feed method you want to use with your printer.

Left and From Top boxes in the Delivery Address box and Return Address box to set the placement of the address on the envelope. Watch the Preview box to see how you're doing.

7. On the Printing Options tab of the Envelope Options dialog box, Word offers options for changing the feed method for the envelope—you have the choice of six different envelope orientations; the choice of placing the envelope Face Up or Face Down in the printer; and the choice of Clockwise Rotation. Again, choose the options you want. Click the OK button when you're satisfied.

> **WARNING**
>
> Don't mess with the printing options unless you have to: If you've set your printer up correctly, Word should be able to make a fair guess at how you'll need to feed the envelope for the printer to print it correctly.

8. You now have the option of printing the envelope you've set up by clicking the Print button in the Envelopes and Labels dialog box or adding it to the current document by clicking the Add to Document button.

If you choose the Add to Document button, Word places the envelope on a new page at the start of the document and formats the page to require a manual envelope feed. When you print the document, you'll need to start the printer off with a manually fed envelope; once the envelope has printed, Word will resume its normal feeding pattern for the rest of the document (unless that too has abnormal paper requirements).

Printing Labels

If you don't want to mess with feeding envelopes into your printer and betting that it won't chew them up, sheets of labels are a good alternative. What's more, Word makes it easy to set up labels.

NOTE

In this section we'll look at how to set up labels for one addressee—either a single label or a whole sheet of labels with the same address on each. For sheets of labels with a different address on each label, see Chapter 10, *Mail Merge.*

1. If the current document contains the address you want to use on the label, select the address.
2. Choose Tools ➤ Envelopes and Labels to display the Envelopes and Labels dialog box (see Figure 8.6). If you selected an address in step 1, Word will display it in the Address box.

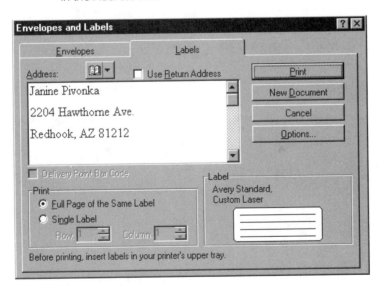

FIGURE 8.6: In the Envelopes and Labels dialog box, click the Labels tab if it isn't displayed.

3. First, choose the type of labels you want. The current type of label is displayed in the Label box in the bottom-right corner of the Envelopes and Labels dialog box. To choose another type of label, click the Options button. You'll see the Label Options dialog box.

- Choose the type of printer you'll be using: Dot Matrix or Laser. (Laser includes inkjets, bubble-jets, and the like.)
- Choose the printer tray that you'll put the label sheets in by using the Tray drop-down list.
- Choose the category of label by using the Label Products drop-down list: Avery Standard, Avery Pan European, or Other. (Other includes labels by manufacturers other than Avery.)
- In the Product Number list box, choose the type of labels you're using—it should be on the box of labels. The Label Information group box will show the details for the type of labels you've selected in the Product Number list box.
- For more details on the labels you've chosen, or to customize them, click the Details button to display the Information dialog box. Click OK when you're done.
- Click the OK button in the Label Options dialog box to return to the Envelopes and Labels dialog box. It will now display the labels you've chosen in the Label box.

4. Add the address (if you haven't already selected one):
   - To include an address from your current address book, click the Insert Address drop-down list button and choose the name from the drop-down list.
   - To include an address from another address book, click the Insert Address button and choose the address book from the *Show Names from the* drop-down list in the Select Name dialog box. Then choose the name, either by typing the first characters of the name into the Type Name or Select from List text box or by selecting it from the list box. Click the OK button to insert the name in the Address box of the Envelopes and Labels dialog box.
   - Alternatively, type the name and address into the Address box.

5. In the Print group box, choose whether to print a full page of the same label or a single label. If you choose to print a single label, set the Row and Column numbers that describe its location on the sheet of labels.

6. If you chose to print a full page of the same label, you can click the New Document button to create a new document containing the labels, then print it and save it for future reference. Alternatively, click the Print button to print the sheet of labels.

TIP

If you want to customize your labels, choose the New Document button, then add any formatting that you like. You can also add graphics by using Word's Insert ➤ Picture command.

Chapter 9

COLUMNS, TABLES, AND SORTING

- **Creating, formatting, and deleting columns**
- **Creating and inserting tables**
- **Editing and formatting tables**
- **Converting tables to text**
- **Arranging your data suitably for sorting**
- **Sorting your data**
- **Using Word's sorting options**

In this chapter, we'll look at two ways of creating multicolumn documents in Word without using large numbers of tabs. Word's *columns* provide a quick way of creating newspaper-style columns of text. *Tables* are for laying out text (or data) in columns made up of rows of cells—and, if necessary, for sorting that text or data.

Columns

To create columns in a document, you can either convert existing text to columns, or you can create columns and then enter the text in them.

Word uses sections (discussed in Chapter 6) to separate text formatted in different numbers of columns from the rest of the document. If the whole of a document contains the same number of columns, Word doesn't use section breaks, but if the document contains one-column and two-column text, Word will divide the text with section breaks; likewise, two-column text will be separated from three-column text, three-column text from four-column text from two-column text, and so on, as shown in Figure 9.1.

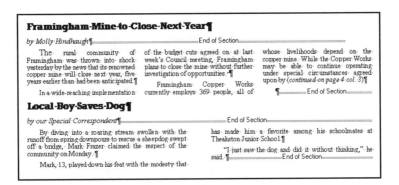

FIGURE 9.1:
Word uses section breaks to separate the sections of text that have different numbers of columns from each other.

> **NOTE** Word displays column layouts only in Page Layout view and in Print Preview. In Normal view and Outline view, Word won't indicate how the columns in your document will look.

Creating Columns Quickly with the Columns Button

To create columns quickly, without worrying about formatting details:

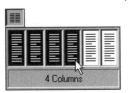

1. To create columns from existing text, select it. To create columns in only one part of your document, select that part.
2. Click the Columns button on the Standard toolbar and drag down and to the right over the grid that appears to indicate how many columns you want. Release the mouse button, and Word will create the columns.

Creating Columns with the Columns Dialog Box

For more control over the columns you create, use the Columns dialog box instead of the Columns button:

1. To create columns from existing text, first select the text. To create columns in only one part of your document, select that part.
2. Choose Format ➢ Columns to display the Columns dialog box (see Figure 9.2).

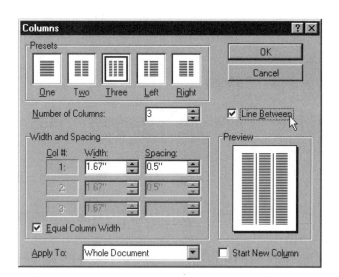

FIGURE 9.2:
The Columns dialog box gives you fine control over the number and formatting of columns.

3. Choose the number of columns you want to create, either by clicking one of the buttons in the Presets list or by entering a number in the Number of Columns box. (These settings affect each other.)
4. If need be, adjust the column width and spacing in the Width and Spacing group box.
   - If you chose One, Two, or Three columns from the Presets box and want to produce columns of varying widths, clear the Equal Column Width check box.
   - In the Width box for each column, enter the column width you want. In the Spacing box, enter the amount of space you want between this column and the column to its right.
5. To add a line between each column on your page, select the Line Between check box.
6. Click the OK button to close the dialog box and create the columns with the settings you chose.

Changing the Number of Columns

Once you've created columns in a document, you can change the number of columns by selecting the relevant text and using either the Columns button or the Columns dialog box:

- Click the Columns button on the Standard toolbar and drag the grid that appears until you've selected the number of columns you want.
- Choose Format ➢ Columns to make adjustments to the columns as described in the previous section, *Creating Columns with the Columns Dialog Box*.

Starting a New Column

To start a new column at the top of the page:

1. Place the insertion point at the beginning of the text that will start the new column.
2. Choose Format ➢ Columns to display the Columns dialog box.
3. In the Apply To drop-down list, choose This Point Forward.
4. Check the Start New Column box.
5. Click the OK button. Word will create a new column from the insertion point forward.

Removing Columns from Text

You don't really remove columns from text—you adjust the number of columns. For example, to "remove" two-column formatting from text, you change the text to a single-column layout.

The easiest way to switch back to a single-column layout is to click the Columns button on the Formatting toolbar and drag through the resulting grid to select the one-column bar, then release the mouse button. Alternatively, choose Format ➢ Columns to display the Columns dialog box, choose One from the Presets group box, and then click the OK button.

> **TIP**
>
> To switch only part of a document back to a single-column format, select that part first. To switch only a section, place the insertion point anywhere within that section.

Tables

Word's tables give you a way to present complex information in vertical columns and horizontal rows of cells. Cells can contain text—a single paragraph or multiple paragraphs—or graphics.

You can create a table from existing text, or you can create a table first and then enter your text into it. Once you've created a table, you can add further columns or rows, or merge several cells in the same row to make one cell.

To embellish your tables, you can use borders, along with font formatting (bold, italic, underline, highlight, and so on), paragraph formatting (indents, line spacing, etc.), and style formatting—not to mention Word's Table AutoFormat feature. We'll briefly look at formatting tables in this section.

Inserting a Table Quickly with the Insert Table Button

The easiest way to insert a table is to click the Insert Table button on the Formatting toolbar. Drag the insertion point down and to the right over the grid that appears to select the size of table (number of rows and columns) you want to create, and then release the mouse button.

> **TIP**
>
> **To create the table from existing text, select the text before clicking the Insert Table button.**

Inserting a Table with the Insert Table Command

You can also insert a table by choosing Table ➤ Insert Table and then choosing the details of the table in the Number of Columns, Number of Rows, and Column Width boxes in the Insert Table dialog box (see Figure 9.3).

Using Table Autoformatting

Formatting your tables can be a slow business, so Word offers a Table AutoFormat feature that can speed up the process. To create a new table and autoformat it, choose

Table ➤ Insert Table and click the AutoFormat button in the Insert Table dialog box to display the Table AutoFormat dialog box (see Figure 9.4).

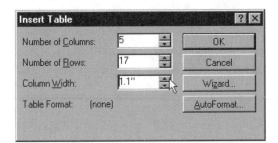

FIGURE 9.3:
In the Insert Table dialog box, set up the table you want to create.

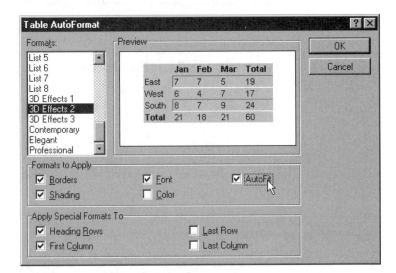

FIGURE 9.4:
The Table AutoFormat dialog box offers quick access to a veritable plethora of predefined table formats, and options to customize them.

TIP
If you're not quite sure what shape and layout your table will take on as you create it, you can also apply autoformatting after creating the table—just click inside the table and choose Table ➤ Table AutoFormat, or right-click in the table and choose Table AutoFormat.

Use the Formats list box and the adjacent Preview box to choose the format that suits you (or your table) best. You'll find that some of the formats (for example, Elegant and Professional) fail to live up to their names, but others (such as 3D Effects 2) are inoffensive and borderline pleasing.

In the Formats to Apply group box, choose whether you want Word to apply Borders, Shading, Font, and Color formatting to the table by selecting or clearing the boxes next to the selections. Make sure you've cleared the check marks next to the formatting selections you don't want. The most important of these formatting options is AutoFit, which causes Word to adjust the column width to suit the text in your table rather than blindly allotting an inappropriate width to each column.

In the Apply Special Formats To group box, check the boxes to choose which rows and columns you want Word to apply special formatting to: Heading Rows, First Column, Last Row, and Last Column. The last two choices are good for emphasizing totals or conclusions.

Once you've made your choices, click the OK button. If you're creating a table, Word will return you to the Insert Table dialog box, where you again click OK to dismiss the dialog box and create the table with the formatting you've chosen; if you're running AutoFormat on a table already created, Word will apply the formatting you chose to the table.

Using the Table Wizard

For creating complex tables, try Word's Table Wizard. Choose Table ➤ Insert Table and click the Wizard button in the Insert Table dialog box that appears. The Wizard will then present you with a number of choices as it walks you through the creation of the table.

> **TIP**
>
> You can also fire up the Table Wizard by choosing File ➤ New and choosing Table Wizard.wiz on the Other Documents tab of the New dialog box. (If you chose not to install the Table Wizard, Agenda Wizard, Resume Wizard, and their sorcerous brethren when you installed Word, you may not have an Other Documents tab in the New dialog box. Look to the Appendix for instructions on installing them.) This is the best choice for creating a table in a new document rather than in an existing document.

Converting Existing Text to a Table

If you've already got the material for a table in a Word document, but it's laid out with tabs, paragraphs, commas, or the like, you can quickly convert it to a table:

1. Select the text.
2. Choose Table ➤ Convert Text to Table. Word will display the Convert Text to Table dialog box with its best guess about how you want to separate the text into table cells.

- If the selected text consists of apparently regular paragraphs of text, Word will suggest separating it at the paragraph marks, so each paragraph will go into a separate cell.
- If the selected text appears to contain tabbed columns, Word will suggest separating it at each tab, so each tabbed column will become a table column.
- If the selected text appears to have commas at regular intervals in each paragraph—as in a list of names and addresses, for example—Word will suggest separating the text at each comma. This is good for database-output information (such as names and addresses) separated by commas.
- If the selected text appears to be divided by other characters (such as hyphens), Word will suggest dividing it at each hyphen (or whatever).

3. If necessary, change the setting in the Separate Text At box. This may change the number of columns and rows that Word has suggested. If you choose Other, enter the separator character in the Other box. This can be any character or any letter.

4. If necessary, manually adjust the number of columns and rows by changing the number in the Number of Columns box; the number of rows will adjust automatically.

5. Adjust the setting in the Column Width box if you want to (Auto usually does a reasonable job, and you can adjust the column widths later if you need to).

6. Click the OK button to convert the text to a table or click the AutoFormat button to have Word walk you through formatting the table (click OK when Word returns you to the Convert Text to Table dialog box after formatting).

Selecting Parts of a Table

When manipulating your tables, first you need to select the parts you want to manipulate. While you can just click and drag with the mouse (or use the keyboard or the shift-click technique discussed in Chapter 5), Word also offers shortcuts for selecting parts of tables.

> **TIP**
>
> One of the keys to understanding how Word selects cells is the hidden end-of-cell marker that each cell contains. Once you drag past this to another cell, you've selected both that cell and the other. The end-of-cell marker is a little circle with pointy corners. To display end-of-cell markers, choose Tools ➢ Options and check the Paragraphs box in the Nonprinting Characters group box on the Options dialog box's View tab, or click the Show/Hide ¶ button on the Standard toolbar.

To select one cell, move the mouse pointer into the thin cell selection bar at the left edge of the cell. You'll know when it's in the right place because the insertion point will change to an arrow pointing north-northeast. Then click to select the cell (including its end-of-cell marker).

To select a row, move the mouse pointer into the table selection bar to the left of the row, and then click. Alternatively, double-click in the cell selection bar at the left edge of any cell in the row.

- To select multiple rows, click in the table selection bar and drag up or down.
- To select a column, Alt-click in it. Alternatively, move the mouse pointer to just above the topmost row of the column where it will turn into a little black arrow pointing straight down, and then click.
- To select multiple columns, click just above the topmost row of any column and drag left or right.
- To select the whole table, Alt–double-click anywhere in it.

Word also offers menu options for selecting parts of tables: Table ➤ Select Column, Table ➤ Select Row, and Table ➤ Select Table. Place the insertion point in the appropriate row or column (or drag through the rows or columns to select cells in multiple rows or columns) and then choose the appropriate command.

Navigating in Tables

You can move easily through tables using the mouse, the arrow keys, or the Tab key. ← moves you backward through the contents of a cell, character by character, and then to the end of the previous cell; → moves you forward and then to the start of the next cell; ↑ moves you up through the lines and paragraphs in a cell and then up to the next row; and ↓ moves you downward. Tab moves you to the next cell, selecting any contents in the process; Shift+Tab moves you to the previous cell and also selects any contents in the cell.

Editing Text in a Table

Once the insertion point is inside a cell, you can enter and edit text (and other elements) as in any Word document, except for entering tabs, for which you need to press Ctrl+Tab.

Row height adjusts automatically as you add more text to a cell or as you increase the height of the text. You can also adjust it manually, as we'll see in a moment.

Adding and Deleting Cells, Rows, and Columns

Often you'll need to change the layout of your table after you create it—for example, you might need to add a column or two, or delete several rows, so your information is presented most effectively.

> **TIP**
>
> Word distinguishes between deleting the *contents* of a cell, row, or column and deleting the cell, row, or column itself. When you delete the contents of a cell, row, or column, the cell, row, or column remains in place, but when you delete the cell, row, or column, both it and any contents in it disappear. To delete just the contents of a cell, row, or column, select your victim and press Delete.

Deleting Cells

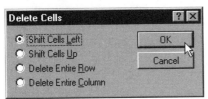

To delete cells and their contents from a table, select the cells and choose Table ➢ Delete Cells (or right-click to bring up the shortcut menu and choose Delete Cells). Word will display the Delete Cells dialog box, offering to move the remaining cells up or to the left to fill the space left by the cells you're deleting. If necessary, choose Shift Cells Left or Shift Cells Up, and then click the OK button.

Adding Cells

To add cells to a table, select the cells above which or to the right of which you want to insert the new cells, then choose Table ➢ Insert Cells (or right-click and choose Insert Cells). In the Insert Cells dialog box, choose Shift Cells Right or Shift Cells Down to specify how the selected cells should move, then click the OK button.

Adding Rows

> **TIP**
>
> To add a row to the end of a table instantly, simply position the insertion point in the last cell of the table and press Tab.

To add a row to a table, click in the row above which you want to add the new row, and then choose Table ➤ Insert Rows (or right-click and choose Insert Rows). Word will insert the row above the one you clicked in.

- To insert multiple rows, select the same number of existing rows, then choose Table ➤ Insert Rows. For example, to add three rows, select three rows.
- Alternatively, after selecting a cell, or cells in a number of rows, choose Table ➤ Insert Cells, select the Insert Entire Row option in the Insert Cells dialog box, and then click OK.

TIP The Insert Table button on the Standard toolbar automagically transforms itself into an Insert Rows button when the insertion point is inside a table, and into an Insert Columns button when one or more columns has been selected.

Deleting Rows

To delete a row of cells from a table, click in the row you want to delete and choose Table ➤ Delete Cells (or right-click and choose Delete Cells). In the Delete Cells dialog box, choose Delete Entire Row and click the OK button.

- To skip the Delete Cells dialog box, select the row and choose Table ➤ Delete Rows (or right-click and choose Delete Rows).
- To delete multiple rows, select the rows you want to delete and choose Table ➤ Delete Rows.

Adding Columns

To add a column to a table, select the column to the left of new column you want to add, and then choose Table ➤ Insert Columns (or right-click and choose Insert Columns).

To insert multiple columns, select the same number of existing columns to the left of the ones you want to add, and then choose Table ➤ Insert Columns. For example, to add three columns, select three columns.

Deleting Columns

To delete a column of cells from a table, click in the column and choose Table ➤ Delete Cells. In the Delete Cells dialog box, choose Delete Entire Column and click the OK button.

- To skip the Delete Cells dialog box, select the column and choose Table ➤ Delete Columns (or right-click and choose Delete Columns).

- To delete multiple columns, select the columns you want to delete and choose Table ➢ Delete Columns.

TIP To delete an entire table, select the table using Table ➢ Select Table, and then choose Table ➢ Delete Rows.

Formatting a Table

As with editing a table, you can use the regular Word formatting features—from the toolbars, the Font and Paragraph dialog boxes, and so on—to format your tables. However, there are a couple of exceptions worth mentioning: alignment and indents.

Setting Alignment in Tables

Alignment in tables is very straightforward once you know that not only can any row of the table be left-aligned, right-aligned, or centered (all relative to the margins set for the page) but also within those rows, the text in each cell can be left-aligned, right-aligned, centered, or justified, relative to the column it's in.

For example, you could center your table horizontally on the page and have the first column left-aligned, the second centered, the third justified, and the fourth right-aligned (though the result would almost certainly look weird). Figure 9.5 shows a table that is more reasonably aligned: The first column is right-aligned to present the numbers in a logical fashion; the second column is right-aligned, and the third left-aligned with the space between the columns reduced to display each first name and last name together while retaining the ability to sort by the last name. The Age column is centered (for aesthetics and this example); and the numbers in the Years of Service column are right-aligned. The table itself is centered on the page.

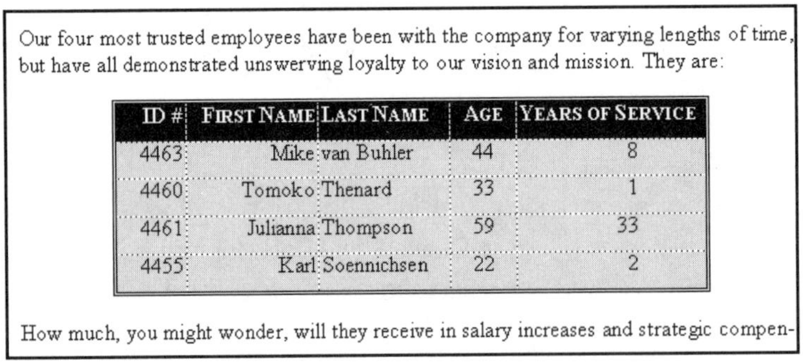

Our four most trusted employees have been with the company for varying lengths of time, but have all demonstrated unswerving loyalty to our vision and mission. They are:

ID #	FIRST NAME	LAST NAME	AGE	YEARS OF SERVICE
4463	Mike	van Buhler	44	8
4460	Tomoko	Thenard	33	1
4461	Julianna	Thompson	59	33
4455	Karl	Soennichsen	22	2

How much, you might wonder, will they receive in salary increases and strategic compen-

FIGURE 9.5:
Use the different types of alignment to display your information clearly.

To set alignment within any cell, use the methods discussed in Chapter 6: the alignment buttons on the Formatting toolbar, the keyboard shortcuts, or the Paragraph dialog box.

To set alignment for a row, choose Table ➢ Cell Height and Width and choose Left, Center, or Right in the Alignment group box on the Row tab of the Cell Height and Width dialog box (see Figure 9.6).

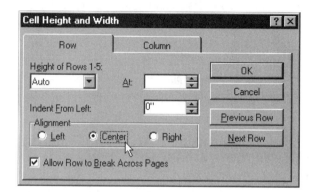

FIGURE 9.6:
Set alignment for a row on the Row tab of the Cell Height and Width dialog box.

Setting Indents in Tables

As with alignment, you can indent the entire table or the contents within each cell. By understanding the difference, you can position your tables precisely where you want them on the page and lay out the table text using suitable indents.

To set indentation for the text in a cell, use the methods you learned in Chapter 6—drag the indentation markers on the ruler or change the settings in the Indentation group box on the Indents and Spacing tab of the Paragraph dialog box. For example, the numbers in the Years of Service column in the table shown in Figure 9.5 have been indented 0.4" from the right margin of the cell to display them more clearly.

To set indentation for a row, choose Table ➢ Cell Height and Width and enter a measurement in the Indent From Left box on the Row tab of the Cell Height and Width dialog box.

Adding Borders and Shading to Your Tables

Adding borders and shading to your tables is a little more complex than you might expect. Because Word lets you add borders and shading to the paragraphs inside the table, to any given cell, or to the whole table, you have to be careful about what you select.

TIP   The quickest way to add borders and shading to a table is to use the Table AutoFormat command, discussed earlier in *Using Table Autoformatting*. If you want more information, read on.

Adding Borders and Shading to the Whole Table To add borders and shading to the whole table, click anywhere in it but don't select anything, then choose Format ➤ Borders and Shading. Word will display the Table Borders and Shading dialog box. Choose the border options you want on the Borders tab and the shading options you want on the Shading tab, then click the OK button.

Adding Borders and Shading to Selected Cells To add borders and shading to selected cells in a table, select the cells by dragging through them or by using the keyboard. (If you're selecting just one cell, make sure you select its end-of-cell mark as well, so that the whole cell is highlighted, not just part of the text.) Then choose Format ➤ Borders and Shading to display the Cell Borders and Shading dialog box. Again, choose the border options you want on the Borders tab and the shading options you want on the Shading tab, and then click the OK button.

Adding Borders and Shading to Paragraphs within Cells To add borders and shading to paragraphs within a cell, select the text you want to format in the cell but don't select the end-of-cell mark. Then choose Format ➤ Borders and Shading. This time Word will display the Paragraph Borders and Shading dialog box. Choose the border and shading options you want; you can also choose how far to position the border from the text by entering a value (in points) in the From Text box.

Merging Cells

Once you've set up your table, you can create special layout effects by merging cells—converting two or more cells in the same row into a single cell. To merge cells, select the cells to merge, then choose Table ➤ Merge Cells. Word will combine the cells into one, putting the contents of each in a separate paragraph in the merged cell; you can then remove the paragraph marks to reduce them to one paragraph.

1994	1995	1996	1997	1998	1999	2000
Western Region Results						
44	48	65	67	71	79	100
Eastern Seaboard Results						
11	12	15	22	23	26	43

Merged cells are especially useful for effects such as table spanner heads. In the example here, the headings "Western Region Results" and "Eastern Seaboard Results" occupy merged cells that span the whole table.

NOTE Word will only merge cells in a horizontal row, not cells in a column, but you can merge several rows worth of cells at once (the cells in each row merging horizontally, but not vertically).

Changing Column Width

The easiest way to change column width is to move the mouse pointer over a column's right-hand border so the insertion point changes into a two-headed arrow pointing east and west. Then click and drag the column border to a suitable position. (You can also click in the column division mark in the horizontal ruler and drag that instead.)

TIP Hold down Shift while you drag the column border to affect only the two columns that share that border. Otherwise, Word changes the width of all the columns to the right of the border you're dragging, as well as the column whose right border you've grabbed.

To change column width more precisely, position the insertion point in the column you want to change, and then choose Table ➤ Cell Height and Width (or select the column, right-click, and choose Cell Height and Width). In the Cell Height and Width dialog box, click the Columns tab to bring it to the front if it isn't already there, and then set the column width in the Width of Column n box.

- If you like, you can also change the amount of space separating columns by entering a different measurement in the Space Between Columns box.
- Use the Previous Column and Next Column buttons to move to different columns and set their width.
- Click the AutoFit button to have Word automatically set a width for the column based on its contents.
- Click the OK button to close the Cell Height and Width dialog box.

Changing Row Height

Word sets row height automatically as you add text to (or remove text from) the cells in any row or adjust the height of the contents of the cells. But you can also set the height of a row manually by placing the insertion point in it and choosing Table ➤ Cell Height and Width (or by selecting the row, right-clicking, and choosing Cell Height and Width). Word will display the Cell Height and Width dialog box. If the Row tab isn't foremost, click it.

From the Height of Row *n* drop-down list, choose At Least to enter a minimum height for the row, or Exactly to enter a precise height. Then enter the measurement in the At box.

- Use the Previous Row and Next Row buttons to move to the previous or next row and set its height.
- Check the Allow Row to Break Across Pages box if you're working with long cells that you can allow to break over pages.
- Click the OK button to close the Cell Height and Width dialog box.

> **TIP** You can also change row height in Page Layout view by clicking and dragging one of the row-break marks (a double horizontal line) on the vertical ruler.

Table Headings

If you're working with tables too long to fit on a single page, you'll probably want to set table headings that repeat automatically on the second page and subsequent pages. To do so, select the row or rows that form the headings, and then choose Table ➤ Headings.

Word will repeat these headings automatically if the table is broken with an automatic page break, but not if you insert a manual page break. Word displays the repeated headings only in Page Layout view and Print Preview, so don't expect to see them in Normal view.

Table Formulas

If you're using tables for numbers—sales targets, net profits, expense reports, or whatever—you may want to use Word's table formulas. These include a variety of mathematical functions, including rounding and averaging, that you may want to get into on your own but which go beyond the scope of this book. The most useful formula for everyday purposes is the SUM formula, which Word offers as the default choice for the last row or column of a table (and for any cell that has cells containing numbers above it or to its left).

To add the numbers in a row or column of cells:

1. Click in a cell in the last row or column of a table (or in any cell that has cells containing numbers above it or to its left).
2. Choose Table ➤ Formula to display the Formula dialog box (see Figure 9.7).
   - If the cell is in the last row of the table (or has cells above it that contain numbers or is the last cell in a table that has numbers in all rows, Word will offer the formula =SUM(ABOVE).
   - If the cell is in the last column of the table (or has cells to its left that contain numbers), Word will suggest =SUM(LEFT).

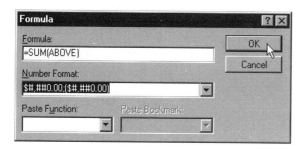

FIGURE 9.7:
Word offers
sum formulas
in the Formula
dialog box.

3. If necessary, choose an appropriate number format from the Number Format drop-down list.

4. Click the OK button to insert the formula in the cell (as a field) and close the Formula dialog box.

    • If you see {=SUM(ABOVE)} or {=SUM(LEFT)} in the cell rather than a pleasantly large total of expenses to be reimbursed (or whatever), turn off the display of field codes by choosing Tools ➤ Options and clearing the Field Codes check box in the Show group box on the Options dialog box's View tab.

> **TIP**
>
> Using table formulas is a bit like building a mini-spreadsheet in Word. If table formulas aren't enough to satisfy you and you need to create a full-fledged spreadsheet in Word, look back to Chapter 4 and the discussion of how you can embed an Excel spreadsheet (or worse) in a Word document.

Copying and Moving within Tables

To copy or move material within a table, either use the mouse and drag to move the selection (or Ctrl-drag to copy it), or use the Cut, Copy, and Paste commands via the Standard toolbar, the Edit menu, or their keyboard shortcuts.

Converting a Table to Text

Sooner or later you're going to need to convert a table back to text. To do so, simply select the table by choosing Table ➤ Select Table or by Alt–double-clicking inside it, and then choose Table ➤ Convert Table to Text. Word will display the Convert Table to Text dialog box with its best guess (based on the contents of the table) at how it should divide the

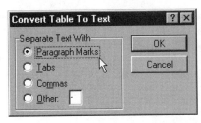

cells when it converts it: with paragraphs, with tabs, with commas, or with another character of your choice. Correct the Separate Text With setting if it's inappropriate, and then click the OK button.

Sorting Information

Once you've created tables of information (or even multicolumn lists formatted using tabs), you'll probably need to sort the information.

Word's sorting feature lets you sort data by up to three types of information at once, such as last name, street name, and zip code. If that doesn't produce fine enough results, you can then sort the same data again using different types of information, such as first name and age—and again, if need be.

How Word Sorts

To make full use of sorting, you need to know *how* Word sorts information. Word sorts by *records* and *fields*, two familiar words that carry quite different meanings in computing. A *record* will typically make up one of the items you want to sort and will consist of a number of *fields*, each of which contain one piece of the information that makes up a record. For example, in a mailing database containing name and address information, each customer and their associated set of data would form a record; that record would consist of a number of fields, such as the customer's first name, middle initial, last name, street address, city, state, zip code, area code, phone number, etc. In Word, this record could be entered in a table (with one field per cell) or as a paragraph, with the fields separated by tabs, commas, or a character of your choice.

Next, you need to know what order Word sorts things in. Here are the details:

- Word can sort alphabetically, numerically, or by date (in a variety of date formats).
- Word can sort in ascending order—from A to Z, from 0 to 9, from early dates to later dates—or in descending order (the opposite).
- Word sorts punctuation marks or symbols (e.g., &, !) first, then numbers, and finally letters. If two items start with the same letter, Word goes on to the next letter and sorts them by that, and so on; if two fields are the same, Word sorts using the next field, etc.

Arranging Your Data for Sorting

If you've already entered all the data in your document or table and are raring to go ahead and sort it, skip to the next section, *Performing a Multilevel Sort*. If you're still in the process of entering your data, or haven't yet started, read on.

The first key to successful sorting is to divide up your records into as many fields as you might possibly want to sort by. Put first names and last names in separate fields, so you can sort by either; likewise, break addresses down into street, city, state, and zip code, so you can sort your data by any one of them. To target customers street by street, break up the street address into the number and the street name, so you can produce a list of customers on Green Street, say, or Hesperian Avenue.

Use a table for complex data or for data that won't all fit on one line of a tabbed document. (You can carry over tabs from the first line of a paragraph onto the second and subsequent lines, but it's visually confusing and rarely worth the effort because table cells can wrap text and keep it visually clear.)

WARNING Above all, before running any complex sorts, save your data and make a backup of it—or even run a practice sort on a noncrucial copy of the data.

Performing a Multilevel Sort

You can perform either a multilevel sort or a single-level sort with paragraph text and with tables. Sorting text in paragraphs is very similar to sorting text in tables, so in this section, we'll look primarily at sorting text in tables, with notes on how to sort text in paragraphs.

Word sorts tables by rows, treating each row as a unit, unless you tell it otherwise. For example, if you select only cells in the first two columns of a four-column table and run a sort operation, Word will rearrange the third and fourth columns according to the sort criteria you chose for the first two columns as well. Likewise, when you sort text in paragraphs, Word treats each paragraph as a unit to be sorted unless you tell it to do otherwise.

NOTE To sort table columns without sorting entire rows, or to sort only part of a number of paragraphs, see *Using Sort Options* later in this chapter.

1. Select the part of the table you want to sort, or select the paragraphs. To sort a whole table, just click anywhere inside the table; Word will select the whole table for you automatically when you choose Table ➤ Sort.

2. Choose Table ➤ Sort to display the Sort dialog box (see Figure 9.8). When sorting paragraphs, you will see the Sort Text dialog box.

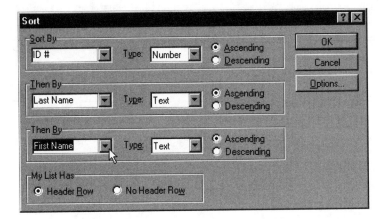

FIGURE 9.8:
Choose options for sorting tables in the Sort dialog box.

3. Look at the My List Has box at the bottom of the dialog box and ensure that Word has correctly identified any header row (i.e., row of headings) at the top of the table or of the rows you're sorting. Word omits the header row from the sort, figuring that you'll still want it at the top of the table. If the text has a header row, make sure the Header Row option button has been selected—otherwise Word will treat the header row as text and sort it along with everything else. You will need to select at least three rows to persuade Word that the rows have a header row.

   • If you've set table headings by using the Table ➤ Headings command, you don't need to worry about the My List Has box—Word knows that the table has headings and dims the options in the My List Has box.

   • When you're sorting paragraphs, Word identifies a header row by the differences in formatting from the rest of the text—a different style, font, font size, bold, italic, etc. (The header row doesn't have to be a bigger font size or boldfaced—it can be smaller than the other text or have no bold to the other text's bold—just so long as Word can recognize it as different.) Be warned that Word may miss your header row if several paragraphs have different formatting, not just the first paragraph; it may also miss the header row for reasons known only to itself.

4. In the Sort By group box, choose the column (i.e., the field) by which to sort the rows of cells first.

- If your table (or your selected rows) has a header row, Word will display the names of the headings (abbreviated if necessary) in the drop-down list to help you identify the sort key you want. If your text has no header row, Word will display Column 1, Column 2, etc. for tables, and Field 1, Field 2, etc., for paragraph text.

- If your text consists of paragraphs with no fields that Word can identify, Word will display Paragraphs in the Sort By box.

5. In the Type box, make sure that Word has chosen the appropriate option: Text, Number, or Date.

6. Next, choose Ascending or Descending for the order in which to sort the rows.

7. If necessary, specify a second sort key in the first Then By box. Again, choose the field by which to sort, check the Type, and choose Ascending or Descending.

8. To sort by a third sort key and produce a more useful sort, repeat step 7 for the second Then By box.

9. Click the OK button to perform the sort and close the Sort dialog box.

Word will leave the table (or the selection of rows, or the paragraphs) highlighted, so if you want to run another sort to get your data into a more precise order, simply repeat steps 2–9.

Using Sort Options

To allow you to direct its sorting capabilities even more precisely, Word offers five sort options in the Sort Options dialog box (see Figure 9.9). Some of these options are available only for particular types of sorts.

To choose sort options, click the Options button in the Sort Text dialog box or the Sort dialog box. The Sort Options group box in the Sort Options dialog box offers the following options:

Sort Column Only sorts only the selected columns of a table or the selected columns of characters in regular text or in a tabbed list (selected by Alt-dragging). This option is not available if you've selected entire paragraphs or columns.

Case Sensitive will sort uppercase before lowercase, all uppercase before initial capitals, initial capitals before sentence case; and sentence case before all lowercase.

The Separate Fields At group box lets you specify which character separates the different fields of text when sorting paragraphs: Tabs, Commas, or Other. Word can usually

FIGURE 9.9:
The Sort Options dialog box provides ways of refining your sorting even further.

identify fields separated by tabs or commas, or even with conventional separators such as hyphens, but if your boss has used, say, em dashes (—) as separators, you'll need to specify that in the Other box.

Once you've made your choices in the Sort Options dialog box, click the OK button to return to the Sort Text dialog box or Sort dialog box.

Chapter 10

MAIL MERGE

- **Creating the main document**
- **Creating the data source**
- **Choosing merge options**
- **Merging the data**
- **Using non-Word documents as data sources**

Mail merge in today's word-processing applications is comparatively friendly and fun. With just a little attention to the details of what you're doing, you can whip together merged letters, forms, envelopes, labels, or catalogs. Word's Mail Merge Helper smoothes out many of the potential speed-bumps in the process.

TIP

You can easily use data sources from other applications—for example, data from Excel spreadsheets or from Access tables, or names of contacts from your Schedule+ address book—with zero complications.

While Word's Mail Merge Helper lets you carry out merges in a variety of different orders, in this chapter we'll look at the most conventional order of proceeding. Once you see what's what, you can mix and match to produce the variations that suit you best. You'll also find that mail merge has a number of different areas, and in some of them, the water gets deep fast—hit a couple of buttons and Word will be expecting you to put together some SQL statements for MS Query to use in hacking a FoxPro database (or worse). In the spirit of cooperation sadly lacking so far in the 1990s, I'll show you how to avoid such predicaments and to steer a path through the pitfalls of mail merge.

Enough mixed metaphors. Let's look first at creating the main document for the merge.

Creating the Main Document

The main document is the file that contains the skeleton into which you fit the variable information from the data file. The skeleton consists of the text that stays the same in each of the letters, catalogs, or whatever, and the *merge fields* that receive the information from the data file. The *data file* contains the information about the recipients of the form letters or the products you're trying to sell them; this data file might be a Word table, an Excel spreadsheet, an Access database, or a Schedule+ address book.

First, if you've got a main document that you want to use, open it and make it the active window. Then choose Tools ➢ Mail Merge to start the merging process. Word will respond by displaying the Mail Merge Helper dialog box (see Figure 10.1).

TIP

The Mail Merge Helper dialog box displays increasing amounts of information and instructions about the merge as you go through the process. If you get confused about which stage you've reached, choose Tools ➢ Mail Merge to display the Mail Merge Helper dialog box and scan the information and instructions it's currently displaying.

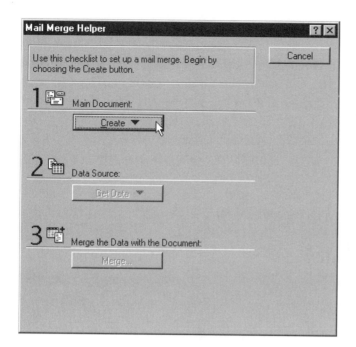

FIGURE 10.1:
The first of many appearances for the Mail Merge Helper dialog box. Click the Create button in the Main Document area to get started.

Click the Create button in the Main Document area and choose the type of document you want to create: Form Letters, Mailing Labels, Envelopes, or Catalogs. (For the example, I chose Form Letters because that still seems to be the most popular option.)

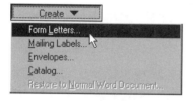

In the message box that appears, choose whether to use the document in the active document window—the document that was open when you started the Mail Merge Helper—or to create a new main document.

• If you choose to use the active document, Word records its name and path underneath the Create button in the Mail Merge Helper dialog box.

• If you choose to create a new main document, Word opens a new document for you.

Specifying the Data Source

The next step is to specify the data source for the mail merge. Click the Get Data button and choose an option from the drop-down list:

• Create Data Source lets you create a new mail merge data source for this merge project.

- Open Data Source lets you open an existing data source (e.g., the one from your last successful mail merge).
- Use Address Book lets you use an existing electronic address book, such as your Schedule+ Contact List or your Personal Address Book, as data for the merge.
- Header Options lets you run a merge in which the data comes from one source and the header information that controls the data comes from another source. This can be useful if you already have a main document with fields defined and a data source with headers that don't match the fields: Instead of changing the headers in the data source (and perhaps thereby rendering it unsuitable for its regular uses), you can choose Header Options, click the Create button, and set up a new set of headers that will bridge the gap between the main document and the data source.

Creating a New Data Source

To create a new data source, click the Get Data button and choose Create Data Source from the drop-down list. Word will display the Create Data Source dialog box (see Figure 10.2).

First, you create the *header row* for the data source—the field names that will head the columns of data and that you'll enter into your main document to tell Word where to put the variable information.

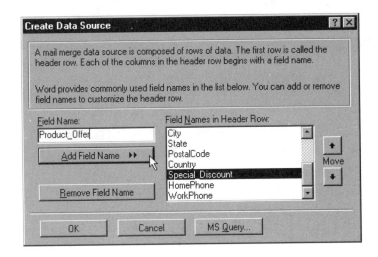

FIGURE 10.2:
Creating a new data source in the Create Data Source dialog box

Word provides a list of commonly used field names for you to customize: Title, FirstName, LastName, JobTitle, and so on. You'll find these more suitable for some projects than others—for example, for a parts catalog, you'll probably want to customize the list extensively, whereas the list is pretty much on target for a business mailing.

- To add a field name to the list, type it in the Field Name box, then click the Add Field Name button. (The most fields you can have is 31, at which point Word will prevent you from adding more.)

> **TIP**
>
> Field names can be up to 40 characters long, but you'll usually do better to keep them as short as possible while making them descriptive—ultra-cryptic names can cause confusion later in the merge process. Names can use both letters and numbers, but each name must start with a letter. You can't include spaces in the names, but you can add underscores instead—*Career_Prospects*, etc.—to make them readable.

- To remove a field name from the list, select it in the Field Names in Header Row list box and click the Remove Field Name button.
- To rearrange the field names in the list, click a field name and then click the Move buttons to move it up or down the list.

> **TIP**
>
> The list of field names in the Field Names in Header Row list box loops around, so you can move the bottom-most field to the top of the list by clicking the down button.

When you've got the list of field names to your liking, click the OK button to close the Create Data Source dialog box and save the data source you're creating.

> **WARNING**
>
> Clicking the MS Query button in the Create Data Source dialog box takes you off into the Twilight Zone of Structured Query Language (SQL, pronounced *sequel* by aficionados). Don't click this unless you're experienced in SQL queries and are happy playing with databases.

Word will now display the Save As dialog box. Save your document in the usual way. Once the document is saved, Word will display a message box telling you that the document contains no data—no surprise, as you've just created it—and inviting you to edit it or to edit the main document. For now, choose the Edit Data Source button.

Word will display the Data Form dialog box (see Figure 10.3), which is a custom dialog box built from the field names you entered in the Create Data Source dialog box.

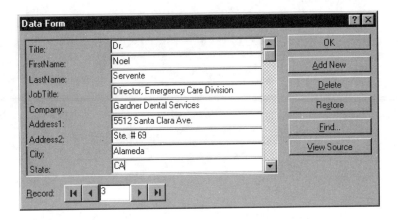

FIGURE 10.3:
In the Data Form dialog box, enter records for the data source you just created.

Add data to the data source: Type information into the fields in the dialog box. Press Enter or Tab to move between fields.

- Click the Add New button to begin a new record after entering the first one.
- Click the Delete button to delete the current record.
- Click the Restore button to restore the record to its previous condition (the information it contained before any changes you just made on screen).
- Click the View Source button to see the kind of data source you're working with in Word.
- Click the Record buttons at the bottom of the Data Form dialog box to see your records: the four buttons call up the first record, previous record, next record, and last record, respectively, and the Record box lets you type in the record number you want to move to.

Click the OK button when you've finished adding records to your data source. Word will close the Data Form dialog box and take you to your main document with the Mail Merge toolbar displayed. Skip ahead to *Adding Merge Fields to the Main Document.*

Using an Existing Data File

To use an existing data file for your mail merge, click the Get Data button in the Mail Merge Helper dialog box and choose Open Data Source. Word will display the Open Data Source dialog box (shown in Figure 10.4). Navigate to the data source document the usual way and open it.

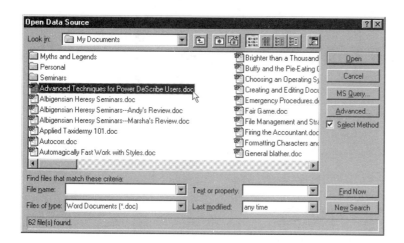

FIGURE 10.4:
Open your existing data source from the Open Data Source dialog box.

Word will now check your purported data source for fields. If it doesn't contain any fields that Word can recognize, Word will display the Header Record Delimiters dialog box for you to indicate how the fields and records are divided (delimited), as shown in Figure 10.5. Pick the delimiter characters in the Field Delimiter and Record Delimiter dropdown lists (you get to choose from paragraphs, tabs, commas, periods, exclamation points, and anything else Word thinks might be a delimiter character in this document), and then click the OK button. (If you opened the wrong file, click the Cancel button to close the Header Record Delimiters dialog box, and then click the Get Data button again for another crack at the Create Data Source dialog box.)

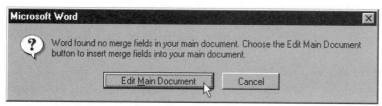

Once Word establishes that your data source contains fields, it will check your main document for merge fields. If it finds none—most likely if you're creating a new main document for the merge—it will display a message box inviting you to insert them.

Click the Edit Main Document button, and Word will return you to your main document. Now it's time to add merge fields to it.

Using Your Address Book

To run a mail merge from the data in your electronic address book, click the Get Data button in the Mail Merge Helper dialog box and choose Use Address Book. Word will display the Use Address Book dialog box. From the Choose Address Book list, choose the address book to use and click the OK button.

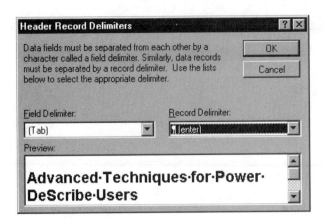

FIGURE 10.5:
If Word displays the Header Record Delimiters dialog box, you may have picked the wrong file by mistake. If not, indicate to Word how the fields and records are divided.

Depending on which address book you select, the next few actions will vary. For example, if you choose your Personal Address Book, Word may invite you to choose a profile for the merge. Play along, and shortly after interrogating you about your social security number and your mother's maiden name, Word will announce in its status bar that it's converting the address book. It will then scan the address book for viable information to use for the merge. Once Word is satisfied that you've picked a suitable address book, it will display a message box telling you that it found no merge fields in your document and inviting you to add some. Click the Edit Main Document button to do so.

Using Excel as a Data Source

To use Excel as a data source for a mail merge, click the Get Data button and choose Open Data Source. In the Open Data Source dialog box, choose *MS Excel Worksheets (*.xls)* from the Files of Type drop-down list in the lower-left corner of the dialog box, navigate to the workbook, and open it in the usual way.

Unless Excel is already open, Word will fire up a copy of it in the background (you'll still see Word on screen) and will open the designated workbook. Word will then display a dialog box in which you select the range of cells to use for the merge (see Figure 10.6).

Once you've done that, Word will put you back into the regular mail-merge loop of editing your main document. When you choose to edit your main document (which we'll look at in a moment), you'll be able to insert any or all of the fields in the workbook by using the Insert Merge Field button, as shown here.

When the merge is finished, Word will close Excel (unless it was already open, in which case Word will close only the workbook it opened).

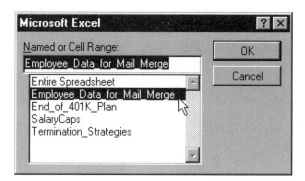

FIGURE 10.6:
When using an Excel spreadsheet as a data source, select a named range or cell range from the Named or Cell Range box to use for the merge.

Using Schedule+ as a Data Source

Your contact database in Schedule+, your Microsoft Office Personal Information Manager, can be a goldmine for mail merges. To use it, click the Get Data button and choose Use Address Book to display the Use Address Book dialog box. Choose Schedule+ Contact List and click OK.

When you choose to edit your main document, you'll be able to insert any or all of the Schedule+ fields by using the Insert Merge Field button, as shown in Figure 10.7.

> **TIP**
> Because you can set them up to meet your specific needs, the four user-defined fields in Schedule+ (User_1 through User_4) can be especially useful for incorporating merge information.

When the merge is finished, Word will close Schedule+ (unless it was already open, in which case Word will close only the schedule you chose).

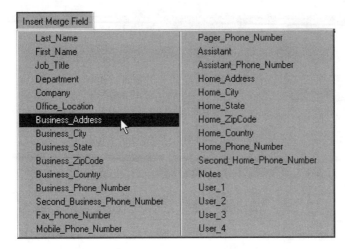

FIGURE 10.7:
Inserting
Schedule+ fields
in a Word mail-
merge document

Adding Merge Fields to the Main Document

Back in the main document, you'll see that Word has opened a Mail Merge toolbar that provides buttons for inserting merge fields and Word fields into the main document.

If you're starting a main document from scratch, add the merge fields as you write it. If you started off with the basis of your merge document already written, you just need to add the merge fields to it.

«First_Name» «Last_Name»
«Job_Title»
«Company»
«Business_Address»
«Business_City», «Business_State» «Business_ZipCode»

To insert a merge field, click the Insert Merge Field button and choose the merge field from the drop-down list of merge fields in the data source you created or chose. For example, to enter an address, choose the Title field; Word will insert a field saying **<<Title>>** in the document. Follow that with a space, insert the FirstName field and another space, and then insert the LastName field. Press ↵ and start entering the address fields. Remember the spaces and punctuation that the words will need—they're easy to forget when you're faced with a large number of fields.

The Insert Word Fields button produces a drop-down list of special fields for use in complex merges, such as Ask, Fill-in, If... Then... Else.... These fields provide you with a way to customize your merge documents so they prompt the user for keyboard input; depending on what kind of data they find in merge fields, they act in different ways. They're beyond the scope of this book, but if you do a lot of complex mail merges, you'll no doubt want to learn how to use them.

At this point, you've got the components of the merge in place—a data source with records, and a main document with field codes that match the header names in the data source. Next, you can specify options for the merge—filtering and sorting, error checking, and more—or just damn the torpedoes and merge the documents.

 If you need to make adjustments to your data source, click the Edit Data Source button on the Mail Merge toolbar—the rightmost button on the toolbar.

 If you suddenly realize you've selected the wrong data source, click the Mail Merge Helper button on the Mail Merge toolbar, click the Get Data source button in the Mail Merge Helper dialog box, and choose the right data source.

Setting Merge Options

In this section, we'll look quickly at how you can sort and filter merge documents so you can perform a merge without producing documents for every single record in your database. If you don't want to try sorting or filtering, go straight on to *Merging Your Data*.

Sorting the Records to Be Merged

By filtering your records, you can restrict the scope of your mail merges to just the appropriate part of your data source rather than creating a label, catalog, or form letter for every single record. For example, you can filter your records so you print labels of only your customers in California and Arizona, or so you send a letter extolling your pine-colored leatherette goblins only to people called Green (first name or last).

That's filtering, but you can use sorting to restrict mail merges, too. Instead of having Word print out your merge documents in the order in which you entered the records on which they're based in the data source, you can sort them by state and by city to gratify the mail room.

To sort your records:

1. Click the Mail Merge Helper button to display the Mail Merge Helper dialog box.

2. Choose the Query Options button to open the Query Options dialog box (see Figure 10.8). Click the Sort Records tab to bring it to the front if it isn't already there. You can also get to the Query Options dialog box by clicking the Query Options button in the Merge dialog box.

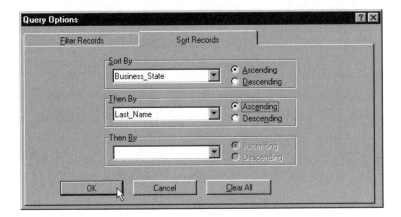

FIGURE 10.8: On the Sort Records tab of the Query Options dialog box, choose how to sort your records.

3. In the Sort By box, choose the first field you want to sort by from the drop-down list, and then choose an Ascending or Descending sort order.

4. To sort more precisely, choose the second field in the first Then By box. (For example, to sort by city within state, choose State in the Sort By box and City in the first Then By box.) Again, choose Ascending or Descending order.

5. Specify another sort field in the second Then By box if necessary (and choose the order).

6. Click the OK button to close the Query Options dialog box.
   - If you want to filter your sorted data, click the Filter Records tab instead and skip to step 3 in the next section.
   - If you choose the wrong sort fields, click the Clear All button to reset the drop-down lists to no field.

Filtering the Records to Be Merged

To filter the records you'll be merging:

1. Select the Mail Merge Helper button to display the Mail Merge Helper dialog box.
2. Click the Query Options button to open the Query Options dialog box. Click the Filter Records tab to bring it to the front if necessary.
3. In the Field drop-down list in the top row, choose the field you want to use as the first filter.
4. In the Comparison drop-down list in the top row, choose the filtering operator to specify how the contents of the field must relate to the contents of the Compare To box:

> Equal to (match)
>
> Not Equal to (not match)
>
> Less Than
>
> Greater Than
>
> Less than or Equal
>
> Greater than or Equal
>
> Is Blank (the merge field must be empty)
>
> Is Not Blank (the merge field must not be empty)

TIP   For the mathematically inclined comparisons, Word evaluates numbers using the conventional manner (1 is less than 11, and so on) and text using the American National Standards Institute (ANSI) sort order: *ax* comes before *blade* alphabetically, so *ax* is "less than" *blade*. You could also use State Is Greater than or Equal to V to filter records for Vermont, Virginia, Washington, and Wyoming. For fields that mix text and numbers, Word treats the numbers as text characters, which means that 11 will be sorted between 1 and 2 (and so on).

5. In the second and subsequent rows, choose And or Or in the unnamed first column before the Field column to add a finer filter to the filter in the previous row or to apply another filter. For example, you could choose *And LastName Is Equal to Green* to restrict your merge to Greens in Vermont.

6. Click the OK button when you've finished defining your filtering criteria. Word will return to the Mail Merge Helper dialog box (unless you got to the Query Options dialog box by clicking the Query Options button in the Merge dialog box, in which case Word will take you back there). Click the Clear All button if you need to reset all the filtering fields.

Merging Your Data

Now you're all set to merge your data source with your main document. In the Mail Merge Helper dialog box, click the Merge button. Word will display the Merge dialog box (see Figure 10.9). To merge your data:

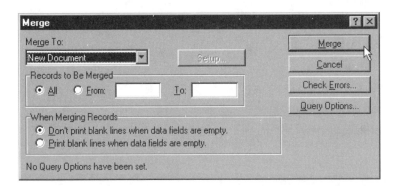

FIGURE 10.9:
In the Merge dialog box, choose whether to merge to a new document, to a printer, or to e-mail.

1. Choose whether to merge to a new document to your printer or to e-mail (if you have Microsoft Exchange installed and correctly configured):
- If you merge to a new document, Word will divide the resulting documents as it thinks best. For example, it will put page breaks between form letters so they're ready for printing, whereas mailing labels will share a page with each other.

TIP

By merging to a new document, you give yourself a chance to check the merged documents for errors—and, if you want, to add a personalized note to particular documents that you didn't want to put into your data source.

- If you merge to your printer, Word simply prints all the documents and doesn't produce an on-screen copy.

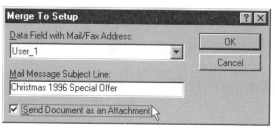

- If you merge to e-mail, click the Setup button to display the strangely named Merge To Setup dialog box. Specify the field that contains the e-mail address in the Data Field with Mail/Fax Address text box, add a subject line for the message in the Mail Message Subject Line text box, and check the Send Document as an Attachment box if the document contains formatting that will not survive transmission as an e-mail message. (This depends on the sophistication of your e-mail package and of the service provider you're using; with basic e-mail, not even bold or italic will make it through unscathed.) Then click the OK button to return to the Merge dialog box.

2. If need be, choose which records to merge in the Records to Be Merged group box: Either accept the default setting of All, or enter record numbers in the From and To boxes. To merge from a specific record to the end of the record set, enter the starting number in the From box and leave the To box blank.

> **WARNING** If you're using sorting or filtering, the records will be in a different order from that in which they were entered in the data source.

3. In the When Merging Records group box, check the *Print blank lines when data fields are empty* option button if you need to track gaps in your data. Usually, though, you'll want to leave the *Don't print blank lines when data fields are empty* option button selected to produce a better-looking result.

4. Click the Check Errors button and verify which option button has been selected in

the Checking and Reporting Errors dialog box (shown here). The default choice is *Complete the merge, pausing to report each error as it occurs*; you can also choose *Simulate the merge and report errors in a new document* if you consider the merge potentially problematic; or you can choose *Complete the merge without pausing. Report errors in a new document.* Click the OK button when you've made your choice.

5. Click the Merge button to run the mail merge.

    - If you're merging to a new document, Word will display it on screen. You can then check the merged documents for errors before printing, and you can save it if you want to keep it for future use.

    - If you're merging to a printer, Word will display the Print dialog box. Choose the page range and number of copies, if necessary, and then click the OK button to print the documents. When Word has finished printing, it will return you to your main document. Word doesn't create the merged documents on disk, so you can't save them.

    - If you're merging to e-mail, Word will check your Exchange settings, and then mail the messages and documents (if you're currently online or connected to the network that handles your e-mail), or Word will place them in your Outbox (if you're not currently online or connected to the network).

Merging Labels and Envelopes

In Chapter 8, we looked at how you can print labels and envelopes with Word. In this section, we won't grind through *all* that information again—we'll just look at the parts that are different when you're running a mail merge to print labels and envelopes.

Merge-Printing Labels

To create labels for a merge-print:

1. Choose Tools ➤ Mail Merge, select Mailing Labels from the Create drop-down list, and then follow the procedures described earlier in this chapter until you've created or selected your data source. Then Word will invite you to set up your main document; accept by clicking the Set Up Main Document button.

2. Word will then display the Label Options dialog box. Choose your labels as discussed in Chapter 8 and click the OK button.

3. Word will then display the Create Labels dialog box (see Figure 10.10), so you can set up a label format. Click the Insert Merge Fields button and choose the fields for the labels from the drop-down list. Word will insert them in the Sample Label box. Include punctuation, spaces, and carriage returns as appropriate.

TIP You can apply formatting to the merge field codes by selecting them and using keyboard shortcuts, such as Ctrl+B for boldface and Ctrl+I for italic.

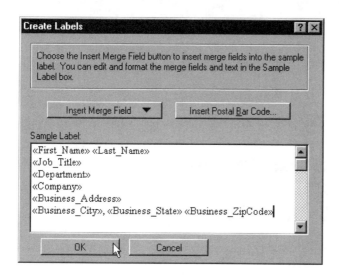

FIGURE 10.10: In the Create Labels dialog box, set up your labels for merge-printing.

4. If you want to include a postal bar code for the address, click the Insert Postal Bar Code button and select the fields from the Merge Field with ZIP Code and Merge Field with Street Address drop-down lists.

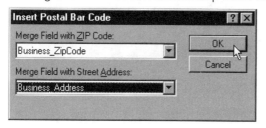

5. Click the OK button to close the Insert Postal Bar Code dialog box. Word will insert a boldfaced line saying **Delivery point bar code will print here!** at the top of the Sample Label box.

6. Click the OK button to close the Create Labels dialog box.

Word will create the main document for the labels from the contents of the Sample Label box and will return you to the Mail Merge Helper dialog box. From there, follow the instructions in *Merging Your Data* to complete the merge.

Merge-Printing Envelopes

To set up envelopes for a merge-print:

1. Choose Tools ➤ Mail Merge, select Envelopes from the Create drop-down list, and then follow the procedures described earlier in this chapter (in *Creating the Main Document* and *Specifying the Data Source*) until you've created or selected your data source. As with labels, Word will display a message box asking you to click the Set Up Main Document button to finish setting up your main document.

2. Click the Set Up Main Document button and Word will display the Envelope Options dialog box that we investigated in Chapter 8.

3. When you've made your choices in the Envelope Options dialog box, click the OK button to display the Envelope Address dialog box (see Figure 10.11).

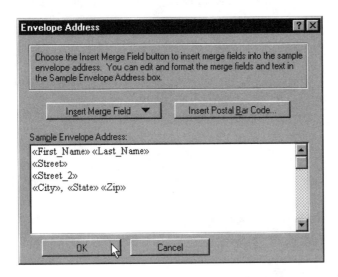

FIGURE 10.11:
In the Envelope Address dialog box, set up the arrangement of fields you want for your envelopes.

4. Click the Insert Merge Fields button and choose the fields for the envelopes from the drop-down list. Word will insert them in the Sample Envelope Address box. Include punctuation, spaces, and carriage returns as appropriate, and add any text that you want on each envelope. Again, you can use keyboard shortcuts to apply formatting to the merge field codes.

5. To include a postal bar code for the address, click the Insert Postal Bar Code button and select the fields from the Merge Field with ZIP Code and the Merge Field with Street Address drop-down lists.

TIP You'll see that in the Insert Postal Bar Code dialog box for envelopes, there's also an FIM-A Courtesy Reply Mail check box that you can select if you want to print a Facing Identification Mark on courtesy reply envelopes.

6.   Click the OK button to close the Insert Postal Bar Code dialog box. Word will insert a boldfaced line saying **Delivery point bar code will print here!** at the top of the Sample Label box.

7.   Click the OK button to close the Envelope Address dialog box.

Word will create the main document for the envelopes from the contents of the Sample Envelope Address box and will return you to the Mail Merge Helper dialog box. From there, follow the instructions *Merging Your Data* to complete the merge. If you choose to merge to a printer, line up the envelopes so they are ready for printing.

Restoring a Main Document to a Regular Document

If you know you won't need to use your main document again for a mail merge, be reassured that it isn't merged forever—you can easily restore it to a regular Word document:

1.   Open the main document.

2.   Choose Tools ➤ Mail Merge to display the Mail Merge Helper dialog box.

3.   Click the Create button and choose Restore to Normal Word Document from the drop-down list. Word will break the main document's attachment to its data file and restore it to normal document status.

Chapter 11

OUTLINES AND ADVANCED FEATURES

- **Working with outlines**
- **Using advanced Find and Replace**
- **Customizing the AutoText feature**
- **Using automatic bullets and numbering**
- **Working with Word as your e-mail editor**

In addition to the Office-wide spelling checker and AutoCorrect features that we looked at in Chapter 3, Word offers several automation features that can greatly increase the speed at which you work with documents. Outlines let you collapse a document to different levels of heading, then reshuffle the headings and their associated text; AutoText lets you create abbreviations for boilerplate text you enter frequently in documents; and automatic bullets and numbering (including heading numbering) lets you format and identify your documents effortlessly. We'll look at each of these features in turn in this chapter. Finally, you can use Word as your e-mail editing program; we'll discuss that at the end of the chapter.

Outlines

Outline view is one of Word's most useful features if you're writing anything longer than a couple of pages. Using Outline view and Word's heading styles, you can collapse a document to an outline showing any number of heading levels from one to eight. For example, you can collapse a document to show three levels of headings, hiding any sub-headings and body text between the headings. You can then zero in on a crucial heading and expand the text underneath it so you can make a strategic addition or two, and then collapse that text again to move quickly to another heading. You can also move blocks of text around your document quickly or promote or demote a whole series of headings in one move.

> **TIP**
>
> You can create a PowerPoint presentation from a Word outline. For details, see Chapter 18.

How Outlines Work

Outlines work by using Word's nine heading styles, Heading 1 to Heading 8. These styles are predefined, so you can't delete them, no matter how hard you try, though you can format them however you like.

> **TIP**
>
> Even if you're creating a short document, Outline view can save you time. As discussed in *Creating a New Style* in Chapter 7, most Heading styles are typically followed by a different paragraph style, on the assumption that you won't want to type several headings in a row—for example, you might want a Heading 1 paragraph to be followed by Body Text, or by some special graphical element that would offset the heading and draw the reader's attention. In Outline view, however, pressing Enter creates another paragraph with the same paragraph style, so you can quickly crank out a full chapter's worth of Heading 1 paragraphs, Heading 2 paragraphs, or whatever.

Creating an Outline

You can create an outline either in a new document or from an existing document.

Creating a New Outline

To create an outline in a new document:

1. Start a new document by choosing File ➤ New and choosing the template you want in the New dialog box.
2. Choose View ➤ Outline to switch to Outline view. Word will display the Outlining toolbar (see Figure 11.1).

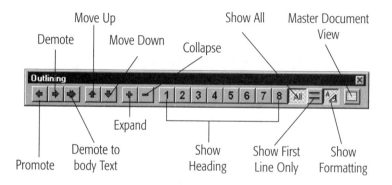

FIGURE 11.1:
The Outlining toolbar provides quick access to the main features of Outline view.

3. Make sure that the paragraph style in the Style drop-down list on the Formatting toolbar is set to Heading 1 style. (Word will usually start the new document with a paragraph in Heading 1 style, depending on which template you chose in step 1.)
4. Enter the first-level headings, pressing Enter after each one. Word will start each new paragraph in Heading 1 style, no matter what the Style for Following Paragraph for the Heading 1 style is set to.
5. To enter a second-level heading, press Tab to switch to Heading 2 style. Type the text for the heading and press Enter; Word will start a new paragraph also based on the Heading 2 style.
   - To enter third-level headings, fourth-level headings, and so on, press Tab to move down through the Heading styles.
   - To move back up through the heading styles, press Shift+Tab.
6. Save the document as usual.

Outlining an Existing Document

To outline an existing document:

1. Open the document.
2. If the document isn't already formatted with styles, apply Heading styles to the headings by using the Formatting toolbar or the Format ➤ Style command.
3. Switch the document to Outline view by choosing View ➤ Outline.

Viewing an Outline

To switch a document to Outline view, choose View ➤ Outline or click the Outline View button on the horizontal scroll bar (if you have it displayed). Word will shuffle your document into Outline view and display the Outlining toolbar.

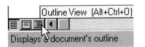

When you choose Outline view, the Outlining toolbar appears, and an outline symbol appears to the left of each paragraph's first line, as shown in Figure 11.2. A fat plus sign appearing next to a heading indicates that the heading has subheadings or text (or both) underneath it; a fat minus sign means that the heading has nothing between it and the next heading. A small empty square indicates a paragraph of non-heading text.

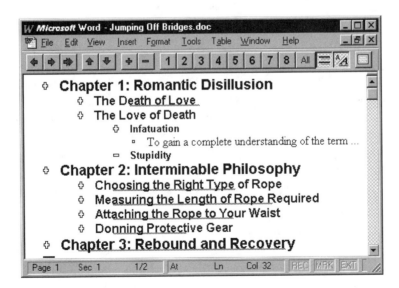

FIGURE 11.2:
In Outline view, Word displays a hierarchy of headings that you can collapse to different levels.

To collapse or expand the outline to different levels, use the Expand and Collapse buttons and the eight numbered buttons on the Outlining toolbar. The Expand button reveals the subtext for the selected heading—for example, if you position the insertion point in a Heading 2 paragraph and click the Expand button, Word will display any Heading 3 paragraphs beneath the Heading 2 paragraph. If there are no Heading 3 paragraphs, Word will display paragraphs with the next Heading level style (Heading 4, then Heading 5, then Heading 6, etc.); if there are no headings at all between the selected Heading paragraph and the end of the document, Word will display body text. The Collapse button reverses the process, collapsing the outline one available level at a time. In other words, outline levels below the one you choose will be hidden.

The eight Show Heading *n* buttons on the Outlining toolbar expand or collapse the whole outline to that level of heading, while the All button toggles the display of all heading levels and body text.

You can also collapse (or expand) all the headings under a heading by double-clicking the fat plus sign next to it.

The Show First Line Only button on the Outlining toolbar shows only the first line of body text paragraphs. This option can be a great help in getting an overview of a large part of your document.

Promoting and Demoting Items

Once you've expanded or collapsed your outline so you can see the appropriate parts of it, you're ready to work with it. Two of the most useful buttons on the Outlining toolbar are the Promote and Demote buttons, which you can use to reorganize the headings in a document quickly. Click these once to promote or demote the current paragraph one level of heading at a time.

When you select a heading using its outline symbol (the fat plus sign), you select all its subheadings as well (whether or not they're displayed). When you promote or demote a heading with its subheadings selected, you promote or demote the subheadings as well. For example, if I demote the Chapter 2 heading shown here from Heading 1 to Heading 2, the

Heading 2 paragraphs will be demoted to Heading 3, the Heading 3 paragraphs to Heading 4, and so on. To promote (or demote) a heading without promoting (or demoting) all its subheadings, first expand the outline to display the sub-headings. Then click in the heading and click the Promote (or Demote) button until the heading has reached the level you want it to be.

> **Chapter 2: Interminable Philosophy**
> ⇩ Choosing the Right Type of Rope
>   ⇩ Nylon
>   ⇩ Manila
>   ⇩ Hemp
> ⇩ Measuring the Length of Rope Required
> ⇩ Donning Protective Gear
> ⇩ Attaching the Rope to Your Waist

TIP   **To select a heading without selecting its subheadings, click in the selection bar next to the heading. To select several headings, click and drag in the selection bar.**

 To demote a heading to text, click the Demote to Body Text button. Word will apply Normal style to it.

TIP   **You can also demote the paragraph you're working in by pressing Tab, or promote it by pressing Shift+Tab (to type a tab, press Ctrl+Tab).**

Moving Items Up and Down

> ⇩ Measuring the Length of Rope Required
> ⇩ Donning Protective Gear
> ◆ Attaching the Rope to Your Waist

Outline view makes reordering the items in an outline speedy and simple. To move a heading up and down the outline, expand or collapse the outline so the heading you want to move is displayed, then click the symbol next to the heading and drag it up or down the outline. You'll see a line move up or down the screen indicating where the paragraph will end up when you let go of it (as shown here).

Alternatively, select the heading (and any subheadings you want to move with it) and click the Move Up or Move Down button to move it up or down the outline one displayed paragraph at a time.

Using Heading Numbering

Heading numbering, which we'll look at later in this chapter, can be a great asset in Outline view. Instead of needing to renumber your chapters as you drag them about the outline, you can let Word take care of the numbering automatically.

Formatting in Outline View

As we saw in *Viewing an Outline* earlier in the chapter, you can click the Show Formatting button on the Outlining toolbar to stop Word from displaying character formatting in Outline view. This feature can help you get more headings on-screen in a readable format.

You can apply character formatting and style formatting as usual in Outline view, but you can't apply paragraph formatting. Bear in mind when applying style formatting to headings that you may not be seeing the effect of the changes you're making. Consider splitting the window (by double-clicking or dragging the Split bar at the top of the vertical scroll bar; see Chapter 5, Figure 5.8) and switching one of the resulting panes to Normal view or Page Layout view.

Printing an Outline

When you print from Outline view, Word prints only the information displayed on screen—for example, to print only the first three levels of headings, click the Show Heading 3 button and choose File ➤ Print.

Advanced Find and Replace

Word's Find and Replace features go far beyond the standard Office Find and Replace features that we looked at in Chapter 3. Not only can you find and replace strings of text and use Find to locate strategic parts of your documents; you can also search for special characters (such as tabs or paragraph marks), for special operators (such as any digit or any character or range of characters), for particular formatting (such as double-underline, bold, and italic in Engravers Gothic font), or for a particular style. You can search for text in a particular language, for paragraphs with particular tab formatting, or for text that sounds like other text. You can even combine many of these elements to conduct searches of truly fiendish complexity that will confound your colleagues and impress your friends.

Finding Text

Word offers a large number of features for finding text. You can search for text without worrying about its formatting; you can search for text with particular formatting, such as bold, double underline, or 44-point Allegro font; or you can search for a particular style.

To find text:

1. Choose Edit ➢ Find to display the Find dialog box (see Figure 11.3).

FIGURE 11.3:
The Find dialog box gives you a quick way to access any combination of characters or formatting in your document.

2. In the Find What box, enter the text you're looking for.
   - You can use *wildcard* characters to find a variety of characters. We'll get into this in a moment in *Finding Special Characters and Special Operators*.
   - Word stores the Find operations from the current session in a drop-down list that you can access by clicking the arrow at the right-hand end of the Find What box.

3. Choose the direction to search from the Search drop-down list: Down, Up, or All. If you choose Down or Up, Word will prompt you to continue when it reaches the end or beginning of the document (unless you started Find at the beginning or end of the document).

4. Choose the options you want from the line of check boxes in the middle of the dialog box. We looked at Match Case and Find Whole Words Only in Chapter 3; Word also offers the following:
   - Use Pattern Matching provides special search options that we'll look at in *Finding Special Characters and Special Operators*, later in this chapter.
   - Sounds Like finds words that Word thinks sound like those in the Find What box. Your mileage may vary depending on your own pronunciation. For example, if you check the Sounds Like check box and enter *meddle* in the

Find What box, Word will find both *middle* and *muddle*, but it won't find rhyming words, such as *peddle* and *pedal*.

- Find All Word Forms attempts to find all forms of the verb or noun in the Find What box. This is particularly useful with Replace operations: Word can change *break*, *broken*, *breaking*, and *breaks* to *fix*, *fixed*, *fixing*, and *fixes*. Enter the basic form of the word in the Find What and Replace With boxes—in this example, you would use *break* and *fix*. Use Find All Word Forms with care, and do not use it with Replace All, which gives it a free hand to wreak havoc on your precious text.

5. Make sure no formatting information appears in the box under the Find What text box. If the No Formatting button at the bottom of the dialog box is displayed, that means Word will look for words only with the selected formatting; click the button to remove the formatting. If the No Formatting button is dimmed, you're OK.

6. Click the Find Next button to find the next instance of your chosen text. If Word finds the text, it will stop; otherwise, it will tell you that it was unable to find the text.

7. Click the Find Next button again to keep searching, or click the Cancel button to close the Find dialog box.

Finding Special Characters and Special Operators

Often, you'll want to search for something more complex than plain text: Perhaps you'll need to search for an em dash (—), or a paragraph mark or any number; or you may want to search for words beginning with one character but not another, or for words that begin with a certain range of letters. For the first three of these, you'll need to use Word's special characters; for the last two, Word's special search operators will do the trick.

Special Characters

To find a special character, such as a paragraph mark, a tab character, or a graphic, click the Special button on the Find dialog box and choose the character from the drop-down list that appears (see Figure 11.4).

You can combine special characters with regular text to make your Find operations more effective. For example, the special character for a paragraph mark is **^p**; to find every instance where "Joanne" appears at the beginning of a paragraph, you could search for **^pJoanne**.

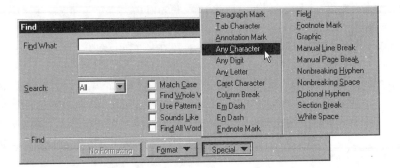

FIGURE 11.4:
You can find special characters, such as page breaks or endnote marks, by using the Special drop-down list in the Find dialog box.

It's usually easiest to enter special characters from the Special drop-down list, but you can also enter them manually for speed's sake. Here's the full list of characters and what they find:

Character	Finds
^?	Any one character
*	A string of characters. Select the Use Pattern Matching check box when you use this.
^p	A paragraph mark
^t	A tab
^a	An annotation mark
^#	Any digit
^$	Any letter
^^	A caret (^)
^n	A column break
^+	An em dash (—)
^=	An en dash (–)
^e	An endnote mark
^d	A field
^f	A footnote mark
^g	A graphic
^l	A manual line break
^m	A manual page break
^~	A nonbreaking hyphen
^s	A nonbreaking space
^-	An optional hyphen
^b	A section break
^w	A white space

Of these, you'll probably find yourself using ^? and * the most. For example, you could use **g^?t** to find "got," "gut," etc., and **f*d** to find "fad," "fatherhood," and "flustered"—not to mention "after the tragic death of Don Quixote."

WARNING	As you can see from the Don Quixote example, you need to be careful when using the * special character, particularly with only one identifying letter on either side of it. (Most any document will contain a *d* somewhere after an *f*.)

Special Operators

Word's special operators let you search for one character out of several specified, one character in a range, any character in a range, any character *except* the given one, and even a string of characters at the beginning or end of a word only. To enter these operators, select the Use Pattern Matching check box, and then click the Special button to display the drop-down list. Here is the list of operators and what they find:

Operator	Finds	Examples
[]	Any one of the given characters	**s[iou]n** finds "sin," "son," and "sun."
[-]	Any one character in the range	**[g-x]ote** finds "note," "mote," "rote," and "tote." Enter the ranges in alphabetical order.
[!]	Any one character except the characters inside the brackets	**[!f][!a]therhood** finds "motherhood" but not "fatherhood."
[!x-z]	Any one character except characters in the range inside the brackets	**a[!b-l]e** finds "ape," "are," and "ate," but not "ace," "age," or "ale."
{x}	Exactly x number of occurrences of the previous character or expression	**we{2}d** finds "weed" but not "wed," because "weed" has two es.
{x,}	At least x occurrences of the previous character or expression	**we{1,}d** finds "weed" and "wed" because both words have at least one *e*.
{x,y}	From x to y occurrences of the previous character or expression	**40{2,4}** finds "400," "4000," and "40000," because each has between two and four zeroes; it won't find "40," because it has only one zero.

Operator	Finds	Examples
@	One or more occurrences of the previous character or expression	**o@h!** finds "oh!" and "ooh!", which both contain one or more *o*s and then an *h*.
<	The following search string (in parentheses) at the beginning of a word	**<(ane)** finds "anesthesia" and "anecdotage," but not "bane."
>	The preceding search string (in parentheses) at the end of a word	**(sin)>** finds "basin" and "moccasin," but not "sinful."

Finding and Replacing Formatting

TIP
When replacing simple text, make sure that Word is displaying no formatting information below the Find What box and Replace With boxes—otherwise Word will find only instances of the text that have the appropriate formatting information (bold, italic, Book Antiqua font, or Heading 4 style, etc.), or it will replace the text in the Find What box with inappropriately formatted text from the Replace With box. To remove formatting information from the boxes below the Find What box and Replace With box, click in the appropriate box and then click the No Formatting button.

There's no need to use text for Replace operations in Word—you can simply find one kind of formatting and replace it with another. For example, say you received an article for your newsletter in which the author had used boldface rather than italic for emphasizing words she intended to explain. To convert these words from bold to italic, you could replace all text that has Bold formatting with text that has No Bold, Italic formatting.

Such replacing sounds suspiciously utopian, but it works well. Alternatively, you can replace particular strings of text that have one kind of formatting with the same strings of text that have different kinds of formatting; or you can replace formatted strings of text with other formatted strings of text.

To replace one kind of formatting with another kind of formatting:

1.   Choose Edit ➤ Replace to display the Replace dialog box.

2.   With the insertion point in the Find What box, click the Format button and choose Font, Paragraph, or Tabs from the drop-down list. Word will display the Find Font, Find Paragraph, or Find Tabs dialog box. These are versions of the Font, Paragraph, and Tabs dialog boxes discussed in Chapter 6.

Format:	Font: Playbill, 20 pt, Italic, Word Underline, Raised 3 pt, Magenta

3.   Choose the formatting you want Word to find, then click the OK button to return to the Replace dialog box. Word will display the formatting you chose in the Format box underneath the Find What box (as shown here).

4.   Add further formatting to the mix by repeating steps 2 and 3 with font, paragraph, or tab formatting.

5.   With the insertion point in the Replace With box, click the Format button and choose Font, Paragraph, or Tabs from the drop-down list. Word will display the Replace Font, Replace Paragraph, or Replace Tabs dialog box. Again, these are versions of the regular Font, Paragraph, and Tabs dialog boxes discussed in Chapter 6.

6.   Choose the replacement formatting, then click the OK button to return to the Replace dialog box. Word will display this formatting in the Format box under the Replace With box.

7.   Again, add further font, paragraph, or tab formatting, this time by repeating steps 5 and 6.

8.   Start the search by clicking the Find Next, Replace, or Replace All buttons.

TIP

Without any text entered in the Find What box and Replace With box, Word will replace all instances of the formatting you chose—for example, all boldface with italic, no boldface. You can also enter text in the Find What box and nothing in the Replace With box to have Word remove that text and put different formatting where it was, or you can enter replacement text in the Replace With box and replace both the text and the formatting at once, for example, replace all boldfaced instances of the word *break* with italicized (without boldface) instances of the word *fix*.

Finding and Replacing Styles

To replace one style with another:

1. Choose Edit ➤ Replace to display the Replace dialog box.

2. Make sure that the Format boxes under the Find What box and the Replace With box don't contain any formatting information. To clear formatting information from the boxes, click in the appropriate box and then click the No Formatting button.

3. With the insertion point in the Find What box, click the Format button and choose Style from the drop-down list. Word will display the Find Style dialog box (see Figure 11.5).

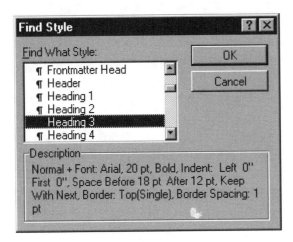

FIGURE 11.5:
In the Find Style dialog box, choose the style you want Word to find.

4. Choose the style you want to find from the Find What Style list, then click the OK button to return to the Replace dialog box. The box underneath the Find What box will display the style you chose.

5. Click in the Replace With box (or press Tab to move the insertion point there), then click the Format button and choose Style once more. Word will display the Replace Style dialog box, which is virtually identical to the Find Style dialog box.

6. Choose the replacement style from the Replace With Style list, and then click the OK button to return to the Replace dialog box. The box underneath the Replace With box will display the style you chose.

7. Choose a search direction from the Search drop-down list if necessary.

8. Start the search by clicking the Find Next, Replace, or Replace All buttons.

TIP

To replace words or characters in one style with words or characters in another style, choose the styles as described above and then enter the appropriate text in the Find What box and Replace With box.

AutoText

Word's AutoText feature is similar to the Office AutoCorrect feature (discussed in Chapter 3) in that it lets you define abbreviations for boilerplate items you want to insert frequently in your documents. The difference is that AutoText does not scan each word you type, looking for a chance to jump in; instead, it lurks in the wings until you summon it to work by pressing the F3 key or by choosing Edit ➤ AutoText.

Creating an AutoText Entry

To create an AutoText entry:

1. Select the text (and/or graphics, etc.) from your document for the AutoText entry. Make sure that it contains all the formatting it needs.
2. Choose Edit ➤ AutoText to open the AutoText dialog box (see Figure 11.6).
3. In the Name box, enter the name you'll use to identify the AutoText entry.
    - Word will automatically display the first couple of words from your selection in the Name box. Usually it's best to think up something catchy that you won't forget in a hurry.
    - Unlike AutoCorrect entries, AutoText entries can have plain-English names that you'll type all the time because they won't trigger AutoText of their own accord.
4. In the Make AutoText Entry Available To list, restrict the AutoText entry to certain templates if you want. Usually, you'll want to do this when the template you're working in needs to have an AutoText entry with the same name as an AutoText entry in Normal.dot (the global template, which is lurking in the wings even when you're working in another template). By making the AutoText entry available only to the other template, you can avoid overwriting the existing AutoText entry in Normal.dot.
5. Click the Add button to add the AutoText entry to the list in the template and close the dialog box. If an AutoText entry with the same name already exists, Word will ask if you want to redefine it. Choose Yes or No; if you choose

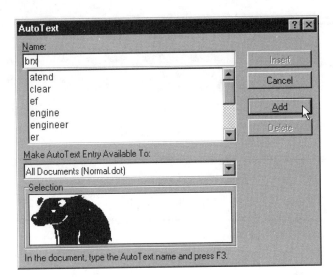

FIGURE 11.6:
The AutoText
dialog box is
used for creating
AutoText entries.

No, Word will let you choose another name for the AutoText entry; if you choose Yes, Word will replace the existing AutoText entry with the new one.

Inserting an AutoText Entry

There are two ways to insert an AutoText entry: the quick way, which involves remembering the name you used for it, and the regular way, which involves looking up the entry up in the AutoText dialog box and inserting it from there.

To insert an AutoText entry quickly, type the name of the entry and press the F3 key. Word will replace the name of the entry with the full text of the entry.

> **TIP**
>
> To insert an AutoText entry even more quickly, type just enough letters of its name for Word to distinguish it from any other AutoText entry name that begins with the same letters, and then press F3.

To insert an AutoText entry whose name you can't remember:

1. Place the insertion point where you want the AutoText entry to appear.
2. Choose Edit ➤ AutoText. Word will display an AutoText dialog box (a different one this time; see Figure 11.7).
3. In the Name list, choose the AutoText entry to insert. Watch the Preview box to make sure you've found the right entry. You can type the first few letters of an entry's name in the Name box to scroll quickly to the right section of the list.

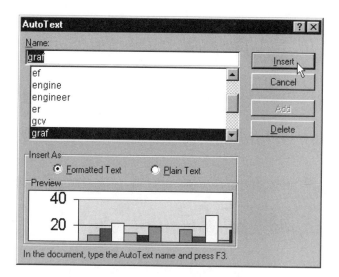

FIGURE 11.7:
To insert an AutoText entry whose name you can't remember, choose Edit ➤ AutoText and then choose the entry from the AutoText dialog box.

4. If the entry has formatting that you don't want in your document, click the Plain Text option button in the Insert As group box to insert the entry as plain text without formatting. On the other hand, if the entry *does* have formatting that you want to appear, make sure the Formatted Text option button has been selected to insert the entry with the same formatting as appears in the Preview box.

5. Click the Insert button to insert the entry and close the AutoText dialog box.

Deleting an AutoText Entry

To delete an AutoText entry, choose Edit ➤ AutoText. In the AutoText dialog box, select the entry from the list of names, and then click the Delete button. You can then delete more AutoText entries while you're at it, or you can click the Close button to exit the AutoText dialog box.

Automatic Bullets and Numbering

In this section, we'll look at Word's features for adding automatic bullets and numbering and heading numbering to your documents. First, though, you need to know that the bullets and numbering that Word applies automatically are paragraph formatting rather than actual characters on the page. Once you've added a bullet to a list, you can't just select the bullet and delete it as you might delete a character—you have to remove it from the paragraph's formatting. We'll look at this process in *Removing Bullets and Numbering*.

Adding Bullets and Numbering

You can add straightforward bullets and numbering to existing text by using the buttons on the Formatting toolbar.

To add bullets, first select the paragraphs you want to add bullets to, and then click the Bullets button on the Formatting toolbar. Word will add the bullets and will apply a hanging indent to each of the paragraphs but will leave them in their current style.

> **TIP**
>
> **To continue a numbered or bulleted list, press ⏎ at the end of the list. To discontinue the list, press Enter ⏎ twice at the end of the list.**

To add numbers, select the paragraphs you want to number, and then click the Numbering button on the Formatting toolbar.

For a variety of styles of bullets and numbering, select your victim paragraphs, and then choose Format ➤ Bullets and Numbering to open the Bullets and Numbering dialog box (see Figure 11.8).

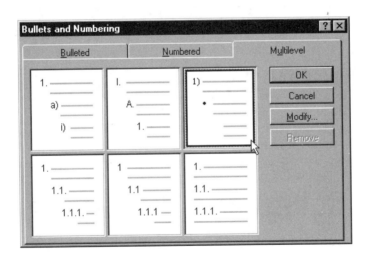

FIGURE 11.8:
The Bullets and Numbering dialog box gives you plenty of choices for bulleting and numbering your lists.

Choose the tab that corresponds to the type of list you want to create: Bulleted, Numbered, or Multilevel, and then click the style that suits you best. Click the OK button to close the Bullets and Numbering dialog box.

Removing Bullets and Numbering

There are three ways to remove bullets or numbering from selected paragraphs:

- Click the Bullets button or the Numbering button.
- Choose Format ➤ Bullets and Numbering and click the Remove button on the tab displayed.
- Right-click the list and choose Stop Numbering from the shortcut menu. (This works for bullets, too.)

Using Heading Numbering

For complex documents that require numbered paragraphs (such as contracts and some manuals), Word's heading numbering feature can prove invaluable.

TIP   Heading numbering applies to the whole of a document—you can't apply it to just one section or use different types of heading numbering for different sections, though you can restart heading numbering for each section if you want.

To number headings:

1. Choose Format ➤ Heading Numbering. Word will display the Heading Numbering dialog box (see Figure 11.9).

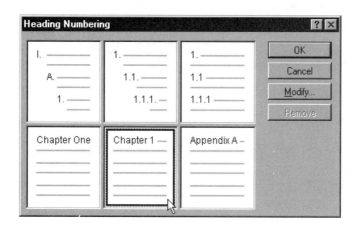

FIGURE 11.9: Choose a style of heading numbering in the Heading Numbering dialog box.

> **TIP**
>
> You can also right-click in any heading and choose Heading Numbering from the shortcut menu to display the Heading Numbering dialog box.

2. Choose a style of heading numbering by clicking one of the pictured styles.
3. Click the OK button to apply the style you chose to your document.

> **TIP**
>
> To remove heading numbering, choose Format ➢ Heading Numbering to display the Heading Numbering dialog box, and then click the Remove button. To modify heading numbering, display the Heading Numbering dialog box and click the Modify button. Word will display the Modify Heading Numbering dialog box with your current heading numbering styles displayed.

Using Word as Your E-mail Editor

The Microsoft Exchange Client for Windows 95 contains an acceptable e-mail editor for general-purpose mail messages, but by using Word as your e-mail editor, you can take advantages of Word features, such as formatting and the Spelling checker.

In WordMail, you can create bulleted and numbered lists in your message, or add tables with cells containing wrapped text. You can also add formatting (such as boldface or italic), or use the highlighter to draw the recipient's attention to the most important points of the message. First, however, you need to tell Windows 95 that you want to use Word as your e-mail editor, which we'll look at in the next section.

Setting Word Up as Your E-mail Editor

To set Word up as your e-mail editor:

Inbox

1. Start the Exchange client by double-clicking on the Inbox icon on the Windows 95 desktop.
2. Choose Compose ➢ WordMail Options to display the WordMail Options dialog box (see Figure 11.10).
3. Select the Enable Word as Email Editor check box at the lower-left corner of the WordMail Options dialog box.

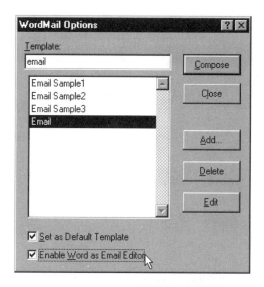

FIGURE 11.10:
In the WordMail Options dialog box, select the Enable Word as Email Editor check box.

4. Choose a template for the mail message from the Template list box. If you want this template to be the default template when you compose e-mail, select the Set as Default Template check box. If you want to be able to choose a different template for each message you compose, clear the Set as Default Template check box.

5. Click Compose to close the WordMail Options dialog box and start writing a message. Read on.

Writing E-mail in Word

To write e-mail messages in Word, enable Word as your e-mail editor as described in the previous section. Once you've done that, when you click the New Message button in Exchange, Exchange will start Word as your e-mail editor.

First, address your message, either by typing an e-mail address into the To box or by clicking the To button and choosing one or more recipients from the Address Book dialog box (see Figure 11.11).

Enter a subject in the Subject box, then enter the text of your message in the main text box (see Figure 11.12). You can use most of the Word features described in Part II of this book for composing your message; for example, you can have heading styles such as Heading 1, Heading 2, and Heading 3 in your message, and you can use the outlining features discussed earlier in this chapter for scrutinizing your message; you can use the Spelling checker; you can use font and paragraph formatting to make the elements of your message stand out; and you can even add pictures to your messages.

To send your message, click the Send button or press Alt+S.

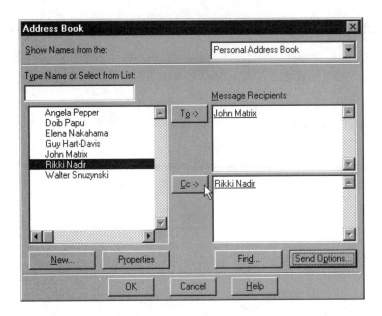

FIGURE 11.11:
Choose one or more recipients for the message in the Address Book dialog box.

FIGURE 11.12:
In the New Message - Microsoft Word window, compose and send your message.

Chapter 12

CREATING MACROS AND CUSTOMIZING WORD

- **Creating macros to speed repetitive tasks**
- **Customizing toolbars, menus, and keyboard shortcuts**
- **Setting environment options**
- **Working with templates**

In this chapter, we'll look at three of Word's most appealing features—easy macro recording in a powerful macro language; a user interface (screens, menus, and keyboard shortcuts) customizable to the *n*th degree; and templates that you can pack with special styles, AutoText entries, toolbars, and macros.

By recording macros, you can automate routine tasks (such as creating or formatting documents) so you can run them with one keystroke or click, thus saving significant amounts of time and effort.

By customizing the Word user interface, you can ensure that the menus and toolbars you or your colleagues use contain the commands most useful to you or them— or you can take commands that might cause problems out of temptation's way. You can also set Word's environment options—such as the Edit and File Locations options—to further simplify your working life.

By using templates, you can use boilerplate text and formatting to greatly speed the creation of documents.

Macros

A macro is a sequence of commands that you can assign to a single key, button, or menu command, and then repeat at will. For example, you might create a macro to automate basic formatting tasks on a type of document you receive regularly in an inappropriate format and which requires a clearly defined sequence of steps to reformat it.

In Word, you can swiftly create macros by turning on Word's macro recorder and performing the sequence of actions you want the macro to contain. (If you're feeling ambitious, you can then open the macro in a macro-editing window and change it by deleting parts of what you've recorded or by typing in extra commands; or you can write a macro from scratch.)

Once you've created a macro, you can assign it to a menu option, a key combination, or a toolbar button and run it at any time.

Recording a Macro

First, start the macro recorder by double-clicking the REC indicator on the status bar. Word will display the Record Macro dialog box (see Figure 12.1).

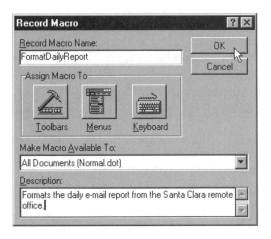

FIGURE 12.1:
In the Record Macro dialog box, enter a name for the macro you're about to record and give it an illuminating write-up in the Description box.

Enter a name for the new macro in the Record Macro Name text box. The macro name can be up to 80 characters long and can contain both letters and numbers, but it must start with a letter. It cannot contain spaces, punctuation, or special characters (such as ! or *).

> **TIP** If you type a space or a forbidden character in the Record Macro Name text box, Word will dim the OK button to keep you from proceeding any further.

Enter a description for the macro in the Description box. This description is to help you (and anyone you share the macro with) identify the macro; it will appear on the status bar when you highlight the macro's menu option or when you move the mouse pointer over the macro's toolbar button. The description can be up to 255 characters long, but only about 100 characters will fit on the status bar at 640x480 screen resolution, so put the important information up front.

If you want to restrict the macro to just the current template, choose the template from the Make Macro Available To drop-down list. If you want the macro to be available no matter which template you're working in, make sure the default setting, *All Documents (Normal.dot),* appears in the drop-down list box.

Next, click one of the buttons in the Assign Macro To box: the Toolbars, Menus, or Keyboard button. Word will display the Customize dialog box with the Toolbars, Menus, or Keyboard tab displayed, respectively (see Figure 12.2).

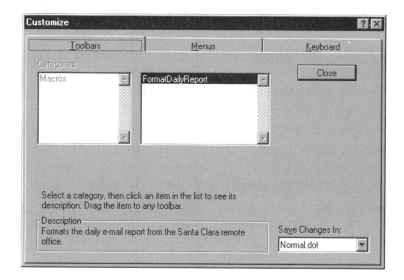

FIGURE 12.2:
Choose a way to run the macro in the Customize dialog box.

- If you chose Toolbars, click the macro name and drag it to any convenient toolbar. Word will display the Custom Button dialog box (see Figure 3.4 in Chapter 3). Choose one of Word's suggested buttons, or leave the Text Button selected and type in a suitable name in the Text Button Name text box. Then click the Assign button to assign the button to the macro and to return to the Customize dialog box.
- If you chose Menus, choose a menu from the Change What Menu drop-down list— Word suggests the Tools menu, but you'll find it rapidly becomes full if you record more than half-a-dozen macros. Then choose a position on the menu for the macro from the Position on Menu drop-down list (or leave Auto selected and let Word put the macro wherever it thinks most suitable on the menu) and edit the menu item for the macro in the Name on Menu text box. Put an ampersand (&) before a letter to produce an underscored access key—for example, **S&witch Printers** will produce the menu entry _Switch Printers_. Then click the Add button to add your choice to the menu (if you made a Position on Menu choice rather than choosing Auto, the button will read Add Below). An access key allows you to select that command by pressing the underscored letter to activate it.

> **TIP**
>
> Two quick things here: First, the menu name for a macro doesn't have to bear any relation to the macro's name. For example, you could give the SwitchPrinters macro a menu item name of Tinker to Evers to Chance if it happened to remind you of triple-plays. Second, you can also create a new menu—for example, Macros—by clicking the Menu Bar button. We'll look at this later in the chapter.

- If you chose Keyboard, click in the Press New Shortcut Key box and enter the key combination you want (see the section _Assigning a Keyboard Shortcut_ later in this chapter for details of what key combinations can be), then click the Assign button.

You can then choose one of the other tabs in the Customize dialog box and assign a second control mechanism to the macro, or click the Close button to dismiss the Customize dialog box and start recording the macro. Word will display the Macro Record toolbar, darken the REC indicator in the status bar, and add a cassette-tape icon to the mouse pointer to remind you that you're recording.

Now record the sequence of actions you want to immortalize. You can use the mouse to select items from menus and to make choices in dialog boxes; but to select items on screen, you must use the keyboard.

To perform any actions you don't want recorded, you can pause the macro recorder at any time by clicking the Pause button on the Macro Record toolbar. Click the Pause button again to resume recording.

 To stop recording, click the Stop button on the Macro Record toolbar. Word has now recorded your macro and assigned it to the control you chose.

Running a Macro

To run a macro, simply click the toolbar button or choose the menu item or press the key combination you assigned to it.

If you chose not to assign a button, menu item, or key combination (perhaps because you have too many macros, as I do), you can run a macro by choosing Tools ➤ Macro to display the Macro dialog box and selecting the macro from the Macro Name list. Click the Run button.

Editing a Macro

If you make a mistake while recording a macro, you can of course always choose to re-record it, but often a better option is to edit the mistakes out of it. If you're prepared to spend a few minutes looking at the WordBasic programming language, you can usually figure out which is the offending line and simply remove it.

To edit a macro:

1. Display the Macro dialog box by choosing Tools ➤ Macro.
2. Choose the macro from the Macro Name list box and click the Edit button. Word will open a macro-editing window containing the text of the macro along with the Macro toolbar.
3. Edit the text of the macro as needed.
4. Choose File ➤ Save Template to save the changes to the macro (and to the template).
5. Choose File ➤ Close to close the macro-editing window.

Recording a New Action

To record a new action in the macro (for example, to replace an action you got wrong before), position the insertion point at the appropriate point in the macro and click the Record Next Command button on the Macro toolbar. Word will display the cassette tape icon on the mouse pointer. Perform the action; Word will record it, writing it into the macro at the point you chose, and will then switch off the recorder.

Getting Help on WordBasic

Word offers comprehensive help on the WordBasic programming language. To view it, choose Help ➤ Microsoft Word Help Topics and choose the WordBasic Reference on the Contents tab. You can then choose WordBasic Statements and Functions by Category to see the WordBasic commands broken up into logical sections (such as Finding and Replacing, Mail Merge, and Paragraph Formatting) or WordBasic Statements and Functions to see an alphabetical listing. Most of the statements and functions have examples, which can be particularly helpful when creating and troubleshooting your macros.

> **TIP**
> If Word doesn't offer you any help on WordBasic, you may need to install the WordBasic files. See the Appendix for details on installation.

Deleting a Macro

To delete a macro that you no longer need, display the Macro dialog box by choosing Tools ➤ Macro. Choose the macro in the Macro Name list box, and click the Delete button. Choose Yes in the warning message box.

Customizing Word

In Word, you can customize the toolbars, the menus, the menu bar, the keyboard shortcuts, and certain environment options that control where Word stores files of different types and so on. The first of these, customizing toolbars, we looked at in Chapter 3; the rest we'll look at here.

Customizing Menus

You can customize menus by adding items to them, or by removing any items that you don't use—or that you don't want other people to use. If that's not enough, you can remove the menus themselves and add menus of your own.

Adding Items to Menus

By strategically adding items to menus, you can have all the commands, styles, macros, and fonts that you need right at hand:

1. Choose Tools ➢ Customize to open the Customize dialog box.
2. Click the Menus tab to bring it to the front (see Figure 12.3).

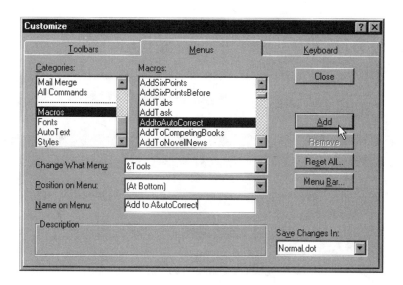

FIGURE 12.3: Adding items to menus on the Menus tab of the Customize dialog box

NOTE To make changes in a template other than Normal.dot, open a document based on that template before starting these steps, and choose the template in the Save Changes In drop-down list in the Customize dialog box.

3. In the Categories list box, select the category of item to add.
4. In the Commands list box, select the command to add.
5. In the Change What Menu drop-down list, choose the menu to which to add the item.
6. If you care about the item's position on the menu, choose a position for it from the Position on Menu drop-down list:
   - *(Auto)* will place the new items wherever Word thinks best.
   - *(At Top)* will place the new item first on the menu.
   - *(At Bottom)* will place the new item last on the menu.
   - Selecting an item already on the menu in the Position on Menu drop-down list will let you place the new item below that item.
7. In the Name on Menu text box, Word will suggest a name for the menu item. Change this name if needed for clarity.

TIP You can add an *access key* (also known as a "hotkey" or—bizarrely—a "mnemonic") for the item by putting an ampersand (&) before the access key letter. For best results, make sure that letter isn't already an access key for any other item on the menu—check the access keys assigned to the existing menu entries in the Position on Menu drop-down list.

8. Click the Add button (or Add Below button, if you chose an existing menu item for positioning in step 6) to add the item.
9. Add more items to any of the menus, or click the Close button to close the Customize dialog box.
10. Choose File ➢ Save All to save the changes to the template.

Removing Items from Menus

To remove one item quickly from a menu, press Ctrl+Alt+− (that's the hyphen key there, but think of it as minus). The mouse pointer will change to a short, thick horizontal line. With this mouse pointer showing, pull down a menu and click the item you want to remove. The menu will close, and the item will be gone from it.

> **TIP** — If you decide not to remove an item, press Esc to restore the mouse pointer to normal.

To remove a number of items from a menu, display the Customize dialog box by choosing Tools ➢ Customize, and then click the Menus tab. In the Change What Menu drop-down list, choose the menu containing the item; in the Position on Menu drop-down list, choose the item itself. Then click the Remove button to remove the item.

Restoring Word's Menus to Their Defaults

You can restore all of Word's predefined menus in any given template to their default state—and at once wipe out any and all changes you've made to them—by clicking the Reset All button on the Menus tab of the Customize dialog box. Check the Save Changes In drop-down list before you do this to make sure you're working in the right template.

Word will display a message box to make sure you know exactly what will happen if you choose to restore the menus. Choose Yes if you're positive you want to make this drastic change.

Customizing the Menu Bar

You can customize Word's menu bar itself by adding menus, removing menus, and renaming menus. To do so, first display the Customize dialog box by choosing Tools ➢ Customize and check the Save Changes In drop-down list to make sure you're working in the right template.

Adding Menus

To add a menu to the menu bar:

1. Click the Menu Bar button in the Customize dialog box to display the Menu Bar dialog box (shown in Figure 12.4).
2. Enter a name for the new menu in the Name on Menu Bar text box. Put an ampersand (&) before the letter you want to use as an access key. Make sure this access key letter isn't already assigned to another menu.
3. Choose a position for the menu in the Position on Menu Bar list: **(First)** and **(Last)** will place it first and last, respectively; or you can choose the name of the existing menu after which you want to put the new menu.

FIGURE 12.4:
Adding a new
menu in the Menu
Bar dialog box

4. Click the Add button (it'll be the Add After button if you chose to place the menu after an existing menu in step 3) to create the new menu.
5. Choose Close to return to the Customize dialog box. Now you can add items to the menu as described in *Adding Items to Menus* earlier in the chapter.
6. After closing the Customize dialog box, choose File ➤ Save All to save the changes to the template.

Removing Menus

To remove a menu from the menu bar:

1. Click the Menu Bar button in the Customize dialog box to display the Menu Bar dialog box.
2. In the Position on Menu Bar, choose the menu to remove.
3. Click the Remove button. Word will display a message box warning you that removing the menu will also remove all the items assigned to the menu.
4. Choose Yes to remove the menu.
5. Choose Close to return to the Customize dialog box.
6. After closing the Customize dialog box, choose File ➤ Save All to save the changes to the template.

Renaming Menus

To rename a menu:

1. Click the Menu Bar button in the Customize dialog box to display the Menu Bar dialog box.
2. In the Position on Menu Bar, choose the menu to rename.
3. Enter the new name for the menu in the Name on Menu Bar box. Put an ampersand (&) before the letter you want to use as the access key.
4. Click the Rename button (see Figure 12.5).
5. Click Close to exit the Menu Bar dialog box and again to close the Customize dialog box.

FIGURE 12.5:
Renaming a menu
in the Menu Bar
dialog box

6. Choose File ➤ Save All to save the changes to the template.

Customizing Keyboard Shortcuts

Even if you're not a die-hard WordStar user who's finally switched to Word, you can speed and simplify your work by customizing the keyboard to suit your needs. While Word comes with an impressive array of preprogrammed keyboard shortcuts, you're likely to find other items that you need to have at hand instead. (If you *are* a former WordStar user, you can remap most of the keyboard... .)

Assigning a Keyboard Shortcut

To set a keyboard shortcut:

1. Choose Tools ➤ Customize to display the Customize dialog box.
2. Click the Keyboard tab to bring it to the front of the dialog box (see Figure 12.6).

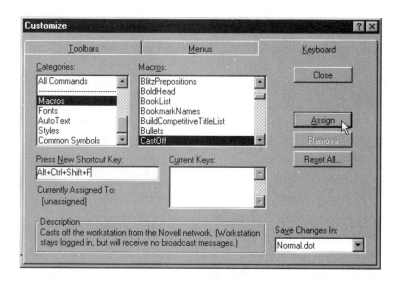

FIGURE 12.6:
Setting keyboard
shortcuts on the
Keyboard tab of
the Customize
dialog box

3. Specify the template to change in the Save Changes In drop-down list if necessary. (Leave Normal.dot selected if you want the changes to apply to all templates that don't have this keyboard combination set to another command.)

4. In the Categories list, select the category of item for the new keyboard shortcut.

5. Choose the item to add in the Commands list box. (If you chose Macros, Fonts, AutoText, Styles, or Common Symbols in the Categories list, the list box will change its name to suit your choice—Macros, Fonts, and so on.)

6. Click in the Press New Shortcut Key box and press the key combination you want; Word will display it in the Press New Shortcut Key box. A key combination can be any of the following:
   - Alt plus a regular key not used for a menu access key
   - Alt plus a function key
   - Ctrl plus a regular key or function key
   - Ctrl+Alt plus a regular key or function key
   - Shift plus a function key
   - Ctrl+Shift plus a regular key or function key
   - Alt+Shift plus a regular key or function key
   - Ctrl+Alt+Shift plus a regular key or function key

   Because this last option involves severe contortions of the carpal tunnels, it's not a great idea for frequent use.

7. Check the Current Keys box to see if that key combination is already assigned. (If it is, and you don't want to overwrite it, press Backspace to clear the Press New Shortcut Key box, and then choose another combination.)

8. Click the Assign button to assign the shortcut.

9. Either assign more keyboard shortcuts or click the Close button to close the Customize dialog box.

10. Choose File ➢ Save All to save the changes to the template.

Removing a Keyboard Shortcut

Usually you remove a keyboard shortcut by assigning that shortcut to another item—for example, if you assign Ctrl+P to a Photograph style you've created, Word will overwrite Ctrl+P as the shortcut for the Print command. But sometimes you may need to remove a shortcut without assigning it to another item—for example, if you want to prevent the user from performing certain actions.

To remove a keyboard shortcut:

1. Choose Tools ➢ Customize to display the Customize dialog box.

2. Click the Keyboard tab to bring it to the front of the dialog box.

3. Specify the template to change in the Save Changes In drop-down list if necessary. (Leave Normal.dot selected if you want the changes to apply to all templates that don't have this keyboard combination set to another command.)
4. In the Press New Shortcut Key box, press the key combination you want to remove.
5. In the Current Keys box, click the key combination you want to remove (there may be several for some commands).
6. Click the Remove button.
7. Either remove more keyboard shortcuts or click the Close button to close the Customize dialog box.
8. Choose File ➢ Save All to save the changes to the template.

Resetting All Keyboard Shortcuts

You can quickly reset all keyboard shortcuts for the template specified in the Save Changes In drop-down list by clicking the Reset All button on the Keyboard tab of the Customize dialog box. Word will display a confirmation message box to make sure you want to take this drastic step.

Choose Yes to reset the keyboard shortcuts, and then click Close to exit the Customize dialog box. Again, choose File ➢ Save All to save the changes to the template in question.

Choosing Environment Options

Word offers any number of options for printing, AutoFormat, spelling, grammar, and the like, all stored on the twelve tabs of the Options dialog box (Tools ➢ Options). In this section, we'll look at the most important options not discussed in other sections of this book.

> **TIP** For more detail on the options not discussed in depth in this section, consult Word's Help files by clicking the Help button (the ? button) in the Options dialog box or by choosing Help ➢ Microsoft Word Help Topics.

View Options

The options on the View tab (see Figure 12.7) let you specify which tools and elements you see on screen.

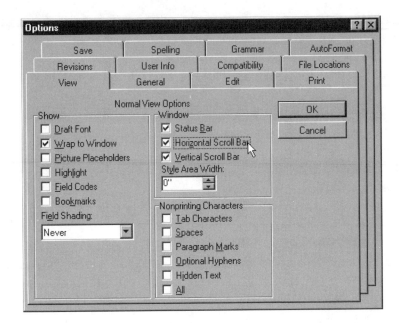

FIGURE 12.7:
Set up your screen with the options on the View tab of the Options dialog box.

NOTE Normal view and Page Layout view offer some different view options— for example, Page Layout view does not offer the Wrap to Window and Draft Font options, but it does offer Text Boundaries (dotted lines around page elements), Drawings (for displaying drawing objects created in Word), and Object Anchors (the anchor symbols that indicate an item is attached to a particular paragraph).

Show Options Check the Picture Placeholders box to have Word display empty boxes instead of graphics. This will let you scroll through your documents faster, particularly when using a slower computer.

Keep the Wrap to Window box checked to have Word adjust the line length to fit the window and make the text more readable.

Select the Field Codes check box to have field codes rather than results displayed in text. Check the Bookmarks check box to have bookmark markers appear in text.

Window Options Choose whether to have the status bar, horizontal scroll bar, and vertical scroll bar displayed. In the Style Area width box, enter a measurement other than 0" if you want to display the style area, a pane on the left side of the Word window that displays the style for each paragraph.

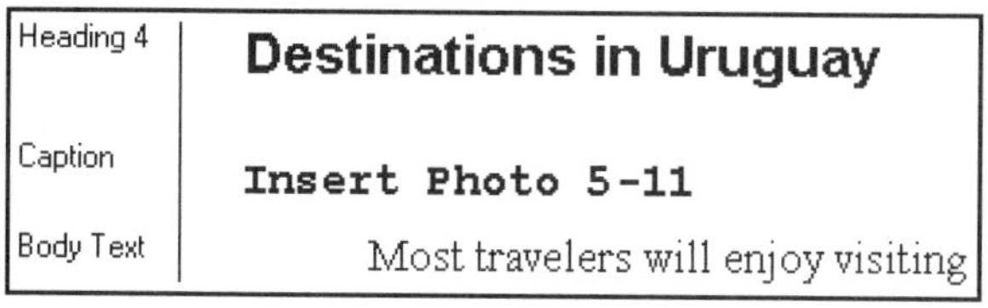

Heading 4	**Destinations in Uruguay**
Caption	`Insert Photo 5-11`
Body Text	Most travelers will enjoy visiting

Nonprinting Characters Choose which characters and items you want to see on screen: tabs, spaces, paragraph marks, optional hyphens, hidden text, or all of the above.

General Options

The options on the General tab of the Options dialog box (see Figure 12.8) offer a mishmash of choices.

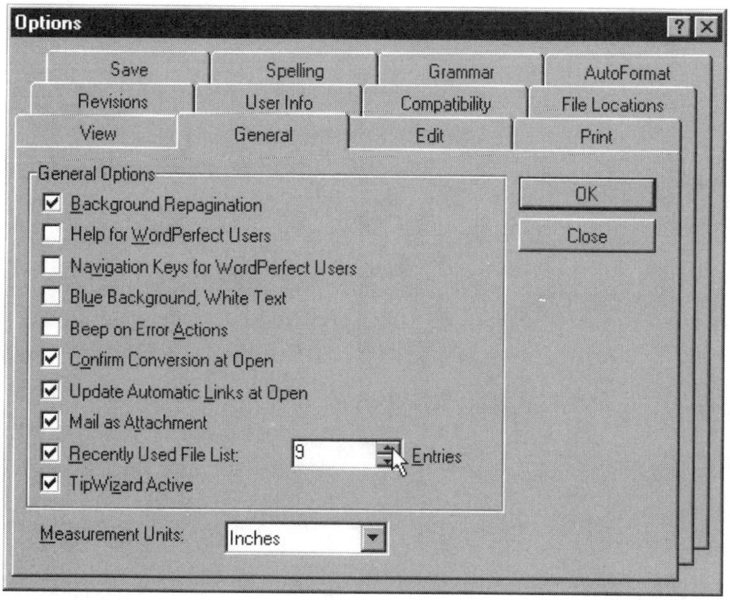

Options

Save | Spelling | Grammar | AutoFormat
Revisions | User Info | Compatibility | File Locations
View | General | Edit | Print

General Options
- ☑ Background Repagination
- ☐ Help for WordPerfect Users
- ☐ Navigation Keys for WordPerfect Users
- ☐ Blue Background, White Text
- ☐ Beep on Error Actions
- ☑ Confirm Conversion at Open
- ☑ Update Automatic Links at Open
- ☑ Mail as Attachment
- ☑ Recently Used File List: 9 Entries
- ☑ TipWizard Active

Measurement Units: Inches

OK
Close

FIGURE 12.8:
The General tab of the Options dialog box

Background Repagination repaginates your documents surreptitiously as you work. On long documents, this may slow down your computer.

> **NOTE** Background Repagination isn't available in Page Layout view, which is always up to date with its pagination.

Help for WordPerfect Users performs equivalent Word commands when you press a WordPerfect key combination. For example, if you type Home Home ↑ with Help for WordPerfect Users on, Word will move to the beginning of the document; if you type Home Home ↑ without Help for WordPerfect Users on, Word will move to the beginning of the line, beep, and then move up one line. When this option is on, **WPH** appears on the status bar.

Navigation Keys for WordPerfect Users makes the PageUp, PageDown, Home, End, and Esc keys behave in Word as they do in WordPerfect. When this option is on, **WPN** appears on the status bar. (If both Help for WordPerfect Users and Navigation Keys for WordPerfect Users are on, **WP** appears on the status bar.)

Blue Background, White Text displays white text on a blue background, which can be visually restful. If you also choose View ➢ Full Screen, you can pretend you're using WordPerfect 5.1 for DOS... .

Beep on Error Actions makes Word beep when you do something it doesn't like. If you find this an irritant rather than a helpful warning, clear the check box.

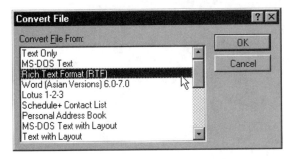

Confirm Conversion at Open displays a Convert File dialog box when you open a file in format other than Word. Select this check box if Word is misconverting your files and you want to try a different conversion.

Update Automatic Links at Open updates any automatic links in a document when you open it.

Mail as Attachment lets you e-mail a document as an attachment (see Chapter 4).

Recently Used File List controls the number of latest-used files that appear at the foot of the File menu. Increase the number in the Entries box to list more files; clear the check box to have none appear at all (for example, for security reasons).

TipWizard Active allows Word to make suggestions in the Tip Wizard toolbar (if you have it displayed). If you find the Tip Wizard annoying, or if it slows down your computer by monitoring your activities, clear this check box.

Measurement Units controls the units in which the rulers, Paragraph dialog box, etc., display measurement: choose Inches, Centimeters, Points, or Picas.

Edit Options

The options on the Edit tab of the Options dialog box (see Figure 12.9) can greatly affect your day-to-day work in Word.

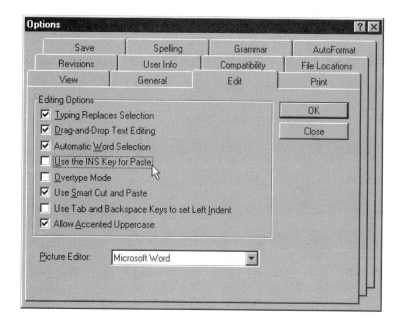

FIGURE 12.9:
Make sure the options on the Edit tab of the Options dialog box are set to suit your preferences.

Typing Replaces Selection causes Word to overwrite any selected item when you start typing. If this disconcerts you, clear the check box, and Word will move the insertion point to the beginning of a selection when you start typing.

Drag-and-Drop Text Editing controls whether you can use drag-and-drop. If you don't use drag-and-drop, turning this off may speed up Word a bit.

Automatic Word Selection lets you quickly select multiple words. (See *Selecting Text with the Mouse* in Chapter 5 for details.)

Use the INS Key for Paste makes the Insert (aka Ins) key perform the Paste command rather than toggle between Insert mode and Overtype mode.

Overtype Mode turns on Overtype mode, discussed in *Insert and Overtype Modes* in Chapter 5.

Use Smart Cut and Paste adds and removes spaces as necessary when you cut, paste, and drag-and-drop text.

Use Tab and Backspace Keys to Set Left Indent lets you indent and outdent the left margin by pressing Tab (after you've entered one tab stop) and Backspace, respectively.

Allow Accented Uppercase is for text formatted in French.

Print Options

The Print tab of the Options dialog box (see Figure 12.10) lets you select the default tray of paper for the printer and specify whether to print just the data when printing a form. Then there are five Printing Options and five Include with Document options.

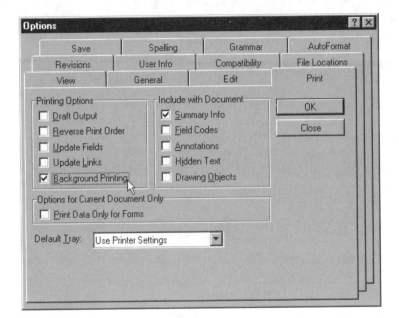

FIGURE 12.10:
Choose how to print your document and what to include with the document on the Print tab of the Options dialog box.

Printing Options *Draft Output* lets you print a stripped-down version of your document on some printers. Your mileage may vary.

Reverse Print Order prints documents from last page to first.

Background Printing lets you keep working (albeit a bit more slowly) while Word is printing your documents.

Include with Document Choose whether to print summary info, field codes, annotations, hidden text, and drawing objects (objects created in Word, including lines) when printing your document. Summary Info and Annotations will each print on a separate page at the end of the document; field codes, annotations, and drawing objects will print where they occur in the document.

User Info

Enter your name, initials, and mailing address on the User Info tab of the Options dialog box (see Figure 12.11). Among other things, Word uses the name for file summary information, the initials for annotations, and the mailing address for envelopes.

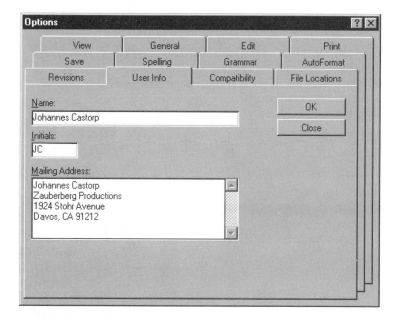

FIGURE 12.11:
Make sure your personal information is correct on the User Info tab of the Options dialog box.

File Locations

The options on the File Locations tab of the Options dialog box (see Figure 12.12) lets you specify where Word should locate documents, clip-art pictures, templates, and other files it maintains.

Documents is the category that can save you the most time: If you want Word to suggest saving documents somewhere other than the My Documents folder, change Documents straight away.

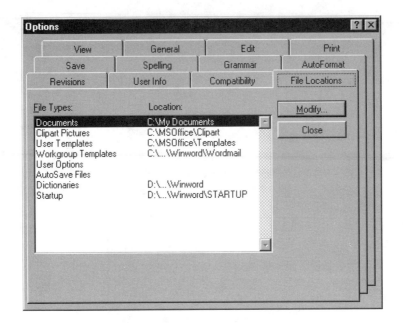

FIGURE 12.12:
Specifiy where Word should keep its various types of documents on the File Locations tab of the Options dialog box.

To change a file location:

1. Choose the item to change in the File Types list box.
2. Click the Modify button to display the Modify Location dialog box (see Figure 12.13).

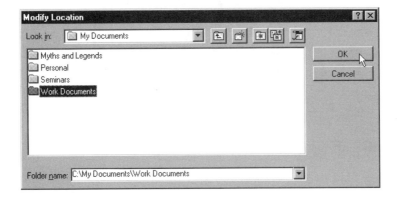

FIGURE 12.13:
In the Modify Location dialog box, choose the new location for the item.

3. Choose the folder for the new location by using standard Windows 95 techniques.
4. Click the OK button to close the Modify Location dialog box.

Save Options

The options on the Save tab of the Options dialog box (see Figure 12.14) can help keep your work safe.

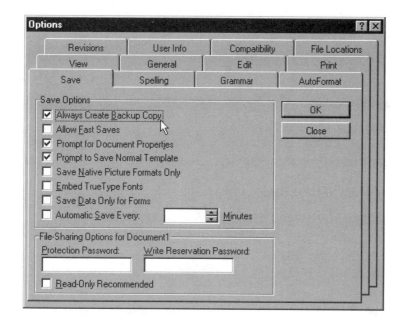

FIGURE 12.14:
Specify how to save your documents on the Save tab of the Options dialog box.

Save Options *Always Create Backup Copy* creates a backup copy each time you save a document by renaming the previously saved version of that document to **Backup of filename** and giving it the extension .WBK. This is a valuable option—with two caveats: First, it will slow down your save operations a little, though usually not enough to worry about; and second, you need to understand that the backup is *not* the same as the currently saved version of the file—if you destroy the latest saved version, the backup will provide you with the previous version.

> **TIP** To make the backups of your documents virtually identical to the currently saved copies, always save twice in immediate succession.

Allow Fast Saves speeds up save operations by saving only the changes to a file, not actually saving the file itself. This option can create bizarre results—if you delete most of a large file (or most of a file containing graphics) and then fast-save it, the file size will still be large; and fast-saved documents will always be somewhat larger than regularly saved documents. Bear this in mind if disk space is at a premium or you're often transferring documents by modem.

TIP
You can't choose both Always Create Backup Copy and Allow Fast Saves at the same time—it's one or the other. Allow Fast Saves saves you only a little time unless you have a very slow computer or you're working with huge documents (or both).

Prompt for Document Properties displays the Properties dialog box automatically the first time you save a document. This is useful if you use the file summary information to identify your documents; if you don't, it rapidly proves tedious.

Prompt to Save Normal Template makes Word check with you before it saves changes to Normal.dot, the global template. Select this option if you spend time customizing Normal.dot and want to be able to escape any embarrassing changes you make by mistake.

Save Native Picture Formats Only saves only the Windows version of a graphic imported from a different format.

Embed TrueType Fonts lets you save the fonts used in a document with the document so the document appears the same on a computer that doesn't have those particular fonts installed.

WARNING
Choosing Embed TrueType Fonts can greatly increase the size of document files. Use it only if you're sharing files and need to ensure they look exactly the same on the other computers.

Automatic Save Every nn Minutes causes Word to save an automatic backup of documents at a specified interval (from one minute to 120 minutes).

NOTE
You can use these automatic backups to recover documents if Word or your computer crashes. When you exit Word normally by choosing File ➢ Exit, Word deletes any automatic backups made in that session. These backups are stored in the Autosave Files location specified on the File Locations tab of the Options dialog box (discussed in the previous section). When you restart Word after a crash, it should open any autosaved files that haven't been deleted and display them to you as (Recovered). Check them carefully and save them under new names.

File-Sharing Options These options are for protecting your documents from intrusion, alteration, and damage. Consult the Help files for details.

Spelling Options The options on the Spelling tab of the Options dialog box—for controlling automatic spell checking, working with dictionaries, and so on—are discussed in Chapter 3.

AutoFormat Options The options on the AutoFormat tab of the Options dialog box—for controlling Word's automatic formatting of your documents—are discussed in Chapter 7.

Templates

As discussed in Chapter 2, Word provides a number of different templates that provide you with shortcuts to creating specific types of documents. You can also create your own

templates by starting a new file and choosing Template in the Create New group box in the New dialog box, then customizing and saving the file.

Any template can contain its own styles (for formatting text), AutoText entries (for inserting text and other elements quickly), toolbars (for quick access to the commands you need), and macros (for performing repetitive actions). You can also copy any of these four types of items between any two templates.

Copying Styles, AutoText, Toolbars, or Macros from One Template to Another

To copy one or more styles, toolbars, AutoText entries, or macros from one template to another, open the Organizer dialog box by choosing File ➢ Templates and clicking the Organizer button in the Templates and Add-ins dialog box. Click the appropriate tab (Styles, AutoText, Toolbars, Macros) to bring it to the front of the Organizer dialog box. Figure 12.15 shows the Organizer dialog box with the Toolbars tab displayed, and the paragraphs below discuss transferring toolbars; the procedure is the same for styles, AutoText entries, and macros.

If you have opened a document based on a template other than Normal.dot or if you have opened a template itself, Word will display the toolbars you created in Normal.dot in one panel and the toolbars from the other template in the other panel; otherwise, Word will display the toolbars you've created in Normal.dot on both sides, which doesn't help much.

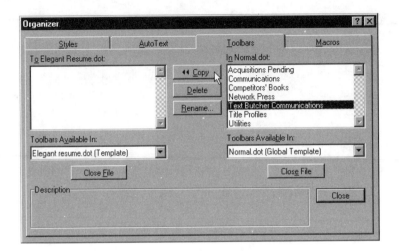

FIGURE 12.15: The Organizer dialog box lets you copy styles, AutoText entries, toolbars, or macros from one template to another quickly.

To open the right templates, click the Close File button on one side to close the currently open file and then click the Open File button (into which the Close File button will have metamorphosed). Choose the template from the Open dialog box that Word then displays.

Copy the toolbar by selecting it from the left-hand or right-hand box and clicking the Copy button. When you click the Close button to exit the Organizer dialog box, Word will invite you to save any changes to affected templates; choose Yes.

Deleting and Renaming Items in the Organizer Dialog Box

You can also use the Organizer dialog box to delete or rename styles, AutoText entries, toolbars, or macros. Open the Organizer dialog box with the appropriate template as described in the previous section and select the tab for the item you want to affect.

Renaming an Item

Choose the item to rename and click the Rename button. Enter the new name for the item in the Rename dialog box and click OK.

Deleting an Item

Choose the item to delete and click the Delete button. Choose Yes in the confirmation message box that Word displays. (To delete more than one item at a time, you can select a range of items by selecting the first, holding down Shift, and clicking the last; or you can select multiple items by selecting the first, then holding down Ctrl as you click on the others.)

When you've finished deleting or renaming items, click the Close button to close the Organizer dialog box.

Part 3

Excel

Chapter 13

CREATING WORKSHEETS

- **What Excel offers**
- **Creating a spreadsheet**
- **Entering data**

Excel is a spreadsheet program that you can use to enter, manipulate, and crunch data to your heart's content. This data can be pretty much anything—deposits in your daughter's bank account and putative interest accrued by 2015, employee hiring and firing information by department, or detailed data on the mating habits of frogs in Borneo.

In this chapter, we'll look briefly at what Excel is and does. Once we've set the scene, we'll look at how to create a spreadsheet and enter data in it. In the next chapter, we'll look at how to work with that data, change it, and format it as appropriate.

Spreadsheets, Worksheets, and Workbooks

First, we need to spend a moment with the terms we'll be using. Excel is a *spreadsheet* program—a program designed to work with numbers (as opposed to a word processor, such as Word, which is designed to work with words). You enter your data in cells arrayed into horizontal rows and vertical columns on a *worksheet*, an arrangement somewhat reminiscent of an accountant's ledger but far more flexible.

Excel organizes worksheets by workbook, on the basis that you may need more than one worksheet for any given project. Each new workbook you open contains 16 worksheets by default, but you can add further worksheets up to 255. (You can also remove worksheets from the original 16 if you prefer to work with fewer worksheets around.)

Each worksheet contains 16384 rows (numbered from 1 to 16384) and 256 columns (numbered from A to IV—the first 26 columns are numbered A to Z, the next 26 AA to AZ, the next 26 BA to BZ, etc.). The worksheets are numbered automatically from Sheet 1 to Sheet 256, but you can change their names to anything that suits you, provided the name contains fewer than 32 characters and doesn't contain any of these characters:

/
\
?
\
:
*

Because this is happening on a computer, the whole thing is virtual as opposed to physical, but imagine these virtual worksheets as being stacked on top of each other, with the first at the top. As a result, you can work with cells in three dimensions—across in the rows, down in the columns, and down *through* the stack of worksheets in the workbook. You can include formulas to automatically perform calculations on the data contained in the workbook; we'll look at formulas in Chapter 16.

For example, consider the worksheet, 1996, shown in Figure 13.1. As you can see from the worksheet tabs at the bottom of the screen, this is the thirteenth worksheet in the workbook and follows worksheets named January through December, each of which tracks one month's sales of the various products foisted on a gullible public by Text Butcher Communications, Inc.

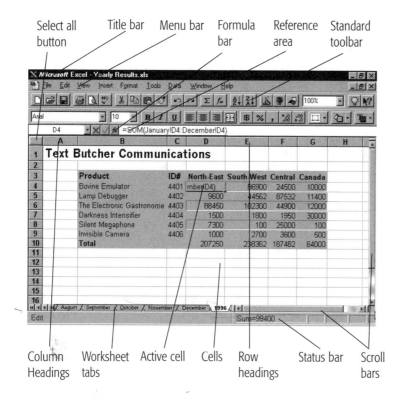

FIGURE 13.1:
The parts of the Excel window, featuring a sample spreadsheet that performs calculations down through the stack of worksheets.

Parts of the Excel Screen

As you can see in Figure 13.1, the Excel screen has standard Windows application items: a title bar, a menu bar, a status bar, toolbars, scroll bars, and more. To these Excel adds the following:

The *reference area* displays the location of the active cell.

The *formula bar* is where you enter and edit data and formulas.

Cells are where you enter data and formulas.

Row headings and *column headings* let you quickly select a row or a column.

Worksheet tabs let you quickly move between worksheets (by clicking on the tab of the worksheet you want).

Working with Worksheets

In this section, we'll look at the basics of working with worksheets in Excel: how to move to different parts of a worksheet; how to select a worksheet; how to add, delete, and rename worksheets; and how to rearrange them in a workbook. Once we've done that, we'll move on to entering data in the cells of a worksheet.

Moving about the Worksheet

You can move from cell to cell using the mouse or the navigation keys (←,→,↑,↓). To move with the mouse, click in the cell you want to make active; use the scroll bars to scroll to other areas of the worksheet.

Here's how you move with the navigation keys:

- The Home key moves the active cell to column A in the current row; Ctrl+Home moves the active cell to cell A1 in the current worksheet.
- Ctrl plus an arrow key moves the active cell to the extreme of the worksheet in that direction—Ctrl+↓ moves the active cell to the last row, Ctrl+← moves the active cell to the last column, etc.
- PgUp and PgDn move the active cell up and down one screen's worth of rows; Alt+PgUp and Alt+PgDn move the active cell left and right one screen's worth of columns, respectively.
- End+Home moves the active cell to the last cell in the worksheet that contains data, and End plus an arrow key moves the active cell to the first cell in that direction that contains data and is next to an empty cell.

Moving among Worksheets

Communications Budget

The easiest way to move from one worksheet to another is to click the worksheet tab of the worksheet you want to move to.

To move to the first worksheet in the workbook, click the Move to First button.

To move to the last worksheet in the workbook, click the Move to Last button.

To move to the next worksheet in the workbook, click the Next button.

To move to the previous worksheet in the workbook, click the Previous button.

TIP

Ctrl+PgUp moves the active cell to the previous sheet; Ctrl+PgDn moves the active cell to the next sheet.

Selecting Worksheets

Use the mouse to select worksheets as follows:

- To select a worksheet, click on its tab at the bottom of the Excel window.
- To choose a range of worksheets, click on the tab for the first worksheet in the range, hold down Shift, and click on the tab for the last.
- To select multiple noncontiguous worksheets, click on the tab for the first worksheet, then hold down Ctrl and click on the tabs for the other worksheets in turn.
- To select all of the worksheets in a workbook, right-click on a worksheet tab and choose Select All Sheets from the shortcut menu.

Adding a Worksheet

To add a worksheet before the worksheet currently selected, choose Insert ➤ Worksheet. To add more than one worksheet at a time, select the same number of worksheet tabs as you want to insert new worksheets, then choose Insert ➤ Worksheet. Excel will add the new worksheets to the left of the leftmost worksheet tab you selected.

Deleting a Worksheet

To delete a worksheet from the workbook, right-click on its tab and choose Delete from the shortcut menu. Choose OK in the confirmation message box.

WARNING

When you delete a worksheet, you delete all the data on it too. You cannot undo this deletion except by closing the file immediately without saving changes, then reopening it. (You'll also lose any other unsaved changes in the workbook, so consider saving the workbook before deleting a worksheet.)

To delete multiple worksheets at once, select their tabs, right-click on one of them, choose Delete from the shortcut menu, and choose OK in the confirmation message box.

Renaming a Worksheet

Sheet1, Sheet2, and so on are not particularly catchy names (though superbly logical and orderly), so you'll probably want to assign the worksheets you use something

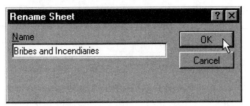

more informative. To rename a worksheet, right-click on its tab and choose Rename from the shortcut menu. Enter the new name for the worksheet in the Rename Sheet dialog box (up to 31 characters) and click OK.

Rearranging the Worksheets in a Workbook

To quickly rearrange the worksheets in a workbook, click on a worksheet tab and drag and drop it to where you want it. An inverted black triangle will indicate the position where it will be dropped between the other tabs.

To copy a worksheet to a different location in a workbook, hold down Ctrl and drag the worksheet tab to the new location.

To move or copy a worksheet between open workbooks:

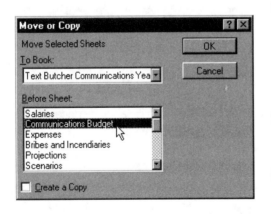

1. Right-click on the worksheet tab and choose Move or Copy from the shortcut menu to display the Move or Copy dialog box. To move or copy multiple worksheets at once, select them first.

2. In the To Book drop-down list, choose the workbook to which you want to move the worksheet.

3. In the Before Sheet list box, select the worksheet before which you want the other worksheet to appear.

4. To copy the worksheet, select the Create a Copy check box.

5. Click OK to close the Move or Copy dialog box and move or copy the worksheet.

Creating a Spreadsheet

In this section, we'll look briefly at starting a new spreadsheet and entering some data in it. Along the way, we'll discuss the different types of data that Excel recognizes, because this affects the data you enter in the cells of any worksheet.

Starting a New Workbook

When you start Excel, it will open a fresh workbook for you on screen with the default 16 blank worksheets.

 To start a new workbook based on the default workbook template, click the New Workbook button on the Standard toolbar. To start a workbook based on a spreadsheet template, choose File ➤ New to display the New dialog box, click the Spreadsheet Solutions tab, choose one of the templates shown there (look at the Preview box to see how the first worksheet in the template looks), and click OK.

Types of Data in Excel

Before you enter data, you need to know how Excel handles it. Excel recognizes five different types of data: numbers, dates, times, text, and formulas.

Numbers

Numbers are values that can be calculated. They can consist of the numerals 0 through 9, with a decimal point (a period) as a separator for decimal places and with commas as separators for thousands.

Numbers can start with a dollar sign ($) or other currency symbol, or with a + or – sign. They can end with a % sign; they can also be enclosed in parentheses (as an alternative to the – sign, for indicating negative numbers).

You control the display of numbers by formatting the cells that contain them—for example, you could format a cell to display currency amounts with two decimal places. We'll look at cell formatting in Chapter 14.

Dates

Excel handles dates as *serial numbers*, which represent the number of days elapsed since 1/1/1900, which is serial number 1 (e.g., 1/31/1900 is serial number 31). With serial numbers, Excel can perform calculations easily—to sort 1/1/97, 3/3/97, and 2/2/97 into reverse order, Excel simply works with the dates 35431, 35492, and 35463 (respectively). The good news is in two parts: First, Excel handles the serial numbers in the background, so you don't need to worry about them; and second, if you enter a date in one of the four formats shown below, Excel will automatically identify it as a date, store it as a serial number, and represent it to you as a date formatted in the way you choose.

Date Format	Example
MM/DD/YY	9/3/96 or 09/03/96
MMM-YY	Sep-96
DD-MMM-YY	03-Sep-96
DD-MMM	03-Sep

Excel uses slashes when displaying dates that need them, but you can use hyphens when entering dates—for example, both **11/28/64** and **11-28-64** will be stored correctly.

Times

Excel uses serial numbers for times as well, representing the 24 hours of the day as values between 0 and 1. So 6 AM is 0.25, noon is 0.5, 6 PM is 0.75, and so on. You can enter time in the formats listed below; specify AM or PM if you don't want Excel to use the 24-hour format.

Time Format	Example
HH:MM	10:15
HH:MM:SS	22:15:17
HH:MM AM/PM	10:15 PM
HH:MM:SS AM/PM	10:15:17 PM

You can combine the date and time values to refer to a given time on a given day: For example, 6 PM on December 25, 1996 would be 35424.75. Enter these date and time values in the following formats:

Date and Time Format	Example
MM/DD/YY HH:MM	9/3/96 10:15 (AM/PM optional)
HH:MM MM/DD/YY	22:15 9-3-96

Formulas

Formulas are mathematical formulas telling Excel to perform calculations on data in cells. For example, to add the data in the cells A1, B2, and C3 and display the result in cell D4, you would enter the formula **+A1+B2+C3** in cell D4. We'll look at formulas in detail in Chapter 16.

Text

Excel considers to be text any data that it does not recognize as a number, date, time, or formula. This is a wide brief; in practice, it means that data containing letters (other than cell addresses, AM or PM, and so on) will be treated as text. For example, if you enter a list of employees' names, positions, and work histories, Excel will treat them as text.

Excel will also treat as text any numeric entries that are formatted outside of its accepted number, date, and time formats—for example, if you type **10%8**, **510,99**, or **11:59AM**, Excel will treat the entry as text because it's not correctly formatted as a percentage, a number, or a time (which needs a space before the **AM**).

Text too long for the cell it's in will be displayed in the cell or cells to the right if they're empty; otherwise only the part that fits in the cell will be displayed, though all of the text is stored. (To see the whole contents of a cell, make it active; Excel will display the contents in the reference area.)

Entering Data

To enter data in the active cell, type it in; alternatively, cut or copy the information from elsewhere, then paste it into the active cell. As you type the first character, it will appear in both the cell and in the reference area, which will display an Enter button, a Cancel button, and a Function button, as shown here from left to right.

Finish typing the entry and press Enter, press one of the arrow keys ($\leftarrow,\rightarrow,\uparrow,\downarrow$), click the Enter button, or click in another cell with the mouse to enter the data in the cell. Excel will enter the data and will hide the Enter, Cancel, and Function buttons that were in the reference area. (Alternatively, click the Cancel button to cancel the entry.) If you pressed one of the arrow keys to enter the information, Excel will move the active cell to the cell in that direction.

> **TIP**
>
> Sometimes you may need to persuade Excel to treat a number as text—for example, you may need a zip code to retain a leading zero rather than being truncated to what Excel considers to be its "true" value. You can do this by entering the *label prefix* for text, an apostrophe ('), in front of the number.

Now move to the next cell and enter information in as appropriate. Two features you can use to speed this process are AutoFill and AutoComplete, which we'll discuss briefly in the next sections.

Using AutoFill

Excel's AutoFill feature lets you quickly enter predefined series of data, such as dates, text, or numbers, in your worksheets. AutoFill works by your entering just enough information to let Excel know what you're trying to enter in the cells, then dragging the *AutoFill handle* to tell Excel which cells you want to affect:

1. Start the series in the first of the cells that will contain the information.
   - For a series of numbers that increase by a given amount, enter the first two numbers in the first two cells. For example, you might enter **1996** in cell A5 and **1997** in cell A6.
   - For a known text series such as the months of the year, enter the first text label. For example, enter **January** in cell A5.
2. Select the cell or cells containing the information.
3. Click the AutoFill handle in the lower-right corner of the rightmost or lower cell and drag the resulting border across or down through the cells that will contain the information. Excel will fill the series with the data given:
   - In the first example in step 1, if you drag from the lower-right corner of cell A6 through cell A16, Excel will input the years 1998–2007 in cells A7 through A16.
   - In the second example, if you drag from the lower-right corner of cell A5 through cell L5, Excel will input the months February through December in cells B5 through L5.

Using AutoComplete

Many times you'll find yourself repeating information in different cells in the same column, and here Excel's AutoComplete feature can help you enter data speedily. AutoComplete monitors the items you've entered in the current block of cells containing entries in a column and suggests a previous item when it thinks you're starting to enter it in another cell. For example, if you enter the months January through December in cells A2 to A13 and then type **F** in cell A1 or A14, AutoComplete will suggest **February**, which you can accept by pressing Enter or one of the arrow keys (or by clicking the Enter button

or another cell). If you type **J** as the first letter of cell A14, AutoComplete will not be able to decide between January, June, and July, and will wait for the second letter. If the second letter is **a**, it will suggest **January**; if not, it will wait for the third letter, whereupon it will suggest **June** or **July** if the third letter matches either.

You can also use AutoComplete to add entries with the mouse by right-clicking in the previous or next adjacent cell to column entries (or in one of the cells already containing an entry), choosing Pick from List from the shortcut menu, and selecting the entry from the resulting drop-down list.

AutoComplete is generally quite helpful—you can ignore any suggestions by typing resolutely through them—but you can turn it on and off as necessary:

1. Choose Tools ➤ Options to display the Options dialog box.
2. On the Edit tab, select or clear the Enable AutoComplete for Cell Values check box.
3. Click OK to close the Options dialog box.

Saving and Closing a Workbook

In the next chapter, we'll look at editing and formatting that information. For the time being, save and close the workbook as described in the next section.

To save a workbook, choose File ➤ Save (or click the Save button) and save the file as described in Chapter 3.

To close a workbook so you can work with another workbook, choose File ➤ Close. If the current workbook contains unsaved changes, Excel will prompt you to save the changes before closing the workbook

To exit Excel, choose File ➤ Exit. Excel will prompt you to save unsaved changes to any workbooks before it shuts down.

Chapter 14

EDITING A WORKBOOK

- **Editing data in a workbook**
- **Formatting cells and worksheets**
- **Sorting data**
- **Working with ranges**
- **Entering series**

In the previous chapter, we saw how you can quickly create a workbook and enter data in its worksheets. In this chapter, we'll look at working with the data you've entered in the worksheets: viewing the worksheet, editing the data, formatting it, and sorting it as appropriate. We'll also look at how you can speed up your work in Excel by working with ranges.

Viewing the Worksheet

First, we'll discuss four features that Excel offers for viewing your spreadsheets: zooming the view, splitting a window, freezing panes of a window, and full-screen view.

Zoom

As in Word and PowerPoint, you can zoom the view in Excel by choosing a zoom percentage in the Zoom Control drop-down list on the Standard toolbar (as shown here). The

drop-down list offers set zoom percentages from 25 to 200, but you can set a percentage of your choosing by typing in any value from 10 to 400 and pressing Enter. The Selection choice on the drop-down list will zoom the view to the max for showing the currently selected cells.

Alternatively, you can set a zoom percentage by choosing View ➢ Zoom to display the Zoom dialog box, making a choice in the Magnification group box, and clicking OK.

Split

You can split the Excel window so you can see nonadjacent parts of one worksheet at once, which makes it easier to compare data spread out over a number of rows or columns.

To split the window, make active the cell above which and to the right of which you want to split the window, then choose Window ➢ Split. You can then scroll each window using its scroll bars.

To adjust the split of the windows, move the mouse pointer over the horizontal or vertical split bar (or over the intersection of the two), click, and drag the split bar or bars to where you want them.

To unsplit a window, choose Window ➢ Remove Split.

Freezing Panes

You may also want to freeze the rows at the top of the screen and the columns on the left of the screen so they do not move when you scroll. By doing this, you can keep row and column headings visible while you scroll to far-flung regions of your worksheets.

To freeze the panes, make active the cell to the left of which and above which you want to freeze the panes, then choose Window ➢ Freeze Panes. Excel will display lines indicating the division.

To unfreeze the panes, choose Window ➢ Unfreeze Panes.

Full-Screen View

To display the maximum amount of spreadsheet on-screen at once, use Excel's full-screen view by choosing View ➤ Full Screen. Excel will maximize its window if it isn't maximized already, maximize the current worksheet if it isn't maximized already, hide all displayed toolbars, and display the Full Screen toolbar.

To return Excel from full-screen to its previous state of display, click the Full Screen button on the Full Screen toolbar or choose View ➤ Full Screen again.

Editing Data in a Worksheet

Editing data in a worksheet is fast and straightforward. First, make the cell you want to edit active by clicking on it or moving the active cell indicator to it using the arrow keys. Then press F2 or double-click in the cell to enter Edit mode, which Excel will indicate by displaying *Edit* at the left end of the status bar. Excel will display the data from the cell in the reference area and will display a blinking insertion point in the cell at the point at which edits will take effect.

> **NOTE** If you prefer to edit in the reference area, click once in the cell you want to edit, then click once in the reference area to place the insertion point in it.

Edit the data in the cell (or in the reference area) as need be by typing the new data into it. You can double-click on a word to select it, and you can use ← to move left, → to move right, Home to move to the beginning of a cell, and End to move to the end of a cell. Alternatively, use the mouse to position the insert point where you want to edit, or to select words for enhancement or deletion.

Copying and Moving Data

You can copy and move data in Excel by using Cut, Copy, and Paste (as discussed in Chapter 3) or drag-and-drop. There are two quick points to note here:

- When pasting a range of data, you need only select the upper-left anchor cell of the destination, but be sure that Excel won't overwrite any important data in the other cells that the range will cover.

- To use drag-and-drop, select the cell or range to move or copy, then move the mouse pointer to one of its borders so the pointer changes from a fat cross to an arrow. Then drag and drop as usual.

Deleting the Contents of Cells

To delete the contents of a cell or a range, select the cell or range and press Delete or right-click and choose Clear Contents from the shortcut menu.

Working with Ranges

A *range* is two or more cells. Ranges can be contiguous (i.e., rectangular blocks of cells, referred to by the cells at their upper-left and lower-right corners) or noncontiguous (irregular blocks of cells, or cells that are not adjacent to each other).

Ranges give you a way of working with a number of cells at once, for example, when formatting cells or entering data in them. You can name ranges so you can easily identify them and move to them (see the next section).

The Name Box at the left end of the formula bar displays the name of the currently selected range.

Selecting a Range

To select a contiguous range of cells:

- Click in the upper-left cell of the range, hold down Shift, then click in the lower-right cell of the range.
- Click in the upper-left cell of the range and drag to the lower-right cell of the range.
- Choose in the upper-left cell of the range, hold down Shift, and use the arrow keys to move to the lower-right cell of the range.

NOTE You don't have to work from upper left to lower right—you can work from upper right to lower left if you prefer, or from either lower corner of a range to the opposite upper corner.

To select a noncontiguous range of cells, click in the first cell, then hold down Ctrl and click in the other cells in the range (scroll to them if necessary).

You can quickly select a row by clicking the row heading, a column by clicking the column heading, and the whole worksheet by clicking the Select All button. To select a row quickly using the keyboard, press Shift+spacebar; to select a column quickly, press Ctrl+spacebar.

To name a cell or a range quickly:

1. Select the cell or range.

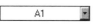

2. Click in the Name drop-down list box at the left end of the formula bar.

3. Enter the name (up to 255 characters with no spaces, and beginning with a letter, a backslash, or an underscore) for the range. Capitalization does not matter for naming.

4. Press Enter.

Changing and Deleting Range Names

Using the Name box is the easiest way of defining range names, but the Define Name dialog box also lets you change and delete range names:

1. Select the cell or range.

2. Chose Insert ➤ Name ➤ Define to display the Define Name dialog box (see Figure 14.1). You'll see the names of currently named ranges in the Names in Workbook list box. If the upper-left anchor cell of the range contains a text label, Excel will suggest it as a range name, replacing any spaces and other unusable characters with underscores.

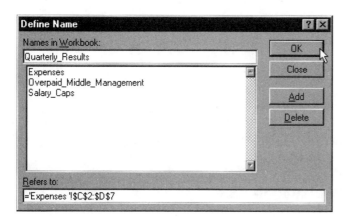

FIGURE 14.1:
Enter the name for the cell or range in the Define Name dialog box.

3. Add, change, or delete the range name:
   - Type a new name for the range into the Names in Workbook text box and click Add.
   - Reuse an existing range name by choosing it in the Names in Workbook list box and clicking on Add.
   - Select the range name in the Names in Workbook list and click Delete.
4. Add, change, or delete further range names as necessary, and click OK.

Going to a Range

To quickly go to and select a named range, select the range name from the Name Box drop-down list.

Formatting Your Data

You can apply formatting to cells using either the Formatting toolbar or the Format Cells dialog box. In this section, we'll look at the easiest ways to apply the most useful types of formatting to your data.

Number Formatting

Because Excel is set up for number crunching, it provides many different number formats for use with different kinds of data. You can quickly apply number formatting by using the Currency Style, Percent Style, and Comma Style buttons on the Formatting toolbar.

Alignment

As we discussed in the previous chapter, Excel identifies any data item as a number, date, time, formula, or text. By default, Excel applies the appropriate horizontal alignment to each of these: For example, Excel right-aligns numbers and left-aligns text. You can overwrite this by applying alignment to the cells as described in the following section; you can also apply vertical alignment to cells for special display effects.

Setting Horizontal Alignment

To apply horizontal alignment, use the four alignment buttons—Align Left, Center, Align Right, and Center Across Columns—on the Formatting toolbar (see Figure 14.2).

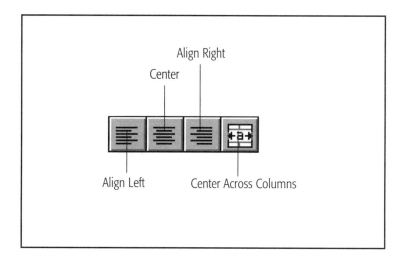

FIGURE 14.2:
Use the four alignment buttons on the Formatting toolbar to apply alignment quickly to cells.

Center Across Columns lets you center the contents of a cell across the columns to its right. Enter the text in the left cell as usual, then select the horizontal range of cells across

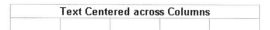

which you want to center the text, and click the Center Across Columns button. The effect is shown here.

Setting Vertical Alignment

To apply more sophisticated alignment options than the above:

1. Choose Format ➤ Cells to display the Format Cells dialog box.
2. Click the Alignment tab to bring it to the front (see Figure 14.3).

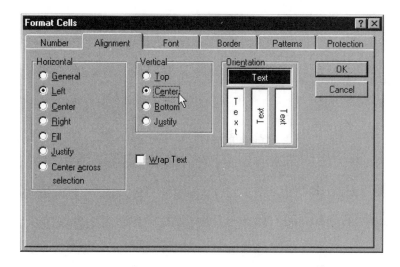

FIGURE 14.3:
Choose alignment options on the Alignment tab of the Format Cells dialog box.

3. In the Horizontal group box, choose the horizontal alignment option you want:
   - General applies Excel's default alignment option for the contents of the cell, such as left alignment for text and right alignment for numbers.
   - Left, Center, and Right we've looked at already.
   - Center Across Selection centers the text across the selected columns.
   - Fill repeats the contents of the cell until it is full.
   - Justify aligns selected text to both the left and the right margins. You'll need to have more than one line of wrapped text (see step 5), and unless your columns are unusually wide, this will look bad.
4. In the Vertical group box, specify the vertical alignment for the selected cells by choosing Top, Center, Bottom, or Justify.
5. If necessary, choose a different orientation for text in the Orientation group box. (The orientation options will be unavailable if you choose Fill or Center Across Selection in the Horizontal group box.)
6. Click OK to apply your choices to the selected cells, or click one of the other tabs in the Format Cells dialog box to make further changes.

Font Formatting

Excel supports a wide range of font formatting that you can use to beautify your worksheets or make the most important information stand out.

To apply font formatting quickly to the selected cells (or selected text with a cell), use the Font drop-down list box, Font Size drop-down list box, Bold, Italic, and Underline buttons, shown here from left to right.

For more complex font formatting, choose Format ➤ Cells to display the Format Cells dialog box, click on the Font tab, make your choices on it, then click OK.

Border Formatting

As well as font formatting, Excel provides a full complement of borders that you can apply to the selected cell or range of cells by clicking the Borders button on the Formatting

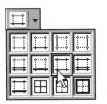

toolbar. You can select from twelve border styles by clicking the drop-down list button on the Borders button and choosing the style of border you want from the drop-down list; this style will stick until you change it, so you can quickly apply it to selected cells by clicking the Borders button.

> **NOTE** You can also apply borders to the active cell or selected cells by choosing Format ≻ Cells to display the Format Cells dialog box, clicking the Border tab, making choices in the Border and Style group boxes, and clicking the OK button.

Using Patterns and Colors

Excel also offers patterns and colors that you can use to make the display of your work-

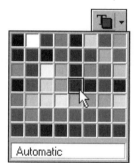

sheets more vibrant and appealing. Unless you're using a color printer, you will probably find colors most useful for on-screen viewing, but patterns can greatly enhance even black-and-white printouts. You can change both the font color (in which the text will display) and the background color of cells, which allows you to make vital information really pop out.

To change the color of the font in selected cells, click the drop-down list button on the Font Color button on the Formatting toolbar and select the color from the drop-down list. This color will stick until you change it, so you can quickly apply it to selected cells by clicking the Font Color button.

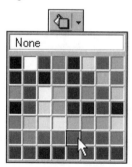

To change the background color of selected cells, click the drop-down list button on the Color button on the Formatting toolbar and choose the new background color from the drop-down list. This color too will stick until you change it.

To change the pattern of selected cells, choose Format ≻ Cells to display the Format Cells dialog box, then click the Patterns tab. Click the Pattern drop-down list and select a pattern. Use the Sample box to see how the pattern will work with the currently selected color. Click OK to close the Format Cells dialog box when you're satisfied.

Protection

Excel's protection is an invisible form of cell formatting. You can format selected cells as either locked (so their contents cannot be changed) or hidden (so their contents are not visible). Then, when you enable protection on the workbook or worksheet, Excel will treat the cells as locked or hidden:

1. Choose Format ➢ Cells to display the Format Cells dialog box.
2. Click the Protection tab.
3. Select the Locked check box or the Hidden check box (or both).
4. Click OK to close the Format Cells dialog box.
5. Choose Tools ➢ Protection ➢ Protect Sheet to display the Protect Sheet dialog box (see Figure 14.4) or Tools ➢ Protection ➢ Protect Workbook to display the Protect Workbook dialog box. These offer different options; follow step 6 for protecting a worksheet, and step 7 for protecting a workbook.

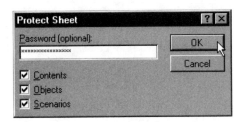

FIGURE 14.4:
Set protection for the active work-sheet in the Protect Sheet dialog box.

6. Choose options for protecting the worksheet in the Protect Worksheet dialog box:
   - Contents prevents the user from changing locked cells or charts.
   - Objects prevents the user from changing graphic objects.
   - Scenarios prevents the user from changing scenarios (an advanced Excel feature).
7. Choose options for protecting the workbook in the Protect Workbook dialog box:
   - Structure prevents the user from moving, deleting, hiding, inserting, or renaming worksheets in the workbook.
   - Windows prevents the user from moving, resizing, hiding, or closing the windows in the workbook.
8. Enter a password in the Password text box if you want to password-protect the worksheet or workbook. This password can be up to 255 characters long and can contain letters, numbers, and symbols; it is also case sensitive, so use uppercase and lowercase as appropriate.
9. Click OK to close the dialog box and enable the protection. If you entered a password in step 8, Excel will display the Confirm Password dialog box; enter the password again and click OK.

TIP To remove protection, choose Tools ➤ Protection ➤ **Unprotect Sheet** or Tools ➤ Protection ➤ **Unprotect Workbook**. If the worksheet or workbook had a password assigned, Excel will display the Unprotect Sheet dialog box or Unprotect Workbook dialog box; enter the password in the Password text box and click OK.

AutoFormatting Worksheets

For formatting tables quickly, try Excel's AutoFormat feature, which (like the Word Table AutoFormat feature we looked at in Chapter 9) offers sundry predefined table formats encompassing all formatting from fonts through borders and shading. To use AutoFormat on selected cells or on a range of cells surrounded by blank cells:

1. Choose Format ➤ AutoFormat to display the AutoFormat dialog box (see Figure 14.5).

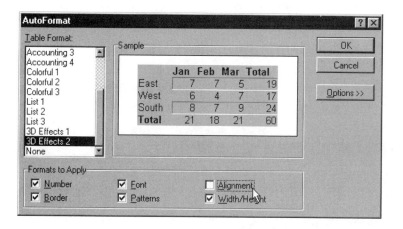

FIGURE 14.5:
In the AutoFormat dialog box, choose the look you want for the selected cells.

2. Choose a format from the Table Format list box. Watch the Sample box for a preview of how your table will look.
3. If you want to apply only some of the formatting characteristics, click the Options button to display six options in the Formats to Apply group box at the bottom of the AutoFormat dialog box. Clear the check boxes for the options you do not want to apply.

4. Click OK to close the AutoFormat dialog box and apply the autoformatting you chose.

> **NOTE** You can change autoformatting once you've applied it by using the normal formatting commands discussed earlier in this chapter.

Styles

In Chapter 7, we looked at the styles that Word provides for quickly formatting your documents consistently. Excel's styles are similar to Word's in that they provide quick access to specific cell formatting, including font, number formatting, color, background color, alignment, patterns, borders, and protection. Like Word, Excel provides a number of predefined styles, and you can add to these any custom formats that you use often and want to keep handy. Also like paragraphs in Word, cells in Excel receive a Normal style by default until you apply another style to them; and you can apply further formatting on top of a style if necessary.

Creating a New Style

You can quickly create a new style from the formatting applied to the active cell:

1. Choose Format ➤ Style to display the Style dialog box (see Figure 14.6).

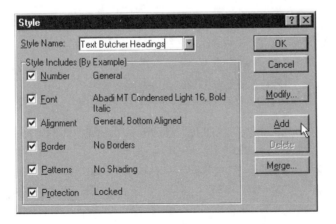

FIGURE 14.6:
To create a new style from the formatting of the active cell, enter the name for the new style in the Style Name drop-down list box in the Style dialog box.

2. Enter the name for the style in the Style Name drop-down list box.
3. In the Style Includes group box, clear the check boxes for any aspects of the active cell's formatting that you do not want to include in the style.
4. Click Add to create the new style.
5. Click OK to close the Style dialog box.

Applying a Style

To apply a style to selected cells:
1. Choose Format ➤ Style to display the Style dialog box.
2. In the Style Name drop-down list box, choose the style to apply.
3. In the Style Includes group box, clear the check boxes for any formatting included in the style that you do not want to apply to the selected cells; for example, you could clear the Number and Alignment check boxes if you wanted the data in the selected cells to retain their original formatting characteristics.
4. Click OK to close the Style dialog box and apply the style.

Modifying a Style

By modifying an existing style, you can instantly make changes to all the cells to which you have assigned that style:
1. Choose Format ➤ Style to display the Style dialog box with the name of the style in the active cell displayed. (You can also choose the style to modify from the Style Name drop-down list.)
2. Click Modify to display the Format Cells dialog box.
3. Use the options on the six tabs of the Format Cells dialog box to change the style to how you want it.
4. Click OK in the Format Cells dialog box to return to the Style dialog box.
5. Choose OK in the Style dialog box to save the changes to the style and apply them to all the cells in the worksheet that have that style.

Deleting a Style

You can quickly delete a style you've created by choosing Format ➤ Style, selecting the style name in the Style Name drop-down list, and clicking Delete. Click OK to close the Style dialog box when you've finished deleting styles.

Merging Styles between Workbooks

You can quickly copy styles between open workbooks using the Merge command:

1. Activate the workbook that will receive the style or styles from the other workbook.
2. Choose Format ➢ Style to display the Style dialog box.
3. Click Merge to display the Merge Styles dialog box (see Figure 14.7).

FIGURE 14.7:
Use the Merge Styles dialog box to copy styles from one workbook to another.

4. In the Merge Styles From list box, select the workbook containing the styles that you want to copy to the current workbook.
5. Click OK to close the Merge Styles dialog box and copy the styles to the first workbook.
6. In the Style dialog box in the first workbook, apply a style from the Style Name drop-down list or click Close to close the Style dialog box.

Restructuring the Worksheet

You can quickly insert (or delete) rows and columns in your worksheet as you need them; you can even delete blocks of cells without deleting entire rows.

NOTE When you delete a cell, a row, or a column, you delete all the data it contains at the same time.

Inserting and Deleting Rows or Columns

To insert complete rows or columns:

1. For rows: Drag through the headings of the rows above which you want to add the new rows. For columns: Drag through the headings of the columns to the left of which you want to add the new columns. Select the same number of row or column headings as you want to insert.

2. Right-click anywhere in the selected rows or columns and choose Insert from the shortcut menu.

To delete complete rows or columns:

1. Drag through the headings of the rows or columns you want to delete.

2. Right-click anywhere in the selected rows or columns and choose Delete from the shortcut menu. Excel moves the remaining rows and columns to fill the space.

Inserting and Deleting Blocks of Cells

When you don't want to insert a whole row or column, you can insert a block of cells and choose to move the existing cells to the right or down:

1. Select the range of cells where you want to insert the block.

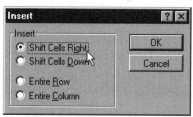

2. Right-click in the selection and choose Insert from the shortcut menu to display the Insert dialog box.

3. Make sure Excel has chosen the most appropriate option in the Insert group box: Shift Cells Right or Shift Cells Down. Select the other option if necessary.

4. Click the OK button to insert the cells.

When you delete a block of cells, you can choose whether to fill the gap with the cells to the right of where the block was or the cells beneath where the block was:

1. Select the range of cells you want to delete.

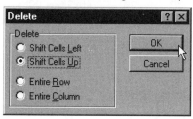

2. Right-click in the selection and choose Delete from the shortcut menu to display the Delete dialog box.

3. Check whether Excel has chosen Shift Cells Left or Shift Cells Up; change this if necessary.

4. Click the OK button to delete the cells.

> **NOTE** You can also choose to insert or delete complete rows or columns in the Insert dialog box and Delete dialog box, but it's faster to work with the row and column headings.

Formatting Rows and Columns

The cells in Excel's worksheets come with a default column width of 8.43 characters and a height of 12.75 points (where one point is $1/72$ of an inch). Excel automatically adjusts row height if you enter taller characters (or graphics) in a cell; you can also adjust both row height and column width manually.

Changing Row Height

To change row height for one row quickly, click on the bottom border of a row heading and drag it up or down until the row is the height you want.

To change row height for several rows at once:

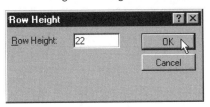

1. Select the rows by dragging through the row headings or through cells in the rows.

2. Choose Format ➤ Row ➤ Height to display the Row Height dialog box.

3. Enter the new height for the row in points in the Row Height text box.

4. Click OK to close the Row Height dialog box.

Changing Column Width

To change column width for one column quickly, click on the right-hand border of a column heading and drag it left or right until the column is the width you want.

To change column width for several columns at once:

1. Select the columns by dragging through the column headings or through cells in them.

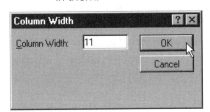

2. Choose Format ➤ Column ➤ Width to display the Column Width dialog box.

3. Enter the new column width in the Column Width text box.

4. Click OK to close the Column Width dialog box.

> **TIP**
>
> You can also set a different default column width in a worksheet by choosing Format ➢ Column ➢ Standard Width and setting a default column width in the Standard Column Width text box in the Standard Width dialog box.

AutoFitting Column Width

Excel's AutoFit feature automatically adjusts column width to fit the widest entry in any selected column. To use AutoFit, select the columns you want to adjust (select the whole worksheet if necessary) and choose Format ➢ Column ➢ AutoFit Selection.

> **TIP**
>
> Wait till you've nearly finished formatting your worksheet before using AutoFormat: If you change the data in a column on which you've used AutoFit, you will need to run AutoFit again to change its width—it won't adjust automatically.

AutoFitting Row Height

Excel automatically autofits row height, but if you override autofitting by setting a row height manually, you can reapply it by choosing Format ➢ Row ➢ AutoFit.

Sorting Data

One of the great advantages of a spreadsheet is that you can manipulate your data easily. Excel offers quick sorting for swiftly arranging the contents of a column into order, and complex sorting for arranging the contents of a table by several sort keys.

Simple Sorting

To sort data in a column or in selected cells quickly, click the Sort Ascending or Sort Descending button on the Standard toolbar. Sort Ascending sorts the cells in the column into alphabetical order or from lowest value to highest; Sort descending sorts the cells into reverse alphabetical order or from highest value to lowest. Selected cells are sorted by the first column.

Complex Sorting

To perform a complex sort on selected cells:

1. Choose Data ➤ Sort to display the Sort dialog box (see Figure 14.8).

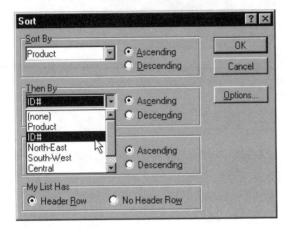

FIGURE 14.8:
In the Sort dialog box, choose up to three sort keys for your data.

2. First, if your data has a header row, make sure that the Header Row option button is selected in the My List Has group box. This will prevent Excel from sorting the headers into their logical alphabetical or numerical position in the data.

3. Choose the first sort key in the Sort by dialog box, then specify Ascending or Descending order.

4. Choose the second sort key in the first Then By box. Again, specify Ascending or Descending order.

5. Choose the third sort key in the second Then By box. Once again, specify Ascending or Descending order.

6. Click OK to close the Sort dialog box and perform the sort according to the sort keys and orders you chose.

Adding Cell Notes

Excel's *cell notes* let you add text or sound notes to any cell to provide extra information to you or your co-workers. Cell notes do not appear in the worksheet; they are indicated by a small red dot in the upper-right corner of the cell to which they are attached.

To add a note to the active cell:

1. Choose Insert ➤ Note to display the Cell Note dialog box (see Figure 14.9).

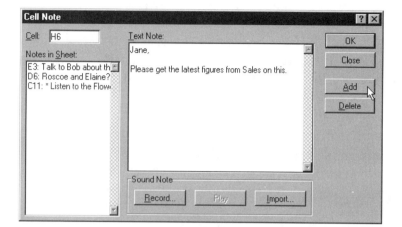

FIGURE 14.9:
In the Cell Note dialog box, you can attach either a text note or a sound note to the active cell.

2. Enter or record your notes:

- For a text note, type the text in the Text Note box.
- For a sound note, you can either click the Record button and record the note using the Record dialog box (shown here) or click the Import button and choose a sound file from the Import Sound dialog box.

WARNING **Recording sound notes can greatly increase the size of a workbook.**

3. Click OK to close the Cell Note dialog box.

To read or listen to a note, move the mouse pointer over the cell that contains it. For a text note, Excel will display a pop-up box containing the text; for a sound note, Excel will play the sound file. (This can be a little creepy if you're mousing about aimlessly in a loaded worksheet.)

To edit a note, choose Insert ➤ Note to display the Cell Note dialog box. In the Notes in Sheet list box, choose the note to edit, then edit it in the Text Note box. (To delete a note, click the Delete button and click OK in the confirmation message box.)

Adding Headers and Footers

To identify the work you print out, you will probably want to change the default header and footer that Excel automatically adds to each worksheet. The default header consists of the worksheet's name from the worksheet tab; the default footer is the page number prefaced by the word *Page*. To change the header and footer to something more informative:

1. Choose File ➤ Page Setup to display the Page Setup dialog box.
2. Click on the Header/Footer tab to bring it to the front (see Figure 14.10). This tab shows previews of both the header and the footer and offers a number of automatic header and footer variants generated from the user information entered when Office was installed on your computer.

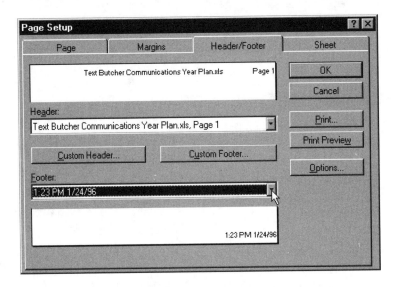

FIGURE 14.10:
Set the header and footer on the Header/Footer tab of the Page Setup dialog box.

3. To use one of the automatically generated headers or footers, choose it from the Header drop-down list or Footer drop-down list. Choose (None) at the top of the list to remove the current header or footer.
4. To create a custom header or footer, click the Custom Header or Custom Footer button to display the Header dialog box (see Figure 14.11) or Footer dialog box, each of which offers Left Section, Center Section, and Right Section boxes.
5. To change a section, click in it and edit the contents using regular editing techniques. To apply font formatting to selected text, click the Font button and choose the formatting as usual in the Font dialog box, then click OK.

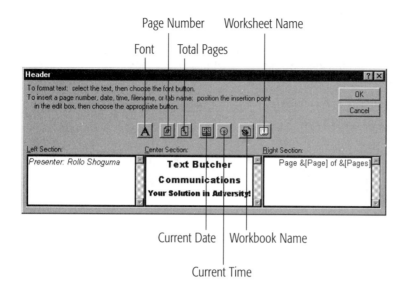

Page Number Worksheet Name

Font Total Pages

Current Date Workbook Name

Current Time

FIGURE 14.11:
Creating a custom header in the Header dialog box

6. To insert the page number, number of pages, current date or time, workbook name or worksheet name, position the insertion point and click the appropriate button to enter the code for the information:

Button	Information Code
Page Number	&[Page]
Number of Pages	&[Pages]
Current Date	&[Date]
Current Time	&[Time]
Workbook Name	&[File]
Worksheet Name	&[Tab]

7. Click OK to return to the Page Setup dialog box.
8. Click OK to close the Page Setup dialog box and return to your worksheet. (Alternatively, you can choose Print Preview to see how your header and footer mesh with the worksheet, or Print to go ahead and print it.)

Printing from Excel

In this section, we'll look quickly at the most important of the many printing options that Excel offers, from straightforward printing of the information in the current worksheet, to carefully laid-out pages containing a selected range of data.

First, though, you can print quickly and simply from Excel:

- To print the currently active worksheet with Excel's default settings, click the Print button on the Standard toolbar.
- To print only a range of data, select that range before clicking the Print button.

Choosing a Paper Type

For more complex printing, first make sure that you and Excel agree on the size and layout of paper you're using:

1. Choose File ➢ Page Setup to display the Page Setup dialog box.
2. If the Page tab isn't displayed, click it to bring it to the front of the Page Setup dialog box (see Figure 14.12).

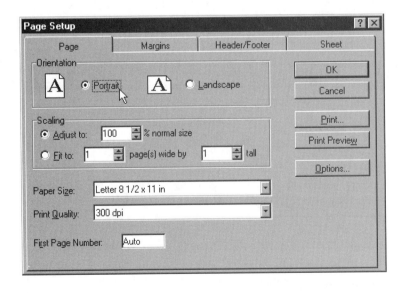

FIGURE 14.12: On the Page tab of the Page Setup dialog box, choose the type of paper you'll be using.

3. In the Orientation box, choose Portrait or Landscape.
4. Use the Scaling group box options to adjust the size of what you're printing if necessary: Either select the Adjust To option button and enter a percentage of

normal size (100% is selected by default) or select the Fit To option button and specify the number of pages wide by the number of pages tall.

5. Choose the paper size from the Paper Size drop-down list.
6. If necessary, change the resolution in the Print Quality drop-down list.
7. To have page numbering start at a number other than 1, enter the number in the First Page Number text box. Otherwise, leave the setting at Auto.
8. Click OK to apply the settings you've chosen, or click one of the other tabs in the Page Setup dialog box to change the margins, header and footer, or worksheet options.

Setting Margins

Next, set margins and header positioning:

1. Choose File ➤ Page Setup to display the Page Setup dialog box.
2. Click the Margins tab to bring it to the front of the Page Setup dialog box (see Figure 14.13).

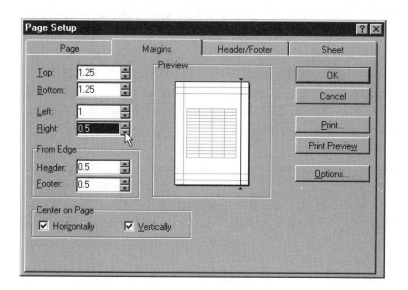

FIGURE 14.13:
Set margin and header placement on the Margins tab of the Page Setup dialog box.

3. In the Top, Bottom, Left, and Right boxes, enter the margin measurements you need. The Preview box will reflect the effects your settings will produce.

4. In the Header and Footer boxes in the From Edge group box, enter the distance that the header and footer should appear from their respective edges of the page.

5. In the Center on Page group box, select the Horizontally or Vertically check boxes as appropriate for the visual effect you want your printout to deliver.

6. Click OK to close the Page Setup dialog box and apply your choices, or click one of the other tabs in the Page Setup dialog box to choose other page setup options.

Setting Worksheet Printing Options

Third, you can also set a number of options for printing worksheets:

1. Choose File ➤ Page Setup to display the Page Setup dialog box.

2. If the Sheet tab isn't displayed, click it to bring it to the front of the Page Setup dialog box.

3. If you will always be printing the same range of cells, set the print area for the worksheet: Click in the Print Area box, then drag in the worksheet to enter the range to print.

TIP At resolutions of less than 1024x768, you'll usually need to click in the title bar of the Page Setup dialog box and drag it out of the way so the worksheet is visible for clicking and dragging; drag the Page Setup dialog box back when you're ready to proceed with it.

4. If you're printing a worksheet that will break onto multiple pages, use the Rows to Repeat at Top and Columns to Repeat at Left boxes in the Print Titles group box to specify which rows and columns to repeat on all pages. Again, click in a box, then click and drag in the worksheet to enter the range.

5. In the Print group box, choose options for printing:
   - Gridlines prints the lines that divide the cells.
   - Notes includes cell notes (on a separate sheet).
   - Draft Quality prints lower-quality output at higher speed.
   - Black and White prints colors as black and white (rather than as gray), making for crisper black-and-white output.
   - Row and Column Headings prints the row numbers and column letters. You'll seldom want this.

6. In the Page Order group box, specify how Excel should divide a spreadsheet onto multiple pages.

7. Click OK to close the Page Setup dialog box and apply your choices, or click another tab in the Page Setup dialog box to set further options.

Using Print Preview

 Before printing any worksheet or workbook, use Print Preview to check quickly that your printout will be close to what you're after: Choose File ➤ Print Preview, click the Print Preview button on the Standard toolbar, or click the Print Preview button in the Page Setup dialog box.

Print Preview displays the current page of the worksheet or workbook (see Figure 14.14):

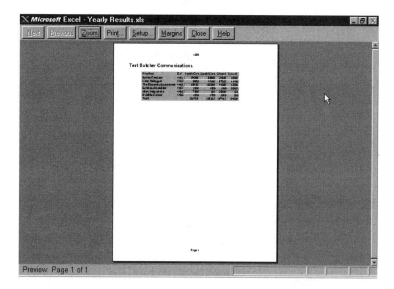

FIGURE 14.14:
Use Print Preview to make sure your documents look the way you want before you print them.

- Zoom the view to and from full-page view by moving the mouse pointer over the page (where it will appear as a magnifying glass) and clicking, or by clicking the Zoom button.
- Click the Next and Previous buttons to move from page to page in a multi-page worksheet.
- Click the Margins button to display margin lines and handles, and column boundary handles, on the preview. Drag a margin handle or a column boundary handle to adjust it.
- Click the Setup button to access the Page Setup dialog box.
- Choose the Close button to exit Print Preview, or click the Print button to display the Print dialog box.

Printing

After checking your prospective printout in Print Preview, print it as follows:

1. Choose File ➤ Print to display the Print dialog box.
2. Specify a printer in the Printer group box.
3. In the Print What group box, make sure Excel has identified what you want to print: Selection (the currently selected cells), Selected Sheet(s), or Entire Workbook.
4. In the Page Range group box, choose whether to print all pages of the item identified in the Print What group box or just the pages you choose.
5. To print more than one copy, set the number in the Number of Copies text box in the Copies group box. Select the Collate check box if you want to collate each copy in order.
6. Click OK to close the Print dialog box and print the item.

Chapter 15

CHARTING

- **The elements of a chart**
- **Creating a chart**
- **Modifying a chart**
- **Using and creating chart AutoFormats**

There's no simpler way to enliven tedious figures than to use a chart. I'm not going to repeat that antique cliché about how many words a picture is worth, because you will know from your own experience how effective charts can be to illustrate trends in data.

In this chapter, we'll look at how to create charts in Excel and to format them so that they present your data to maximum advantage.

Chart Terms and Basics

Before we get into the specific types of charts that Excel offers, let's look quickly at the different parts that make up a chart. A typical chart such as the one shown in Figure 15.1 includes the following elements:

Axes	Two-dimensional charts have an X-axis (the horizontal axis) and a Y-axis (the vertical axis); three-dimensional charts have a Z-axis (the depth axis).
Titles	A chart will typically have a chart title and a title for each axis.
Legend	The legend identifies each data series (for example, by color or pattern).
Data Series	A data series is one of the sets of data from which the chart is drawn. A pie chart has only one data series, but most types of charts can have two or more data series.
Grid lines	The grid lines are lines drawn across the charts from the axes for visual reference.
Categories	Categories are the items by which the data series is separated. For example, if a chart showed the years 1992–1999, each category would be one of those years.

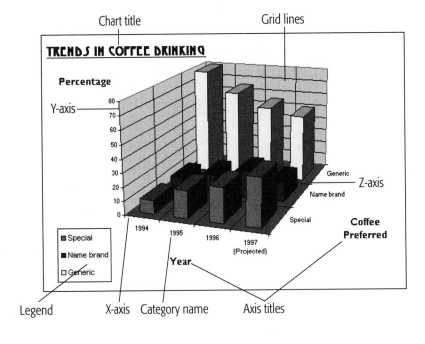

FIGURE 15.1:
The elements of a typical chart

Choosing the Right Type of Chart

Excel offers a wide variety of different types of charts, and choosing the right chart for your data can be a tough call. In this section, we'll look at the basic chart types and discuss what they're usually most useful for. The good news is that once you've created a chart in Excel, you can quickly modify it (by adding legends, titles, and so on) or even switch it to a different and more suitable chart type without losing any data.

Area charts are good for showing how much different series of data contribute to a whole. These charts use connected points to map each series, and the space between the series is filled in with a color or pattern.

Bar charts are the type of chart typically used for showing performance against benchmarks. Each data point is marked by a horizontal bar that extends to the left or right of the baseline.

Column charts, which are similar to bar charts but use vertical bars instead of horizontal bars, are typically used for showing sales figures, rainfall, and the like.

Line charts are good for showing changes in series over time; a typical use would be for charting temperature or changes in stock prices. The data points in each data series are connected by a line.

Pie charts are notorious enough from math class to need neither introduction nor illustration: A single data series is divided up into pie slices showing the relative contribution of the various data points. Pie charts are great for showing market share, survey results, and the like.

Doughnut charts are mutant pie charts that can show more than one data series. You might use a single doughnut chart instead of two pie charts to show changes in market share over two years.

Radar charts represent data points as symbols around a central point (the putative radar scanner), with the value of each data point represented by its symbol's distance from the scanner. Radar charts can be confusing when misused; use them with care.

XY or *scatter charts*, typically used for charting the results of surveys or experiments, plot a series of data pairs against XY coordinates. The result typically resembles a line chart that's lost its lines (some formats do have lines).

Combination charts add a line chart to a column chart or bar chart, plotting one or more data series as lines and the others as bars or columns. You can use combination charts either to demonstrate two trends at once or to severely confuse your audience (or both).

3-D charts include 3-D area charts, 3-D bar charts, 3-D column charts, 3-D line charts, 3-D pie charts, and 3-D surface charts. Use them when the complexity of your data overwhelms two dimensions.

Creating a Chart

Excel lets you create a chart either on a separate worksheet (a *chart sheet*) or embedded on the current worksheet. The procedures for creating the two are the same apart from the second step:

1.  Select the range whose data you want to chart. To create a chart on a separate worksheet, choose Insert ➢ Chart ➢ As New Sheet. To create an embedded chart, select Insert ➢ Chart ➢ On This Sheet or click the ChartWizard button on the Standard toolbar, then drag the area on the worksheet where you want the chart to appear.

2. Excel will display the first ChartWizard dialog box, displaying the range of data you selected in step 1. Click Next to display the second ChartWizard dialog box (see Figure 15.2).

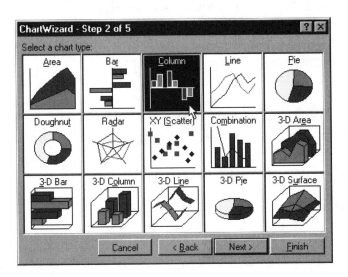

FIGURE 15.2:
In the second ChartWizard dialog box, choose the type of chart you want, then click Next.

3. Choose the chart best suited to your data and click Next to display the third ChartWizard dialog box (see Figure 15.3), which displays various formats for the type of chart you chose.

4. Choose a format for the chart type you chose and click OK to display the fourth ChartWizard dialog box (see Figure 15.4).

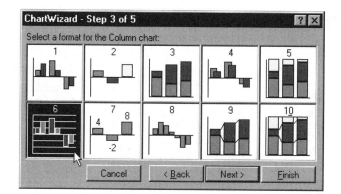

FIGURE 15.3:
In the third ChartWizard dialog box, choose a format for the chart type you chose, then click Next.

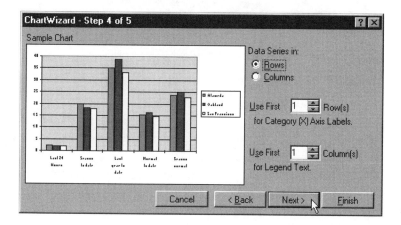

FIGURE 15.4:
In the fourth ChartWizard dialog box, specify details about your chart, then click Next.

5. Enter the details for your chart, then click Next to display the fifth and final ChartWizard dialog box (see Figure 15.5). The details vary with different types of chart, but typically you will do the following:
   - Choose whether the data series is in rows or columns.
   - Choose how many rows or columns to use for Category Labels.
   - Choose how many columns or rows to use for Legend Text.

6. Choose the final options for your chart: Choose whether to add a legend; enter a chart title; and enter axis titles for X and Y (and for second Y for 3-D charts). Click Finish to create the chart and embed it in your worksheet (see Figure 15.6) or place it on a separate worksheet. Excel will also display the Chart toolbar shown in the figure.

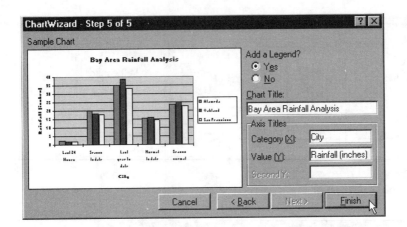

FIGURE 15.5:
In the fifth ChartWizard dialog box, add the chart title and axis titles, then click Finish.

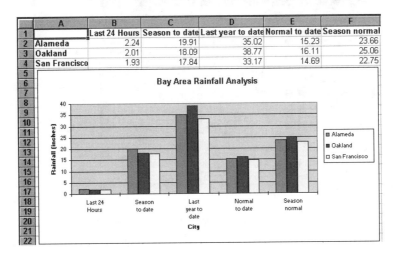

FIGURE 15.6:
The chart embedded in the worksheet

Modifying a Chart

Once you've created a chart, you can easily modify it so that it presents your data most effectively. In this section, we'll look at how you can resize and reposition a chart, edit its component parts, and even change it swiftly and painlessly to another chart type.

Moving a Chart

The easiest way to move an embedded chart to a different position on a worksheet is to click anywhere in it and drag it to the position you want it on the worksheet.

To move a chart from one worksheet to another, right-click in it and choose Cut from the shortcut menu. Navigate to the worksheet on which you want to position the chart, then right-click where you want the upper-left corner of the chart to appear and choose Paste from the shortcut menu.

NOTE You cannot move a chart on a chart sheet, but you can click the chart sheet tab and drag it to a different position in the workbook.

Resizing a Chart

To resize an embedded chart, click anywhere in it to select it, then move the mouse pointer over one of its handles to display a double-headed arrow. Click and drag until the dotted outline is the size you want:

- The side handles resize the chart in only one dimension, while the corner handles resize the chart in two dimensions.
- Hold down Shift as you drag a corner handle to resize the chart proportionally to how it was before.

NOTE You cannot resize a chart sheet.

Deleting a Chart

To delete an embedded chart, either click in it and press Delete, or right-click in it and choose Cut from the shortcut menu.

To delete a chart sheet, right-click the sheet tab and choose Delete from the shortcut menu, then choose OK in the warning message box. You won't be able to undo this deletion.

Editing a Chart

You can edit many of the elements of a chart to change its appearance or highlight certain elements at the expense of others.

To edit a chart, first activate it by double-clicking anywhere in it so that it grows a thick, shaded border (see Figure 15.7). You can then edit any of the elements of the chart by clicking it so it displays handles and its name appears at the left end of the formula bar (see the figure).

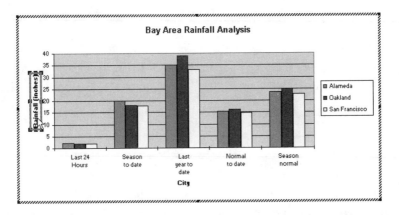

NOTE You can also select elements in a chart by using ←, →, ↑, and ↓, to move from element to element. Press Esc to deselect a selection.

To edit the text of an element such as an axis title you've selected, click in it and use regular editing methods to change the text. Click elsewhere in the chart to enter the change.

To format an element that you've selected, either double-click it or right-click it and choose the Format option from the shortcut menu. (This will vary depending on the item you have selected: Format Chart Title, Format 3-D Area Group, Format Axis, and so on.) Choose options as appropriate and click OK when you're satisfied.

Removing an Element from a Chart

To remove an element from a chart, activate the chart, then right-click in the element you want to delete and choose Clear. (Alternatively, click in the element to select it, then press Delete.)

Inserting Elements in a Chart

You can insert a variety of elements in a chart, depending on what type of chart it is. For example, most charts (including radar charts and scatter charts) can have axes and gridlines, but pie charts and doughnut charts cannot.

To insert elements in a chart, right-click in it and choose the item to insert from the shortcut menu: Insert Titles, Insert Axes, Insert Gridlines, or Insert Data Labels.

To add a legend to a chart, click the Legend button on the Chart toolbar or choose Insert ➤ Legend.

Changing a Chart to Another Type

Excel lets you easily change a chart from one type to another, so when you're creating a chart from your data, feel free to mess around with different chart types until you find one that really suits your data and displays it to maximum advantage. You can change either an entire chart to a different type, or you can change a selected data series to a different chart type to create a combination chart.

To change a chart from one type to another:

1. Double-click in the chart to activate it. To change just one data series, select it by clicking on it in the active chart.
2. Right-click in open space in the chart and choose Chart Type from the shortcut menu to display the Chart Type dialog box (see Figure 15.8). The central area of the dialog box will show the chart's primary type, and the Apply To group box will have Selected Series, Group, or Entire Chart highlighted, depending on what you selected in step 1.

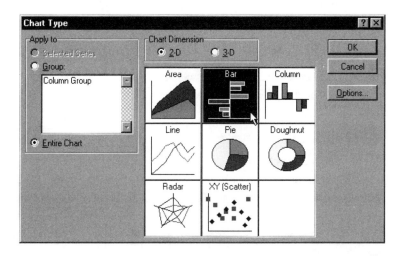

FIGURE 15.8:
In the Chart Type dialog box, choose the type of chart into which you want to morph the current chart.

3. If necessary, change the selection in the Apply To group box. Selected Series will be available only if you selected a data series in step 1. Group will be available if the chart includes two or more types of data series, such as area and column.
4. In the Chart Dimension group box, choose 2-D or 3-D.
5. In the central area of the dialog box, choose the type of chart into which you want to change the selected series, group, or chart. Different options will be

available depending on the type of chart you're starting from and whether you have a series, group, or the whole chart selected.

6. For more options on the type of chart you're choosing, click the Options button and choose options in the dialog box displayed, then click Chart Type to return to the Chart Type dialog box or OK to apply your choices.

7. If you skipped step 6 or chose Chart Type in it, click OK to close the Chart Type dialog box and apply the chart you chose to your selection.

You can also change a chart quickly from one type to another by selecting the chart, clicking the Chart Type drop-down button on the Chart toolbar, and selecting the type of chart you want from the drop-down list.

AutoFormatting a Chart

If you're familiar with the AutoFormat features in Word, Excel's Chart AutoFormat features will make a lot of sense to you. Each AutoFormat is tailored to a particular type of chart (e.g., bar, pie, or doughnut) and contains predefined formatting that you can quickly apply to your chart instead of applying formatting manually. Some of the AutoFormats provide specifications for chart elements such as gridlines, labels, colors, and patters.

You can also create your own AutoFormats, which we'll look at in a minute.

Applying an AutoFormat

To apply an AutoFormat, first create the chart and activate it. Then:

1. Right-click in the chart and choose AutoFormat from the shortcut menu to display the AutoFormat dialog box (see Figure 15.9).

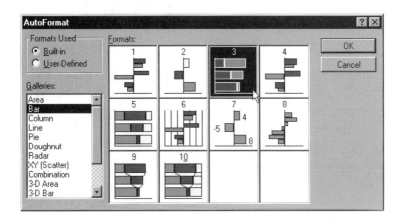

FIGURE 15.9:
In the AutoFormat dialog box, choose the AutoFormat you want for the chart and click OK.

2. In the Formats Used group box, select Built-In to use Excel's built-in AutoFormats or User-Defined to use AutoFormats you've defined (as described in the next section).

3. Choose the AutoFormat you want:
   - If you're using Excel's built-in AutoFormats, choose the type of chart you want in the Galleries list box, then select the format you want in the Formats box.
   - If you're using user-defined AutoFormats, choose the format you want in the Formats list box that replaces the Galleries list box.

4. Click OK to apply the AutoFormat you chose.

Creating Your Own AutoFormats

By creating your own AutoFormats, you can quickly apply your lovingly developed formatting to all your charts:

1. First, create a chart and apply to it all the formatting that you want the AutoFormat to contain.

2. Activate the chart.

3. Right-click in the chart and choose AutoFormat from the shortcut menu to display the AutoFormat dialog box.

4. In the Formats Used group box, select the User-Defined option button.

5. Click Customize to display the User-Defined AutoFormats dialog box.

6. Click Add to display the Add Custom AutoFormat dialog box.

7. Enter a name for the AutoFormat in the Format Name dialog box. This name can be up to 31 characters long, but you won't be able to see more than about 16 characters in the Formats list in the AutoFormat dialog box.

8. Enter a description of the format in the Description box. This can be up to 32 characters, and you'll be able to see all of them.

9. Click OK to close the Add Custom AutoFormat dialog box and add the AutoFormat to the Formats list.

10. Click Close to close the User-Defined AutoFormats dialog box

Chapter 16

USING FORMULAS AND FUNCTIONS

FEATURING

- **What are formulas and functions?**
- **Creating formulas**
- **Entering functions**
- **Dealing with error messages**

Excel was built to crunch numbers as you do granola, and formulas and functions are its raison d'être. As you might imagine, Excel provides enough calculating power to sink the proverbial battlecruiser. The good news is that formulas and functions can be extremely simple to use, and if you want to create a simple formula that, say, adds the contents of the cells in a column or divides the contents of one cell by the contents of another, it'll take no more than a few clicks of your mouse.

In this chapter we'll concentrate on the practical rather than the esoteric. We'll look at what formulas and functions actually are (and what the difference between the two is), what they consist of, and how you can enter them in your spreadsheets quickly and easily.

What Are Formulas and Functions?

A formula, as you'll remember from those blissful days in math class, is a recipe for performing a calculation on numerical data. A formula can be anything from simple addition (such as the hours on an invoice) to complex calculations on how to build a bigger and more robust Hubble.

This chapter promised you both formulas and functions—so what's the difference? Simply put, a function is a predefined formula built into Excel. Excel ships with enough functions to satisfy most computing needs—everything from a straightforward SUM to an ugly DSTDEVP for calculating standard deviation (don't ask) based on all the entries in a database. But for specialized projects, you can create powerful formulas of your own swiftly and safely.

The Parts of a Formula

To create a formula in Excel, you need to indicate the data to be used in the computation and the operation or operations to be performed. Data can consist of constants (numbers) and references to cells, as we'll see in the next section. Operations use three categories of operators: arithmetic, logical, and text.

Constants

A *constant* is a number entered directly in the formula—it uses a constant value in every calculation (unless you change the formula). As an example of using constants in a formula, you could enter the following formula in a cell to subtract 31 from 33:

    =33-31

When you press Enter, the cell will display **2**. The initial = sign tells Excel that you're entering a formula in the cell; 33 and 31 are constants, and the minus sign is the operator for subtraction.

This example probably seems pretty pointless: You'd do better to enter **2** in the cell and be done with it. And as you can imagine, using constants for all the values of a calculation in Excel is about as slow (and accurate) as punching them into a calculator. Usually you will want to use references in your formulas instead of constants. Read on.

References

A *reference* indicates to Excel the location of the information you want to use in a formula. By using references instead of constants, you can build formulas that you don't need to change when the data in your worksheet changes. For example, to perform the calculation **33-31**, you could enter **33** in cell B4 and **31** in cell B5 and then enter this formula in cell B6:

```
=B4-B5
```

This tells Excel to subtract the contents of cell B5 from the contents of cell B4. Now you can change the data in cells B4 and B5, and Excel will automatically recalculate the value of the result of the calculation in cell B6.

When you're referring to the current worksheet in a formula, you can use cell references without specifying the worksheet name: Excel will assume you mean the current sheet. To reference cells on another worksheet, enter the worksheet name and an exclamation point before the cell reference:

```
=Sheet11!B4-Sheet11!B5
```

If you rename a worksheet, Excel will automatically change the references in your formulas. For example, if you renamed Sheet11 to **Dresden China**, Excel would change the above formula as follows:

```
=`Dresden China`!B4-`Dresden China`!B5
```

Notice that Excel encloses the name of the worksheet in single quotation marks.

One of the easiest ways to enter the references to a formula is to use range names, which we looked at in Chapter 14. For example, if you've assigned the name TotalIncome to one cell and the name TotalOutgoings to another, you could use this formula to calculate the net:

```
=TotalIncome-TotalOutgoings
```

By using range names, you avoid having to specify which sheet the information is currently residing on.

Operators

The operator is the way in which you tell Excel which operation to perform with the data you've supplied by using constants and references. As we mentioned earlier, Excel uses three types of operators: arithmetic, logical, and text.

Arithmetic Operators

Excel's six arithmetic operators are the old standbys from math adapted slightly for the computer keyboard:

Operator	Action	Example
+	Addition	=D4+E4
/	Division	=20/E4
^	Exponentiation	5^2
*	Multiplication	=E5*24
%	Percent	20%
-	Subtraction	=D4-E4

As you will remember from that math class, exponentiation raises the specified number to the given power (for example, **2^2** is 2 to the power of 2—in other words, 2x2, or two squared). The percent operator divides the number preceding it by 100 to produce a percentage, so 20% is expressed as 0.2.

Logical Operators

Straight math is all very well, but you also need to be able to compare values, and for this you need to use Excel's *logical* operators:

Operator	Meaning	Example
=	Equal to	=D5=6
>	Greater than	=D5>6
<	Less than	=6<5]
>=	Greater than or equal to	=Sheet4!A33>=250
<=	Less than or equal to	=88<=10000
<>	Not equal to	=A5<>"Penguin"

As you can see from the examples, these operators compare one value or text string (such as *Penguin* in the sixth example) to another. They return a result of TRUE if the condition is true and a result of FALSE if the condition is false; TRUE is represented as a mathematical 1 and FALSE as a mathematical 0. This means that, while a cell will display TRUE or FALSE, if you use the result of the cell in a formula, it will be treated as a 1 or a 0.

Text Operator

Excel uses one text operator—the ampersand (&)—for joining two labels together. For example, if cell C47 contains the label *1994* and cell D47 contains the label *Results* (with a blank space before it), you could use the formula **=C47&D47** to produce the result *1994 Results* in another cell. You can use the & operator with a value and a text string, as in the example here; with two values; or with two text strings. If you use & to concatenate (which is computer Latin for "slam together") two values, bear in mind that Excel joins the two values together rather than adding them: If cell A11 contains the value 50 and cell B11 contains the value 100, the formula **=A11&B11** will produce the result 50100 rather than 150.

How Excel Uses Operators

So far the examples we've looked at have been agreeably simple, using only one operator apiece; but when any formula contains more than one operator, the order in which Excel evaluates the operators becomes important. For example, **=50*100-20** could mean either that you multiply 50 by 100 and then subtract 20 from the result (giving 4980), or that you subtract 20 from 100 and then multiply 50 by the result (80), giving 4000.

Excel evaluates operators in the order of precedence shown in the following list. Where two operators have the same precedence, Excel evaluates them from left to right.

Operator	Action
-	Negation (negative numbers)
%	Percent
^	Exponentiation
* and /	Multiplication and division
+ and -	Addition and subtraction
=, >, <, <=, >=, <>	Comparison

You'll see from this that in the example above (**=50*100-20**), Excel will evaluate the multiplication operator before the negation operator, giving 4980 as the result.

If you want to perform the calculation the other way, read the next section for instructions on how to use parentheses to change the order in which Excel evaluates operators.

Changing Precedence in a Formula

Memorizing Excel's operator precedence list and applying it effectively can be tricky. To alleviate this, Excel lets you use parentheses to change the order in which it evaluates the operators in a formula. Excel evaluates the contents of parentheses in a formula first, ignoring its otherwise slavish devotion to operator precedence. For example, you could change our example formula from **=50*100-20** to **=50*(100-20)** to force Excel to evaluate the contents of the parentheses before the multiplication (and thus produce the result 4000).

Excel insists on your using parentheses in pairs—each left (opening) parenthesis must be matched by a right (closing) parenthesis. If you try to enter a formula that's missing a right parenthesis, Excel will display a message box complaining that *Parentheses do not match* and will return you to the reference area to fix the formula; if your formula is missing a left parenthesis or otherwise running a surplus of right parentheses, Excel will display a message box complaining *Error in formula* and likewise return you to the reference area.

To help you in pairing your parentheses, Excel flashes each opening or closing parenthesis you enter in bold, together with its matching parenthesis if it has one. When you enter a closing parenthesis and see no opening parenthesis flash in acknowledgment, look closely for a missing opening parenthesis. When you enter it correctly, you should see its paired closing parenthesis flash.

Pairing parentheses becomes even more important when you *nest* parentheses, putting one pair of parentheses inside another. Excel will evaluate the nested parentheses first. For example, in the formula **=400-(44/A2)+(3*(C3+1))**, Excel will evaluate **C3+1** first.

If you find that entering grouped values in parentheses helps you understand what your formulas are doing, you can use parentheses even when they are not strictly necessary for telling Excel how you want a formula to be calculated.

Creating a Formula

As you might have guessed, you can simply type a formula straight into the active cell or the reference area of the formula bar, then click the Enter button (or press Enter, or click in another cell) to enter the formula. But (as you'll also have guessed) you can use the mouse to quickly indicate references (cells and ranges).

To enter a reference in a formula, you can simply point to the cell or range with the mouse and click on it. To do so, start typing the formula as usual. Then, when you've reached the point where you want to enter the first reference, move the mouse pointer to the cell you want to reference and click on it. (To reference a range, click and drag through it. To reference a cell or range on another worksheet, click on the worksheet tab to move to the worksheet first.) Excel will enter the reference in the formula, will display a shimmering dotted border around the referenced cell or range, and will display *Point* in the status bar to indicate that you've just used Point mode. You can then continue typing your formula in the reference area.

TIP

You can also use the keyboard to enter a reference in a formula by using ↑, ↓, ←, and → to navigate to the cell. To select a range, hold down Shift and use the arrow keys to select the range.

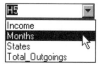

To enter a range name in a formula, you can either type it in or select it from the name drop-down list at the left end of the formula bar, then continue typing the formula in the reference area.

NOTE

Instead of using the name drop-down list, you can press F3 to display the Paste Name dialog box. Choose the range name from it and click OK. (Pressing F3 won't display the Paste Name dialog box if the workbook contains no range names.)

Working with Functions

As we discussed at the beginning of this chapter, a function is one of Excel's built-in formulas. For example, the SUM formula mentioned earlier adds the contents of the specified range. To add the contents of cells B5 through B10, you could use the function **=SUM(B5:B10)** rather than the formula **=B5+B6+B7+B8+B9+B10**.

First, some terminology. Each function consists of a *name* and one or more *arguments* indicating the data to be used. In the above example, the name is **SUM** and the single argument it uses is **B5:B10**. The arguments for a function can be constants, references, range names, or other functions; for functions that use multiple arguments, the arguments are separated by commas. A function returns a *result*.

NOTE

I just lied: Excel has a few functions that take no arguments at all. One is NA, which returns *#N/A*, an error value indicating that a result is not available. (In case you're wondering, this can be useful for troubleshooting problems in your formulas.)

Entering a Function by Hand

As with formulas, you can enter functions in your worksheets by hand by simply typing them in. You can use Point mode to select references, and you can enter range names by using the name drop-down list or by pressing F3 and using the Paste Name dialog box. But for most functions you will do better to use the help provided by the Function Wizard, as described in the next section.

The main exception to this is the SUM function, for which Excel provides an AutoSum button on the Standard toolbar. To quickly create a sum with AutoSum:

1. Make active the cell that will contain the function.

2. Click the AutoSum button. Excel will enter the function **=SUM()** and will suggest within the parentheses the cells in the current row or column that it identifies as most likely contenders for summing. For example, if the active cell is immediately below a column of figures, AutoSum will suggest summing that range; if the active cell is to the right of a row of figures, AutoSum will suggest summing that range.

3. If the range is not correct, click and drag with the mouse to indicate the correct range.

4. Press Enter, click the Enter button, or click elsewhere in the worksheet to enter the function.

Entering a Function with the Function Wizard

Excel's Function Wizard provides an easy way to select the function you need and supply it with the arguments it wants:

1. Make active the cell that you want to contain the function.

2. Click the Function Wizard button on the Standard toolbar to display the Function Wizard dialog box (see Figure 16.1).

> **NOTE** If you don't have the Standard toolbar displayed, type = to start the function, then click the Function Wizard button on the formula bar.

3. In the Function Category list box, choose the category of functions you want.
   - Click the Most Recently Used item at the top of the list to see which functions you've used most recently.
   - Choose All if you're not sure which category the function you're looking for fits into.

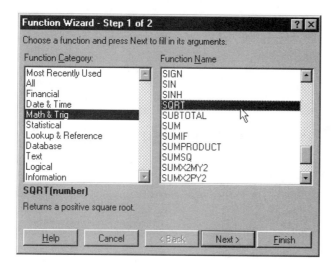

FIGURE 16.1:
To enter a function, click the Function Wizard button to display the first Function Wizard dialog box.

4. Choose the function from the Function Name list. Use the description at the bottom of the Function Wizard dialog box to check that this is the function you want. (Click Help to find out more about the function you've selected.)

5. Click Next to move to the second Function Wizard dialog box (see Figure 16.2). This dialog box is different for each function: It contains a description of the function and descriptions of the arguments required for it.

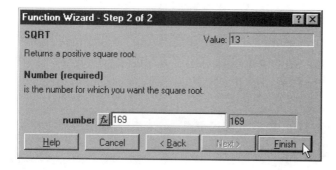

FIGURE 16.2:
Choose arguments for the function in the second Function Wizard dialog box.

6. Choose the arguments for the function in the text boxes:
   - Type in a constant, a reference, a range, or a function.
   - Use Point mode to enter a reference or a range by clicking (and dragging if necessary) outside the dialog box.
   - Use the Name drop-down list to enter a range name (or press F3 and select the name in the Paste Name dialog box).

- Click a Function Wizard button next to an argument to enter a nested function as an argument (a *nested* function is one you enter inside another function).

7. Click Finish to close the Function Wizard dialog box and enter the function in the worksheet.

Copying and Moving Formulas

You can copy or move formulas about a workbook by using the regular Cut, Copy, and Paste commands. But with formulas that contain cell references, you need to consider the effect that copying or moving the formula will have on the references.

First, you need to know what absolute references and relative references are, and the distinction between the two.

Absolute, Relative, and Mixed References

By default, Excel uses relative references in your workbooks, which work relative to the cell containing the formula. For example, say you have three columns of numbers—A, B, and C—and you want to subtract the value in each B cell from the value in the corresponding A cell and then multiply the result by the value in the corresponding C cell. You could enter in cell D1 the formula **=(A1-B1)*C1**, copy it, and paste it into the remaining cells in column D. With relative references, Excel will adjust the formula it enters in each cell so each performs the same relative operation: Subtract the value in the cell three columns to the left by the value in the cell two columns to the left, and multiply the result by the value in the cell one column to the left. So cell D2 will contain the formula **=(A2-B2)*C2**, cell D4 will have **=(A4-B4)*D4**, and so on.

> | **TIP** | You can also copy a formula by using the AutoFill handle as discussed in Chapter 13. |

Relative references are widely useful in creating worksheets quickly, but sometimes you'll want to use absolute references instead. An absolute reference in a formula refers to the same place in a workbook no matter where you copy or paste it to. For example, suppose you wanted to add your beloved state sales tax to the calculation in the previous example, and cell E10 held the current tax rate. If you used the relative reference **E10** in the first formula (**=(A1-B1)*C1*E10**), Excel would change **E10** to **E11**, **E12**, and so on when you pasted into another cell. But when you use an absolute reference, Excel will not change the reference: Cells D2, D3, and so on will still use E10 as the reference.

Excel uses the dollar sign ($) to denote absolute references, so the absolute reference for cell E10 would be **E10**. As you can see, both the column and the row need the dollar sign for the reference to be absolute. This is because you can also create *mixed* references—references with either the column fixed and the row relative (**$E10**), or with the column relative and the row fixed (**E$10**).

To quickly create an absolute reference or a mixed reference from a relative reference, select the reference using Point mode, then press F4 once, twice or thrice:

- Once produces an absolute reference (e.g., A1)
- Twice produces a mixed reference relative in column and absolute in row (e.g., A$1)
- Thrice produces a mixed reference absolute in column and relative in row (e.g., $A1).

Pressing F4 a fourth time returns you to a relative reference. If you start with an absolute reference or a mixed reference, each press of F4 moves you on to the next type of reference listed above.

NOTE	Two quick notes here: First, when you use Cut and Paste to move a formula (rather than Copy and Paste to copy it), Excel does not change its references. Second, when you move a range of data referenced in a formula, Excel modifies the reference in the formula (whether absolute, mixed, or relative) to reflect the new location. (This only happens when you move the whole range of data referenced, not if you move just part of it.)

Recalculating Formulas

Every time you change the numbers in a workbook that contains formulas, Excel needs to recalculate them. By default, Excel recalculates all formulas whenever you change the workbook, keeping everything up to date. Usually this will happen fast enough not to slow down your work, so you'll have no reason to change it. But if you're regularly working with large spreadsheets or with a slow computer, you can turn automatic recalculation off (or back on) as follows:

1. Choose Tools ➤ Options to display the Options dialog box.
2. Click the Calculation tab to bring it to the front of the Options dialog box.
3. In the Calculation group box, choose the option you want:
   - Automatic turns automatic recalculation on (as described above).
   - Automatic Except Tables calculates all dependent formulas except data tables.
   - Manual recalculates formulas only when you choose to do so by pressing F9 in the workbook or clicking the Calc Now button on the Calculation tab of the Options dialog box. Select the Recalculate Before Save check box if you want Excel to recalculate the workbook when you save it.
4. Click OK to close the Options dialog box and save your choices.

> **TIP**
> When you're using manual calculation, Excel will display *Calculate* in the status bar when the workbook contains a change that requires recalculation.

Viewing Formulas in the Workbook

As we've seen so far in this chapter, Excel by default displays the result of any formula in the cell the formula occupies, letting you view and work with the result as if it were a regular number and displaying the formula only in the reference area when the cell that contains it is active.

For working out problems in your workbooks, use the Ctrl+` toggle (that's the single left quotation mark found to left of 1 on full-size keyboards and in weird places on notebook keyboards, *not* the single-quote key) to display all formulas in the worksheet instead of their results.

Understanding and Dealing with Errors in Formulas

As you'll have guessed from reading this chapter, the power and flexibility that Excel's formulas offer gives you plenty of latitude for getting things wrong. Here are the top eight error messages that you'll see when you've done something wrong in a formula and Excel doesn't like it:

Message	Meaning	What to Do
#####	The formula result is too long to fit in the cell.	Increase the column width.
#DIV/0!	The formula is trying to divide by zero.	Locate the reference or formula that provides the zero and change it.
#N/A	No value is available for the value to which the formula refers.	Nothing. (Enter #N/A in cells that do not have data yet to mark the lack of data.)
#NAME?	The formula references a range name that Excel cannot find.	Make sure the range exists and that its name is correctly spelled. Redesignate the range if necessary.
#NULL!	The formula references a range incorrectly.	Check that the range is specified correctly. Use a comma (,) to refer to two areas that do not intersect.
#NUM!	The formula cannot use the number supplied. For example, a function that requires a positive number cannot use a negative number.	Check for unsuitable numbers and correct them.
#REF!	The formula refers to an invalid cell. For example, you may have deleted a cell that the formula refers to, or pasted something over it.	Change the formula to correct the invalid reference.
#VALUE!	The formula uses the wrong type of argument—for example, if you specify text where Excel expects to find a number.	Make sure that all arguments are valid.

Chapter 17

CREATING MACROS AND CUSTOMIZING EXCEL

- **Creating a macro**
- **Editing a macro**
- **Customizing Excel**
- **Creating templates**

Excel offers almost as many customization features as does Word to make your everyday work smoother, faster, and simpler. In this chapter, we'll first discuss Excel's macro-recording and macro-editing features before moving on to look at how you can customize Excel to provide a suitable working environment. Finally, we'll look at how you can use templates in Excel to speed your creation of workbooks.

Macros

As we mentioned in Chapter 3, Excel includes a powerful macro language called Visual Basic for Applications, or VBA for short. Like Word, whose macro features we looked at in Chapter 12, Excel lets you record a macro simply by switching on the macro recorder, performing the actions you want to record, and then turning the recorder off. Once you've recorded a macro, you can open it in a macro-editing window and edit it by adding, deleting, or altering the instructions it contains.

Recording a Macro

Before you start recording a macro, you need to decide whether you want the macro to use *relative references* or *absolute references*. As you'll remember from Chapter 16, a relative reference is a reference relative to where the active cell currently is, whereas an absolute reference is fixed no matter where the active cell happens to be. If you choose to use relative references, the macro will record how you move the active cell from the cell you start recording in and will work from whichever cell is active when you start replaying it. If you do not use relative references, the macro will use absolute references and will record the specific cells that you use when recording the macro; when you play back the macro, it will use those cells, no matter which cell is active. Use relative references for any macro that you want to be able to use on different worksheets; use absolute references for any macro that will always work with the same cells.

To record a macro with relative references, choose Tools ➤ Record Macro to display the Record Macro submenu. If the Use Relative References menu item has a check mark by it, Excel will record the macro with relative references; if there is no check mark, Excel will use absolute references. To add or remove the check mark, select the Use Relative References option from the Record Macro submenu.

To record a macro:

1. Choose Tools ➤ Record Macro ➤ Record New Macro to display the Record New Macro dialog box.
2. Enter a name for the macro in the Macro Name box. The name must begin with a letter and can be up to 255 characters long; it can contain underscores, but cannot contain spaces or punctuation marks.
3. Enter a description for the macro in the Description box. Excel will propose by default a description involving your user name and the date: *Macro recorded 1/28/97 by Rikki Nadir* or something similar. You can enter several lines of text here, but later you will thank yourself for being concise.

4. To set further options for the macro, click the Options button to reveal the nether reaches of the Record New Macro dialog box (see Figure 17.1). Choose options as follows:

- To assign the macro to a command on the Tools menu, select the Menu Item on Tools menu check box and enter the name in the text box. Enter an ampersand (&) before the letter that you want to use as an access key; for example, enter **Ind&ustrial Average** to produce a menu item of *Indu̱strial Average* that you can trigger by pressing **u**.

- To assign the macro to a shortcut key, select the Shortcut Key check box and press the key that you want to use with Ctrl as a shortcut key. Press Shift if you want to add that to the key combination: You can use Ctrl+k and Ctrl+Shift+K to run different macros in the same workbook if you want.

- If you want to store the macro somewhere other than in the current workbook, choose Personal Macro Workbook or New Workbook in the Store In group box. Storing the macro in your Personal Macro Workbook means that you will be able to use the macro in any workbook. Storing the macro in the current workbook means that you will be able to use the macro only in this workbook, and any Tools menu option or shortcut key you create will apply only to this workbook.

- If you want to record the macro in the Excel 4.0 macro language (for example, so that you can use it with an old copy of Excel) instead of in VBA, select the Microsoft Excel 4.0 Macro option button in the Language group box.

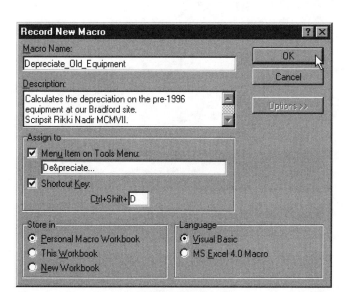

FIGURE 17.1:
Enter a name for the macro in the Record New Macro dialog box; enter a description and choose options if you like.

5. Click OK to close the Record New Macro dialog box and start recording the macro. Excel will display the Stop Recording toolbar (shown here), and the status bar will display *Recording*.

6. Perform the actions that you want to record in the macro.

7. Click the Stop Macro button on the Stop Recording toolbar to stop recording.

Running a Macro

Once you've recorded a macro, the first thing to do is to make sure that it works as you intended. If you didn't assign a shortcut key or a menu option to the macro when you recorded it, you can quickly run it by making an appropriate cell active, choosing Tools ➢ Macro to display the Macro dialog box, selecting the name of your macro, and clicking Run. Excel will perform the actions you recorded.

Assigning a Macro to a Tools Menu Item or a Shortcut Key

If you didn't assign an option on the Tools menu or a shortcut key to a macro when you recorded it, you can assign one afterwards easily enough:

1. Choose Tools ➢ Macro to display the Macro dialog box.

2. Select the macro in the Macro Name/Reference list box.

3. Click the Options button to display the Macro Options dialog box (see Figure 17.2).

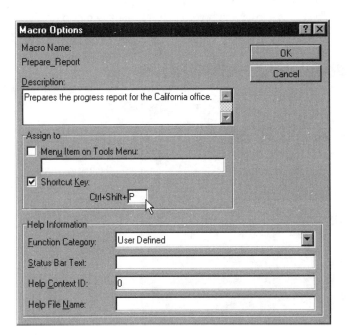

FIGURE 17.2:
In the Macro Options dialog box, you can quickly add (or change) a macro's menu item or shortcut key.

4. In the Assign To text box, choose the new assignments you want:
   - To assign the macro to a shortcut key, select the Shortcut Key check box and press the key that you want to use with Ctrl as a shortcut key. Press Shift if you want to add that to the key combination.
   - To assign the macro to a command on the Tools menu, select the Menu Item on Tools menu check box and enter the name in the text box. Enter an ampersand (&) before the letter that you want to use as an accelerator key.

5. Click OK to close the Macro Options dialog box and return to the Macro dialog box.

6. Repeat the process for another macro, or click Close to close the Macro dialog box.

Assigning a Macro to a Toolbar Button

You can also run a macro by assigning it to a toolbar button:

1. Choose View ➤ Toolbars to display the Toolbars dialog box.

2. Make sure the toolbar to which you want to add the macro is displayed. If it's not displayed, select it in the Toolbars list box.

3. Click the Customize button to display the Customize dialog box.

4. In the Categories list, choose a category of buttons. Custom is usually the best choice, because it contains 28 buttons as yet unassigned to any other command.

 **WARNING** The Macro option in the Categories list shows the buttons available for working with macros, not buttons that you can freely assign to your own macros. (The buttons are assigned to commands that start and stop macros, insert VBA modules, and so on.)

5. Click a button in the Buttons group box and drag it to the toolbar to which you want to add it. When you drop it there, Excel will display the Assign Macro dialog box (see Figure 17.3).

6. Select the macro in the Macro Name/Reference list box and click OK to assign it to the toolbar button. Excel will return you to the Customize dialog box.

7. Repeat steps 4 through 6 as appropriate or click Close.

Running a Macro from a Worksheet Button

You can also create a worksheet button for running macros. A worksheet button (as you might well guess) is a button that sits on a worksheet rather than being part of a

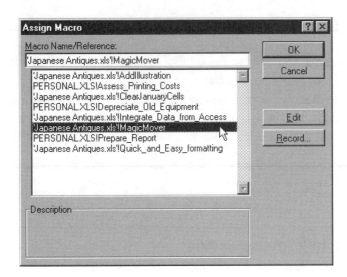

FIGURE 17.3:
In the Assign
Macro dialog box,
choose the macro
to assign to the
toolbar button,
then click OK.

toolbar. By using a worksheet button rather than a toolbar button, you can make sure that a macro is available to your users right where they need it.

To create a worksheet button:

1. Display the Drawing toolbar by right-clicking on any displayed toolbar and choosing Drawing from the shortcut menu. (If you have the Standard toolbar displayed, you can click on the Drawing button instead.)

2. Click the Create Button button on the Drawing toolbar. The mouse pointer will change to a small cross.

3. Click and drag a button-shaped box where you want the button to appear on the worksheet. When you release the mouse button, Excel will display the Assign Macro dialog box (see Figure 17.3 above).

4. Choose the macro to assign to the button:

   - To assign an existing macro to the button, select the macro in the Macro Name/Reference list box and click OK to close the Assign Macro dialog box.
   - To record a new macro, click Record and record the macro as described in steps 2 through 7 of *Recording a Macro*, earlier in this chapter.

5. To rename the button from the generic Button *n* name Excel gives it, drag through the text on the button, type in the name you want (press Enter to create more than one line of text), and then click elsewhere in the worksheet.

You can now run the macro associated with the worksheet button by clicking the button.

TIP

To modify a worksheet button, first Ctrl-click to select it. Once it's selected, you can: change its name by dragging through its text and typing in changes; resize it by dragging one of its handles; move it by dragging one of its edges; or copy it by Ctrl-dragging one of its edges. To assign a different macro to it, right-click the button, choose Assign Macro from the shortcut menu, select the macro in the Assign Macro dialog box, and click OK.

Editing a Macro

If you make a mistake when recording one of your macros, you have the choice of recording the macro again from scratch or braving the rigors of VBA and editing the macro to fix the problem. All the macros you create in a workbook in any one editing session are stored on a tab named Module1, which Excel places after the last worksheet in a workbook; you can get to them either by clicking the Last Sheet button at the lower-left corner of the Excel window or by choosing Tools ➤ Macro, selecting the name of the macro in the Macro Name/Reference list box in the Macro dialog box, and clicking the Edit button. (On subsequent editing sessions, Excel will store macros on tabs named Module2, Module3, and so on.)

We don't have space in this book to get into editing Excel macros, though I would encourage you to explore the possibilities here in a positive spirit if you're at all interested, because macros in Excel can save you a great deal of time. When you look at the Module*x* worksheet, you will see that each macro is prefaced by comment lines (indicated by a comment character, the single quotation mark) consisting of the name of the macro and the description you gave it:

```
'Integrate Data_from_Access Macro
'Incorporates Access data in the daily report for Head
 Office
```

Beyond that, each macro starts with a **Sub** statement and ends with an **End Sub** statement:

```
Sub Integrate_Data_from_Access
  ActiveCell.FormulaR1C1 = "Daily Report for Head
  Office"
End Sub
```

The instructions between the **Sub** and **End Sub** statements are what you can edit, add, or delete. As a simple example, in the above macro one could change the text within quotation marks to change what the macro enters in the active cell.

Global Macros

As we mentioned in *Recording a Macro* earlier in the chapter, Excel can store macros either in a workbook (so the macros are available only in that workbook) or in the personal macro workbook, Personal.xls. The personal macro workbook is always loaded when you run Excel, but in the background, so that you don't see it unless you deliberately display it. Because the personal macro workbook is always loaded, any macros that you create in it will be available in any workbook you have open.

To record a macro in the personal macro workbook, select the Personal Macro Workbook option button in the Store In group box in the Record New Macro dialog box when recording a macro. Excel creates the personal macro workbook automatically the first time you choose to store a macro there, so you don't need to worry about creating it or finding it. Once Excel has created the personal macro workbook, it will load it every time you start Excel.

You can edit your global macros by displaying the personal macro workbook. To do so, choose Window ➢ Unhide to display the Unhide dialog box, select Personal.xls in the Unhide Workbook list, and click OK. Excel will display Personal.xls with the Module1 tab showing. Edit the macros as described in the previous section, then choose Window ➢ Hide to hide the personal macro workbook again.

Customizing Toolbars and Menus

By customizing Excel's toolbars and menus, you can make sure that all the commands you need for either a particular workbook or for all your workbooks are right at hand.

Customizing Toolbars

Excel lets you create toolbars and customize them as well as its standard toolbars as discussed in *Customizing Toolbars* in Chapter 3. You can also add your Excel macros to new or existing toolbars as discussed in *Assigning a Macro to a Toolbar Button* earlier in this chapter.

Customizing Menus

Earlier in this chapter, we saw how you can add a macro you're recording to Excel's Tools menu so that you can run it quickly and conveniently. You can also use Excel's Menu Editor to add and delete menu items and menus themselves.

Adding a Menu, Menu Item, Submenu, or Submenu Item

Here's how to create a new menu, menu item, submenu, or submenu item in Excel:

1. Switch to the Module1 worksheet at the end of the current workbook to affect the menus in the current workbook, or display the personal macro workbook (by choosing Window ➤ Unhide and selecting Personal.xls in the Unhide dialog box) if you want to affect the menus in all workbooks.
2. Choose Tools ➤ Menu Editor to display the Menu Editor dialog box (see Figure 17.4).

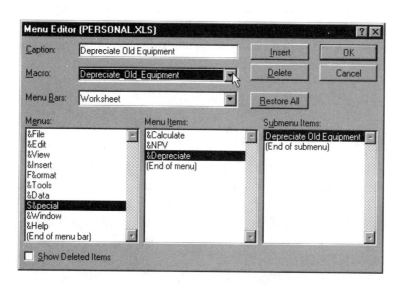

FIGURE 17.4:
You can create menus and submenus in the Menu Editor dialog box. Here we're changing the menus in the personal macro workbook, Personal.xls.

3. In the Menu Bars drop-down list, choose which menu bar you want to change: Usually this will be Worksheet, but you may also want to change the Chart menu bar or one of the Shortcut Menus.
4. Choose where to place your menu, menu item, submenu, or submenu item:
    *   To create a menu: In the Menus list box, select the menu to the left of which you want to add a new menu. (Choose End of Menu Bar to add the new menu after all the existing menus.)

- To create a menu item: In the Menus list box, select the menu to which you want to add the new item. Then, in the Menu Items list box, select the menu item before which the new item is to appear.
- To create a submenu: In the Menus list box, select the menu to which you want to add the new item. Then, in the Menu Items list box, select the item before which the item should appear.
- To create a submenu item: In the Menus list box, select the menu that contains the relevant submenu. Then, in the Menu Items list box, choose the submenu. In the Submenu Items list box, select the submenu to which you want to add the new item.

5. Click Insert.
6. In the Caption text box, enter the name for the new menu, menu item, submenu, or submenu item. Put an ampersand (&) before one letter to make it an accelerator key (e.g., **&Macros** to produce a menu that appears as <u>M</u>acros).
7. If you're creating a menu item or submenu item: In the Macro drop-down list, select the macro that the menu item or submenu item will run.
8. Click elsewhere in the Menu Editor dialog box to add the menu, menu item, submenu, or submenu item.
9. Repeat steps 3 through 8 to add more menus or menu items.
10. Click OK to close the Menu Editor dialog box.

Removing Menus or Menu Items

To remove a menu, menu item, submenu, or submenu item in Excel:

1. Switch to a Module worksheet as described in step 1 in the previous section.
2. Choose Tools ➤ Menu Editor to display the Menu Editor dialog box.
3. In the Menus box, Menu Items box, or Submenu Items box, choose the item you want to delete.
4. Click Delete to delete the item.
5. Delete more items or click OK to close the Menu Editor dialog box.

> **TIP**
> To restore the menus, menu items, submenus, and submenu items to Excel's defaults, click the Restore All button in the Menu Editor dialog box. Excel doesn't confirm this change with you, but if you realize that you made it by mistake, you can click Cancel to exit the Menu Editor dialog box without saving changes.

Using Templates to Save Time

As discussed in Chapter 3, you can use templates to quickly create workbooks based on a common design or on common formatting. We saw in Chapter 13 how you can start a workbook based on one of the dozen templates (for invoices, car leases, timecards, and the like) with which Excel ships; here we'll look at how you can create your own templates for your specific work needs.

By creating a template from a workbook that you've painstakingly set up, you can reuse the workbook and save yourself time and effort. First, make sure the workbook is set up perfectly for reuse. This may mean removing from it data that you'll enter for each new workbook you create based on the template, or entering date formulas into cells rather than specific dates.

Once the workbook is ready:

1. Choose File ➤ Save As to display the Save As dialog box.
2. In the Save As Type drop-down list, choose Template (*.xlt). Excel will switch to the Templates folder.
   - Templates you save in the Templates folder will appear on the General tab of the New dialog box. Alternatively, you can save your templates in the Spreadsheet Solutions folder by double-clicking that folder at this point.
    - You can also create a new folder for your templates by clicking the Create New Folder button, entering a name for the folder in the New Folder dialog box, clicking OK, and then selecting that folder. This new folder will appear as another tab in the New dialog box.
3. Enter the name for your template in the File Name box.
4. Click Save to save the template.
5. If Excel displays the Properties dialog box, enter property information as appropriate. Select the Save Preview Picture check box if you want your template to be able to display a preview in the New dialog box.
6. Choose File ➤ Close to close your template.

To create a new workbook based on the template, choose File ➤ New and select the template in the New dialog box.

Part 4

PowerPoint

Chapter 18

GETTING STARTED IN POWERPOINT

FEATURING

- **What can you create with PowerPoint?**
- **Starting PowerPoint**
- **Creating a presentation**
- **Creating and editing slides**

PowerPoint provides you with all the tools you need to put together moving and persuasive presentations suitable for sales pitches, conferences, or even (in a pinch) entertaining the in-laws over some sodden pseudo-religious holiday. You can create presentations either from scratch or by drawing material from your Word documents or your Excel spreadsheets. You can mix in sound and video to vary the pace, and you can either run the presentation manually or have it run itself automatically while you catch up on your e-mail or knitting in a dark corner.

What Can You Do with PowerPoint?

With PowerPoint, you can put together all the materials you need for a presentation, whether a traditional presentation involving physical slides (or overhead-projector transparencies) or a sizzling computer-based multimedia presentation featuring virtual slides, sounds, and real-time video clips. For your presentation, you can create these materials:

- *Slides* are the images that make up your presentation. Each slide can contain text, graphics, charts, sound, video, and more—even organization charts. You can have celluloid slides created from your PowerPoint slides, but usually you will want to present them by computer. (Alternatively, you can print out the slides on paper or transparency sheets.)
- *Speaker's notes* are speaking aids that consist of an image of each slide together with any notes that you need for that slide. Your audience won't see these notes.
- *Audience handouts* are documents containing images of your slides, several per page. You can add text to clarify the slides.
- *Outline pages* are print-outs of the text of the presentation.

In this chapter, we'll look at how you start creating a presentation and create slides for it. In the next few chapters, we'll look at adding visual elements to your slides and producing the other items described in the list above. Finally we'll discuss how to give the presentation itself.

Creating a Presentation

To start creating a presentation:

1. Launch PowerPoint from the Windows 95 Start menu or from an icon. You should see the PowerPoint startup dialog box (see Figure 18.1). If you don't see the PowerPoint startup dialog box and want to see it, choose Tools ➢ Options to display the Options dialog box, then select the Show Startup Dialog check box on the General tab and click OK. Choose File ➢ Exit, then restart PowerPoint, and the startup dialog box will appear.

> **NOTE**
>
> You may see a Tip of the Day dialog box before the PowerPoint startup dialog box; click OK to dismiss it. (If you don't want to see this dialog box again, clear the Show Tips at Startup check box before clicking OK.)

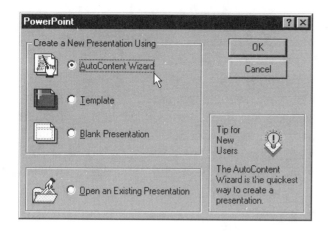

FIGURE 18.1:
In the PowerPoint startup dialog box, choose whether to create a new presentation or open an existing presentation.

2. Choose how to create a new presentation:
   - Select AutoContent Wizard to create a new presentation using advice from PowerPoint. The AutoContent Wizard will help you choose an appropriate template and set up the presentation.
   - Choose Template to create a presentation using one of PowerPoint's templates.
   - Select Blank Presentation to create a presentation from scratch, using PowerPoint's default settings rather than the special settings in one of the templates.
3. Click OK to close the PowerPoint startup dialog box and start creating your presentation. Go on to read the section that corresponds to the choice you made in step 2.

Using the AutoContent Wizard

When you choose the AutoContent Wizard option in the PowerPoint startup dialog box, the AutoContent Wizard will walk you through setting up the presentation.

> **TIP**
>
> To run the AutoContent Wizard without restarting PowerPoint, choose File ➤ New to display the New Presentation dialog box, click the Presentations tab, select AutoContent Wizard, and click OK.

In the first AutoContent Wizard dialog box, which explains what the Wizard will do, click the Next button.

In the second AutoContent Wizard dialog box, enter information for your title slide and click Next.

TIP You can click the Back button to move to the previous AutoContent Wizard dialog box at any point from here on.

In the third AutoContent Wizard, choose the type of presentation you want to create. PowerPoint offers Recommending a Strategy; Selling a Product, Service, or Idea; Training; Reporting Progress; Communicating Bad News; or General. Click the Next button.

If none of these seems appropriate, click the Other button to display the Select Presentation Template dialog box (see Figure 18.2). Choose the template you want (use the Preview button to display a preview of the selected template) and click OK. Click the Next button and skip the next two steps.

Preview

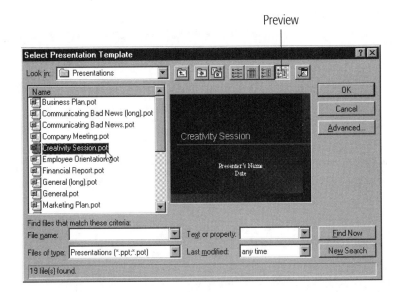

FIGURE 18.2:
In the Select Presentation Template, choose the type of presentation you want to create. Click the Preview button to see a preview of the selected template.

In the fourth AutoContent Wizard dialog box, make your choices in the Select Visual Style for the Presentation group box and the How Long Do You Want to Present? group box. The first setting controls which design PowerPoint will apply to your presentation; the second controls how many slides PowerPoint starts you off with. Again, click the Next button.

In the fifth AutoCorrect dialog box, make your choices in the What Type of Output Will You Use? and Will You Print Handouts? group boxes. Click Next.

In the sixth AutoContent Wizard dialog box, click Finish to have PowerPoint create your presentation with the specifications you chose.

Using a Template

When you choose the Template option in the PowerPoint startup dialog box, PowerPoint will display the New Presentation dialog box (see Figure 18.3) for you to choose the template you want.

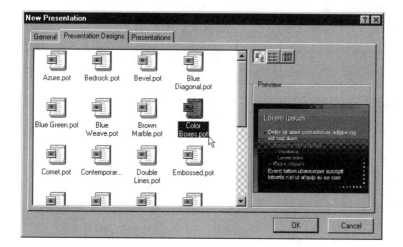

FIGURE 18.3:
In the New Presentation dialog box, choose the template for the type of presentation you want to create.

You have three choices at this point:

- Start a blank presentation by choosing the Blank Presentation icon on the General tab. You get to choose a slide layout for each slide you create, and you can apply a different color scheme to each slide if you want.
- Start a new presentation based on an existing PowerPoint design (color scheme) by choosing an icon on the Presentation Designs tab. You get to choose a layout for each new slide you create.
- Start a new presentation based on an existing PowerPoint theme (including an existing design and slide layout) by choosing an icon on the Presentations tab. PowerPoint will create a number of slides for you, all with the theme's layout and color scheme.

NOTE Any extra folder containing presentation templates that you or your colleagues have created will show up in the New Presentation dialog box as another tab.

Use the Preview box to help you select the type of presentation you want to create, then click OK to start creating the presentation. If you chose one of the first two options, PowerPoint will display the New Slide dialog box (see Figure 18.4). Choose the AutoLayout for the type of slide you want to create and click OK to create it.

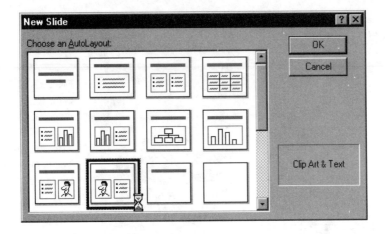

FIGURE 18.4:
Choose the type of slide you want to create by selecting an AutoLayout in the New Slide dialog box.

Creating a Blank Presentation

If you chose Blank Presentation in the PowerPoint startup dialog box, PowerPoint will display the New Slide dialog box (shown in Figure 18.4, above). Choose the AutoLayout for the type of slide you want to create and click OK to create it.

NOTE　If PowerPoint does not display the New Slide dialog box, choose Tools ≻ Options to display the Options dialog box and select the Show New Slide Dialog check box on the General tab. Click OK to close the Options dialog box. In the future, PowerPoint will display the New Slide dialog box automatically; for now, click the New Slide button on the PowerPoint status bar to display this dialog box.

Saving the Presentation

By now, you should have a presentation of some description started, with a new slide on screen. Next, we'll look briefly at the five views that PowerPoint offers; then we'll look at creating and editing slides. First, though, save your presentation by choosing File ➢ Save or by clicking the Save button on the Standard toolbar.

> **TIP**
>
> Before you save your presentation, you may want to set the default file location to a specific folder so that PowerPoint does not automatically save each file to the last folder you used. To do so, choose Tools ➢ Options to display the Options dialog box, click on the Advanced tab, enter the name of the folder in the Default Location text box, and click OK. PowerPoint will search in this folder when opening presentations as well as suggesting this folder as the place to save them.

PowerPoint's Five Views

PowerPoint offers five different views for working with your presentations: Slide, Outline, Slide Sorter, Notes Pages, and Slide Show. You can switch among them by using the five view buttons at the left end of the horizontal scroll bar (see Figure 18.5) or by using View menu commands (View ➢ Slides, View ➢ Outline, etc.). The name of the view you're in appears in the status bar if you have it displayed (to display it, choose Tools ➢ Options, select the Status Bar check box on the View tab, and click OK). We'll look at the features these views provide as we work on slides and presentations in the coming pages.

Creating and Editing Slides

When creating and editing individual slides, use Slide view (see Figure 18.6). To switch to Slide view, click the Slide View button on the horizontal scroll bar or choose View ➢ Slides.

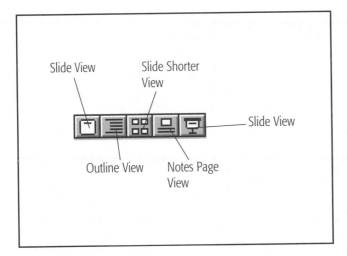

FIGURE 18.5:
Use the view buttons on the horizontal scroll bar to switch among PowerPoint's five views.

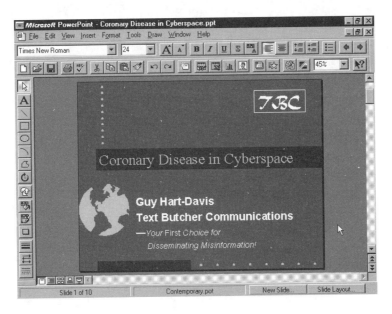

FIGURE 18.6:
Slide view shows you one slide at a time. Use Slide view to create and modify individual slides.

To move to the previous slide or next slide, use the Previous Slide and Next Slide buttons on the vertical scroll bar. To zoom the view of the slide, use the Zoom Control box on the Standard toolbar.

To create a new slide, click the New Slide button on the status bar (or choose Insert ➤ New Slide), choose the slide layout you want in the New Slide dialog box (shown in Figure 18.4, earlier), and click OK.

Entering Text in a Slide

Most of the PowerPoint slide layout schemes contain *placeholders* for text, labeled "Click to add title" or "Click to add text." (Others contain placeholders for other elements—e.g., "Double-click to add org chart," "Double-click to add table," and so on.) You can have up to five different levels of text in a text placeholder, as illustrated in Figure 18.6 earlier.

The placeholders make for a quick and convenient way to add text to slides, but you can also add text to any part of a slide by using the Text Tool, as we'll see in a moment.

Entering Text in a Placeholder

To enter text in a placeholder, click in it and type the text. Use the Enter key to start a new paragraph where necessary; use ←, →, ↑, and ↓, to move around; and use 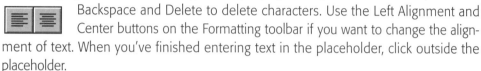 Backspace and Delete to delete characters. Use the Left Alignment and Center buttons on the Formatting toolbar if you want to change the alignment of text. When you've finished entering text in the placeholder, click outside the placeholder.

Entering Text with the Text Tool

By using the Text Tool, you can add text to any area of slide (with no need for a existing placeholder):

1. Click the Text Tool button on the Drawing toolbar. The mouse pointer will change to a downward-pointing arrow when it's not in a placeholder box.
2. To enter a one-line paragraph, click with the downward-pointing arrow where you want the paragraph to start. To enter a multiline paragraph, click and drag to place a box of the size you need.
3. Enter your text, then click outside the box when you've finished.

Pasting In Text from Another Application

You can easily paste in text from another application (such as Word, Excel, or Schedule+) by copying it in that application, switching back to PowerPoint, and issuing a Paste command by clicking on the Paste button or right-clicking and choosing Paste from the shortcut menu. Multiple cells from Excel spreadsheets will be separated by tabs in PowerPoint.

TIP You can also paste in other objects, such as charts from Excel or tables from Word.

Promoting and Demoting Paragraphs

By using the five levels of text available in text placeholders, you can create an effective hierarchy on your slides. To promote and demote paragraphs of text one level at a time, use the Promote and Demote buttons on the Formatting toolbar.

Selecting Text

To select text in a PowerPoint slide, you can do the following:
- Click and drag to select text.
- Double-click in a word to select it.
- Triple-click in a placeholder box or text box to select it.
- Hold down Shift and use the cursor-movement keys (←, →, ↑, ↓, PageUp, PageDown, End, Home, Ctrl+End, and Ctrl+Home).
- Click at the start of a block, hold down Shift, and click at the end of the block.

Press Esc or click elsewhere on a slide to deselect your selection.

Formatting Text

You can format text in PowerPoint using a variety of fonts, font sizes, emphasis (bold, italic, underline), shadow, color, bullets, and line-spacing. You can most easily apply formatting to selected text by using the buttons on the Formatting toolbar (see Figure 18.7).
- Select the Font Face box to quickly choose a different font.
- Use the Increase Font Size and Decrease Font Size buttons to increase and decrease the font size in 4-point jumps.
- Choose the Font Size box to specify a point size (if the size you want isn't listed, type it in the Font Size box and press Enter).
- Use the Bold, Italic, and Underline buttons to apply or remove boldface, italics, and underlining.
- Press the Text Shadow button to apply a shadow.

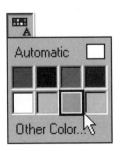

- Click the Text Color button and choose a color from the drop-down list; if you don't see the color you want, click the Other Color button and choose a color on the Standard or Custom tab of the Colors dialog box, then click OK.
- Use the Left Alignment and Center Alignment buttons to left-align and center text, respectively.
- Use the Increase Paragraph Spacing and Decrease Paragraph Spacing buttons to adjust the spacing of the current paragraph.

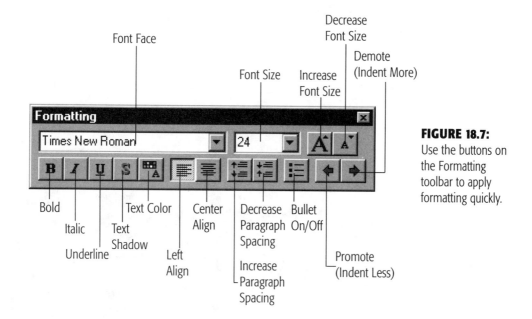

FIGURE 18.7:
Use the buttons on the Formatting toolbar to apply formatting quickly.

That's it for this chapter. Save your presentation, and you will be ready to quit PowerPoint by choosing File ➤ Exit. In the next chapter, we'll look at how to develop a presentation in PowerPoint.

Chapter 19

DEVELOPING YOUR PRESENTATION

FEATURING

- **Outlining a presentation**
- **Creating a presentation from a Word outline**
- **Rearranging the slides in the presentation**
- **Creating notes pages**
- **Modifying the Slide Master and Notes Master**
- **Previewing a slide show**

In this chapter, we'll look at developing a presentation in PowerPoint: How to change the layout of a single slide; how to change the look of all the slides in the presentation; how to develop an outline of the slides in the presentation and rearrange them as necessary; how to add notes pages for the presenter; and how to preview the way the slide show looks. We'll also look at two of the various *masters* in PowerPoint: the Slide Master and Notes Master, and how you can modify them to change the appearance of all the slides or notes pages in your presentation. (The other two masters, the Title Master and the Handout Master, we'll encounter when we look at creating your own templates in PowerPoint in Chapter 21.)

Changing the Layout of a Slide

If you're using one of PowerPoint's presentation templates, PowerPoint will be providing you with a suitable structure for the slides it assumes you want to create. If you're creating a presentation slide by slide, you will be choosing the layout of each new slide you create. Either way, you're likely to want to change the layout of a slide as you progress in developing the presentation.

You can quickly change the layout of the current slide in Slide view or Slide Sorter view by clicking the Slide Layout button on the horizontal scroll bar, choosing the layout you want in the Slide Layout dialog box, and clicking the Apply button (which will be named Reapply until you choose a different layout).

When you choose a new layout, PowerPoint will add to it new placeholders for any objects included on the current slide but not accommodated in the new design. You won't lose any elements that were on the slide before you changed its layout, but things may be a mess, with elements overlapping and obscuring each other. Drag the elements to suitable positions or resize them as appropriate.

Modifying a Slide Master

If you find yourself changing the formatting for more than half the slides in a presentation, you should probably modify the Slide Master. The Slide Master is a kind of mini-template the defines the default format for the title and text objects of all the slides in the presentation. By changing the title and five levels of text on the Slide Master for a presentation, you can ensure a consistent look for the titles and text on all your slides, no matter which layout each individual slide happens to use. You can also add to the Slide Master elements that you want to appear on each slide, such as your company's name and logo, or your photo, URL, and phone number.

> **NOTE**   You can change the Slide Master at any time—when you're starting to create the slides for your presentation, when you've created some of them, or even after you've finished—and PowerPoint will update all the slides automatically with the formatting you choose.

To modify the Slide Master:

1. Choose View ➤ Master ➤ Slide Master to display the Slide Master (see Figure 19.1).

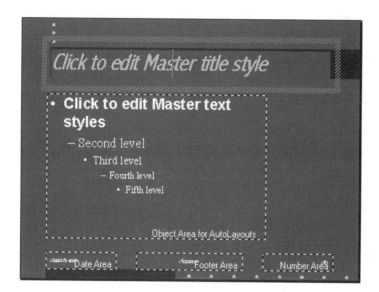

FIGURE 19.1:
By changing the Slide Master (View ➤ Master ➤ Slide Master), you can quickly change the title and text elements for all the slides in your presentation.

2. Click in the Title Area for AutoLayouts box at the top of the slide and apply the formatting you want for the title. This text (and the other text on the Slide Master) is dummy text for you to format, so don't bother editing it—PowerPoint will not retain the changes.

3. Click in the Object Area for AutoLayouts box and apply the formatting you want to the five levels of text.

4. To change the date, footer, or number, click in the Date Area, Footer Area, or Number Area, drag to select the code (e.g., **<<date/time>>**), and apply the formatting you want for it.

5. To add an object to the background of each slide, insert it using the techniques described in Chapter 18 (for a text box) and Chapter 20 (for objects such as pictures).

6. Click the Slide View button to close the Slide Master and return to Slide View.

Your slides will take on the formatting you applied to the Slide Master, except for slides to which you apply individual formatting.

Changing the Design Template

PowerPoint's *design templates* let you impart a consistent appearance to the slides in your presentations. Each design template consists of color schemes, slide masters, title masters, and fonts designed to work together in whichever slide layout you may choose.

To change the design template for the presentation:

1. Choose Format ➤ Apply Design Template to display the Apply Design Template dialog box, which you will recognize as another mild mutation of the Open dialog box.

2. Choose the design template you want. (If PowerPoint is not displaying a preview of the selected template, click the Preview button in the Apply Design Template dialog box.)

3. Click the Apply button to close the Apply Design Template dialog box and apply the chosen design template to your presentation.

Outlining Your Presentation

The first thing to do when creating a presentation is to decide what you're going to include in it. For short and simple presentations, you may be able to get away with working from one slide to the next; but for complex presentations, it's best to use Outline view (see Figure 19.2) to build your presentation and arrange the slides in the most effective order. If you've used Outline view in Word, Outline view in PowerPoint will look familiar: Outline view displays only the text on slides, with no pictures or other graphical elements, and you can collapse the outline so you see only the titles.

> **NOTE**   You can use a Word outline as the basis for a PowerPoint presentation; we'll look at this in the next section.

Switch to Outline view by clicking the Outline View button on the horizontal scroll bar (or by choosing View ➤ Outline), then use the buttons on the Outlining toolbar (see Figure 19.3) to work with the outline:

- The Promote and Demote buttons promote and demote titles and text one level at a time.

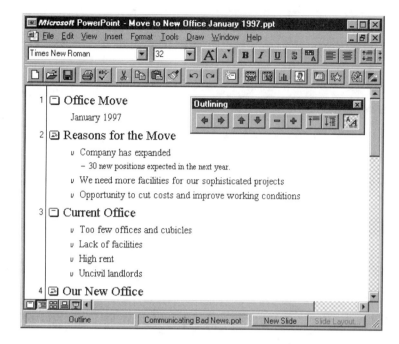

FIGURE 19.2:
In Outline view in PowerPoint, you can quickly rearrange your slides and their contents. The small numbers in the left panel are the slide numbers.

- The Move Up and Move Down buttons move items up and down the outline one displayed line at a time.
- The Collapse Selection and Expand Selection buttons collapse and expand the current slide, respectively.
- The Show Titles and Show All buttons switch the display between only the titles of slides and the full text of slides.
- The Show Formatting button toggles the display of formatting in Outline view. By switching off formatting, you can display the text of more slides on screen at the same time.

Creating a Presentation from a Word Document

You can easily create a presentation from an existing Word outline. This is especially useful for whipping together a quick presentation on the fly (or in the air) from a proposal you've created in Word.

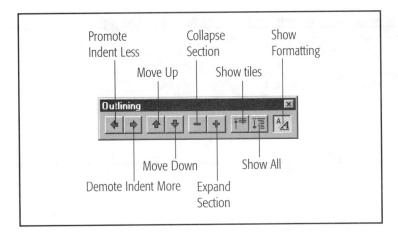

FIGURE 19.3:
Use the Outlining toolbar to quickly develop the outline of a presentation.

To create a presentation from a Word outline:

1. In PowerPoint, choose Insert ➤ Slides from Outline to display the Insert Outline dialog box (see Figure 19.4).

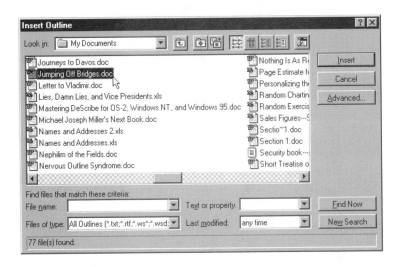

FIGURE 19.4:
In the Insert Outline dialog box, choose the Word document containing the outline you want to insert.

2. Choose the Word document containing the outline and click the Insert button. PowerPoint will convert the Word document as follows:

• Heading 1 paragraphs will become slide titles, so that each Heading 1 appears on a new slide.

- Heading 2 paragraphs will become main bullet points.
- Heading 3, 4, 5, and 6 paragraphs will become sub-points with increasing levels of indent and decreasing font sizes. (Heading 7, 8, and 9 paragraphs will be mushed together with the Heading 6 paragraphs, so you probably won't want to use them.)
- Any paragraph that isn't a heading will be rudely ignored.

Figure 19.5 shows a Word outline and the first PowerPoint slide created from it.

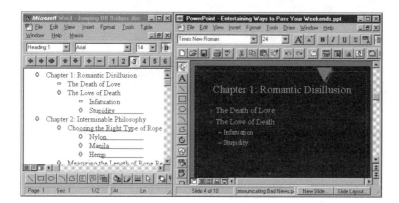

FIGURE 19.5:
Creating a Power-Point presentation from a Word outline

Rearranging Your Slides

Once you've outlined your presentation and created your slides (as discussed in the previous chapter), check that the visual effects you've added to them work well in sequence. To quickly view the order of your slides and reshuffle them as necessary for maximum effect, use Slide Sorter view (see Figure 19.6). In Slide Sorter view (reached by clicking the Slide Sorter view button on the horizontal scroll bar or by choosing View ➤ Slide Sorter), PowerPoint displays thumbnail sketches of a number of slides at once. (How many slides PowerPoint displays depends on how many slides are in your presentation and what screen resolution you're working at.)

To rearrange slides in Slide Sorter view, click on the slide you want to move and drag it to the left of the slide before which it should appear; you will see a vertical line indicating where the slide will land when you drop it.

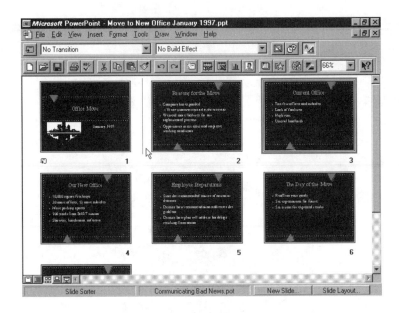

FIGURE 19.6:
Use Slide Sorter view to quickly drag your slides into the order that'll be most effective for your presentation.

Creating Notes Pages

As mentioned in Chapter 18, PowerPoint lets you create speaker's notes to accompany your presentations. Each notes page contains a miniature of a slide accompanied by whatever notes you feel will help you deliver its information cogently and effectively.

To compose and edit speaker's notes, first switch to Notes Page view (see Figure 19.7) by clicking the Notes Page View button on the horizontal scroll bar or choosing View ➤ Notes Pages.

In Notes Page view, you will see the current slide positioned at the top of a page, with space for notes underneath. Enter your notes here, then apply formatting to them as needed using the techniques described in Chapter 18.

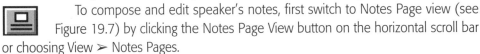

TIP One way of quickly entering the text on a notes page is to copy and paste it across from a Word document (or an Excel spreadsheet).

You can format the placeholder for the text (for example, by adding a border to it) or reposition it and the slide more amenably on the notes page. You can also add clip art, AutoShapes, and other elements to the speaker's notes; we'll look at these three items in the next chapter.

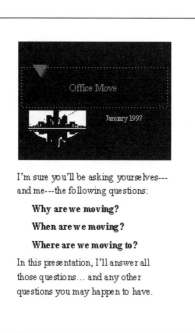

FIGURE 19.7:
Use Notes Page view for composing and editing your speaker's notes for each slide.

Use the Previous Slide and Next Slide buttons on the vertical scroll bar (or PageUp and PageDown, respectively) to move to notes pages for other slides. To zoom the view of the current notes page so you can see clearly what you're working on, use the Zoom Control box on the Standard toolbar.

Use the Promote and Demote buttons to promote and demote the current paragraph or selected paragraphs. You can use the same five levels of text (differentiated by size, bullets, and indentation) on the notes pages as on the slides.

Modifying the Notes Master

If you find yourself frequently changing the layout of your speaker's notes pages, you may want to change the layout of the Notes Master, which controls the formatting of the notes pages in a template. For example, you might want to set up your notes pages with a font you could read on a barn door at twenty paces, or to set up your five points for each slide as bullet points.

To modify the Notes Master:

1. Choose View ➤ Master ➤ Notes Master to display the Notes Master for the current template (see Figure 19.8).

FIGURE 19.8: By changing the layout of the Notes Master, you can quickly change the default layout for the notes pages of all the slides in the current template.

2. Change the five levels of text to the formatting you want them to have on your notes pages:
   - Zoom the display to a comfortable size by using the Zoom Control drop-down list on the Formatting toolbar.
   - Use the Font Face and Font Size drop-down lists on the Formatting toolbar to set font formatting (or choose Format ➢ Font to display the Font dialog box, select the formatting you want, and click OK).
   - Use the Increase Paragraph Spacing and Decrease Paragraph Spacing buttons on the Formatting toolbar to set line spacing (or choose Format ➢ Line Spacing to display the Line Spacing dialog box, select the spacing you want, and click OK).
   - Use the Bullet On/Off button to add or remove bullets from the selection or the current paragraph.
   - Drag an indentation marker on the ruler to alter the indentation of the current paragraph. (If the ruler is not currently displayed, choose View ➢ Ruler to display it.)

3. Change the layout of the notes page to how you want your notes pages to appear. (For example, you could add a border to the notes text box, or you could reposition it and the slide on the notes page.)

4. Click the Notes Page View button to close the Notes Master and return to the notes page for the current slide.

All your notes pages will now have the formatting you chose for the Notes Master unless you change them individually.

Previewing Your Slide Show

You can preview your slide show at any point by using Slide Show view (see Figure 19.9), which is the view you will use for giving your presentation—and for practicing giving it. In Slide Show view, PowerPoint displays your slides one at a time, taking up the full screen. If you've set timing and transitions for your slides (which we'll look at in Chapter 21), the slide show will run automatically; otherwise, you can press **n** to display the next slide, **p** to display the previous slide, and Esc to cancel the slide show.

To switch to Slide Show view, click the Slide Show View button; PowerPoint will start showing the slides from the one on which you were working. (To run the whole slide show, hold down Shift as you click on the Slide Show View button to display the Slide Show dialog box; make sure All is selected in the Slides group box, and click Show to run the presentation.)

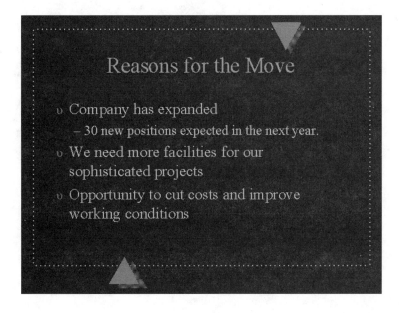

FIGURE 19.9:
Use Slide Show view to give your presentation—and to practice giving it.

Chapter 20

BRINGING A PRESENTATION TO LIFE

FEATURING

- **Adding pictures and graphs to slides**
- **Adding sound and video to slides**
- **Adding AutoShapes to slides**
- **Drawing objects in PowerPoint**
- **Animating objects**

All text and no glitz makes Jack a sorely dull presentation, and one unlikely to edify your audience even if they fail to fall asleep. In this chapter, we'll look at one of PowerPoint's most appealing features: the ability to add to your presentation just about any element your computer can handle, from simple pictures through charts and sounds to full-motion video—and to do it without causing you to break a sweat.

Inserting Objects in Your Presentation

In this section, we'll look at the various *objects* that you can add to a presentation. For this discussion, think of an object as being a chunk of data created in one application, but which you can place in another application. For example, you can take a chart created in Excel or a sound file created with the Sound Recorder and add it to a PowerPoint slide. (This is technically OLE—Object Linking and Embedding—which Chapter 4 examined in more depth; refer back if you need a refresher. However, you don't need to understand OLE to be able to use it.)

Inserting a Graph or Chart

Graphs or charts are a classic way of conveying information in a presentation, particularly when you use them to dramatize otherwise yawn-inducing statistics. PowerPoint offers two ways for you to add a graph or chart to your presentation: You can use the Microsoft Graph applet to create a graph from scratch, or you can create a chart in Excel and copy it across to a slide. The former procedure is useful for quick graphs, while the latter is better for detailed information and for data you already have in Excel.

> **TIP**
>
> You can also *link* an Excel chart to a presentation so the chart in the presentation is automatically updated whenever you update the chart in Excel. Look back at Chapter 4 for more information on linking.

Creating a Graph from Scratch

To create a graph from scratch on the current slide:

1. If the slide has a graph placeholder, double-click it. Otherwise, click the Insert Graph button on the Standard toolbar. PowerPoint will display the Graph sample datasheet and graph (see Figure 20.1).
2. Drag through the rows in the datasheet that contain the sample data and delete it by pressing Delete or by right-clicking and choosing Delete from the shortcut menu.
3. Enter your own data in the datasheet just as you would in an Excel spreadsheet.

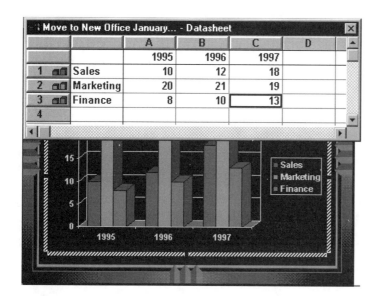

FIGURE 20.1:
To insert a graph
of your design,
change the data
in the sample
datasheet.

 The graph window will graph your data as you enter it. (You can switch between viewing the datasheet and viewing the graph by clicking the View Datasheet button.)

4. Format your graph by using the menus and the toolbars. Graph works like a stripped-down version of Excel.

5. Close the datasheet by clicking its Close button.

6. To return to the slide, click elsewhere in it.

Figure 20.2 shows a graph inserted in a PowerPoint slide.

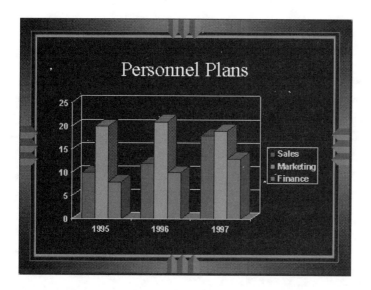

FIGURE 20.2:
A graph inserted in
a PowerPoint slide

Inserting a Chart from Excel

To add a chart you've already created in Excel to a slide, right-click in the chart in Excel and choose Copy from the shortcut menu. Then switch back to PowerPoint by using Alt+Tab or by clicking the Taskbar button, right-click in the graph placeholder on the slide, and choose Paste from the shortcut menu.

> **TIP** To link the Excel chart so that it will be updated in the PowerPoint slide when you edit the chart in Excel, copy the chart, switch to PowerPoint, and select the graph placeholder. Then choose Edit ➢ Paste Special to display the Paste Special dialog box. Click the Paste Link option button and click OK.

Inserting a Picture

To add visual interest to a slide, you can quickly insert a clip-art picture from Office's extensive collection:

1. If the current slide has a clip-art placeholder, double-click it to display the Microsoft ClipArt Gallery dialog box (see Figure 20.3). If not, click the Insert Clip Art button on the Standard toolbar.
2. Choose the category of pictures in the Categories list box.
3. Choose the picture you want in the Pictures box.
4. Click OK to close the Microsoft ClipArt Gallery dialog box and insert the picture in your slide.
5. Reposition and format the picture as necessary.

Inserting a Sound

You can use sounds in two ways in PowerPoint: You can insert a sound in a slide so that it displays as an icon, and plays either automatically or manually; and you can use sounds to mark the transition between two slides. The former we'll look at here; the latter we'll look at in *Assigning Transitions and Timings* in Chapter 21.

To insert a sound in a slide:

1. Choose Insert ➢ Sound to display the Insert Sound dialog box (see Figure 20.4).

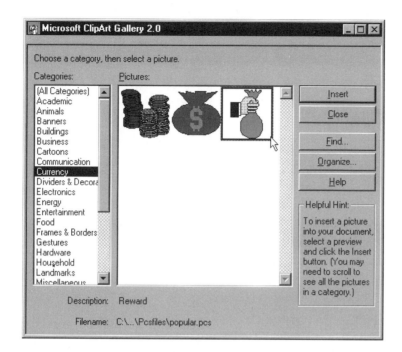

FIGURE 20.3:
In the Microsoft
ClipArt Gallery
dialog box, choose
the picture to insert
in the current slide
and click Insert.

FIGURE 20.4:
In the Insert Sound
dialog box, choose
the sound to add
to the slide.

2. Select the sound to add.

3. Click OK to close the Insert Sound dialog box.

 The sound will appear as an icon on the slide; you can drag it to a new position and resize it as appropriate.

To have the sound play automatically when you reach the slide it's on, select the icon, choose Tools ➢ Animation Settings to display the Animation Settings dialog box, and select Play in the Play Options drop-down list, then click OK.

To play the sound manually during your presentation, double-click it.

Inserting a Video Clip

A video clip can work wonders to make a slide really come alive for the audience: Instead of showing mere words or grainy stills of the new manufacturing plant in Tennessee, you can show its grimy machinery grinding away and its workers milling happily inside to the tune of the Marseillaise.

To insert a video clip in the current slide:

1. Choose Insert ➢ Movie to display the Insert Movie dialog box.
2. Select the video clip or movie file.
3. Click OK to close the Insert Movie dialog box.

The video clip will appear as an icon on the slide; you can drag it to a new position and resize it as appropriate.

To have the video play automatically when you reach the slide it's on, select the icon, choose Tools ➢ Animation Settings to display the Animation Settings dialog box, and select Play in the Play Options drop-down list, then click OK. To play it manually at your convenience, double-click it.

Inserting an Org Chart

An org chart is as indispensable for any humble human-resources presentation as it is when you're preparing a serious corporate raid. Here's how to add one to a slide:

1. Double-click the org chart placeholder on a slide to open the Microsoft Organization Chart applet (see Figure 20.5), or choose Insert ➢ Object to open the Insert Object dialog box, then choose MS Organization Chart 2.0 and click OK.
2. Create your chart in the Organization Chart applet.
3. Choose File ➢ Exit and Return to close Microsoft Organization Chart. It will display a message box asking if you want to update the object in your presentation.
4. Choose Yes to add the new org chart to your slide (see Figure 20.6).

NOTE   To edit the org chart, double-click it in the PowerPoint slide to launch Microsoft Organization Chart.

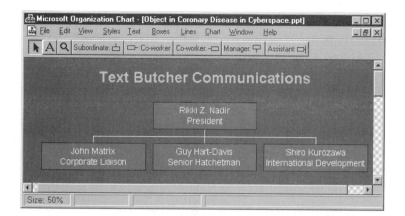

FIGURE 20.5:
Create your org chart in the Microsoft Organization Chart applet, then choose File ➤ Exit and Return.

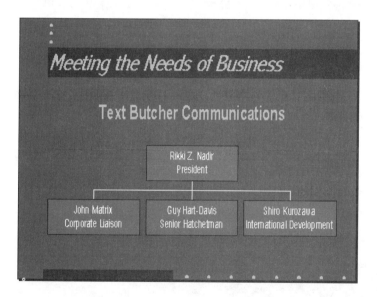

FIGURE 20.6:
Add an org chart to a slide to help size up the competition.

Drawing Objects in PowerPoint

Pictures, graphs, sound clips, video clips—those are all well and good, but many times you will need something a tad simpler to enliven your presentation. In this section, we'll look first at the AutoShape drawing shapes that PowerPoint provides and then at the more conventional drawing tools.

AutoShapes

For the hard of drawing, PowerPoint's AutoShapes are a godsend: There's no need to laboriously kludge together a clumsy arrow, 3-D cube, or speech balloon, because you can insert one of these AutoShapes with a click and drag of your mouse. Once you've inserted the AutoShape, you can add text to it, format it, move it, or even change it into another AutoShape in moments.

To insert an AutoShape:

1. Click on the AutoShapes button on the Drawing toolbar to display the AutoShapes toolbar. For ellipses and rectangles, you don't need to display the AutoShapes toolbar—just use the Rectangle Tool and Ellipse Tool buttons on the Drawing toolbar.

2. Click on the AutoShape button for the shape you want.

3. Click on the slide and drag the AutoShape to the size you want, then release the mouse button. (You can drag in any direction from your starting point.)

- Hold down Shift as you drag if you want to draw a *regular* shape—one that fits in a square. For example, you can draw a true square by clicking on the Rectangle Tool, holding down Shift, and clicking and dragging.

- Hold down Ctrl as you drag to draw a shape from the center rather than from one corner or point. (Hold down Shift as well to drag a regular shape from the center.)

4. Double-click in the AutoShape and type in any text you want in it. Format the text as needed.

5. Click outside the AutoShape to return to your slide. Figure 20.7 shows one use of an AutoShape.

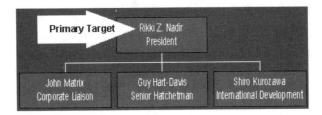

FIGURE 20.7: Use AutoShapes to jazz up your presentations.

To move an AutoShape to another part of your slide, select it and drag it to where you want it. To resize an AutoShape, drag one of its sizing handles.

To change one AutoShape into another AutoShape, select the AutoShape, choose Draw ➢ Change AutoShape, and select the new AutoShape from the submenu. The AutoShape will retain its contents and formatting.

Other Objects

If the AutoShapes don't supply the drawing object you need, try one of the other drawing tools on the Drawing toolbar:

 • Click the Line Tool button, then click and drag on the slide to draw a straight line.

 • Click the Arc Tool button, then click and drag on the slide to draw an arc.

 • Click the Freeform Tool button, then click and drag on the slide to draw a freeform object.

NOTE **To draw a polygon with the Freeform Tool, click to place each vertex (don't drag between clicks), and double-click to place the final vertex. A vertex is (as it were) a corner in the sort of shape that doesn't have corners as squares understand them.**

Repositioning, Resizing, and Aligning Objects

 You can reposition any object on a PowerPoint slide by clicking in it (if it's a text object, click in its border) and dragging it to where you want it.

You can resize any selected object by dragging one of its sizing handles to the required size. Dragging a side handle resizes the object in only that dimension, while dragging a corner handle resizes the object both horizontally and vertically.

TIP **Hold down Ctrl as you drag if you want to resize the object about its center (i.e., so that the center remains still and the edges move).**

To align two or more selected objects with each other, choose Draw ➤ Align and choose Lefts, Centers, Rights, Tops, Middles, or Bottoms from the menu as appropriate.

 To rotate an object, click on the Free Rotate tool on the Drawing toolbar, then click on one handle of the object you want to rotate and drag it in the direction of rotation. Hold down Shift if you want to make the object rotate in 45-degree jumps rather than smoothly.

Adding Borders, Fills, and Shadows

You can add borders, fills, and shadows to any object on a slide. To add or modify borders and fills:

1. Select the object or objects.
2. Choose Format ➤ Colors and Lines to display the Colors and Lines dialog box (see Figure 20.8).

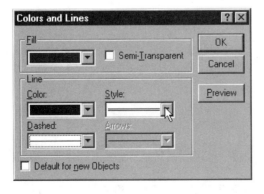

FIGURE 20.8: Choose settings for the selected object's border and fill in the Colors and Lines dialog box.

3. Choose a fill color from the Fill drop-down list. The Shaded, Patterned, and Textured choices on the Fill drop-down list display the Shaded Fill dialog box, Pattern Fill dialog box, and Textured Fill dialog box, respectively. The Other Color choice displays the Colors dialog box. Select the choice you want and click OK.

4. Choose a border color from the Color drop-down list.

5. Choose a border line weight from the Style drop-down list. If you want the line to be dashed, make a choice from the Dashed drop-down list as well; to position an arrowhead (where appropriate), choose from the Arrows drop-down list.

6. Click the Preview button to see the effect of the fill and border you've chosen, then click OK to close the dialog box.

To add or modify a shadow for the selected object:

1. Choose Format ➤ Shadow to display the Shadow dialog box (see Figure 20.9).

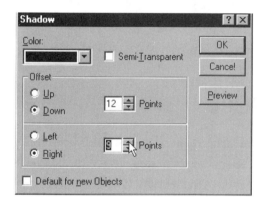

FIGURE 20.9:
Create an appealing shadow for an important object in the Shadow dialog box.

2. Choose a color from the Color drop-down list.

3. In the Offset group box, choose whether to offset the shadow up or down, and left or right, and specify the number of points to offset it in each dimension.

4. Click the Preview button to see the effect of the shadow you've chosen, then click OK to close the dialog box.

Selecting Objects

To work on objects in PowerPoint, you need to select them. By selecting several objects, you can format and position them all at once.

• To select one object, click on it. PowerPoint will display a border around it with handles on each corner and on the middle of each side.

• To select further objects, hold down Shift while you click on each subsequent object. (Alternatively, drag the mouse around the objects you want to select.)

• To deselect an object, click elsewhere in the slide (or outside it) or press Esc.

• To deselect one of a number of objects selected, hold down Shift and click on the object to deselect.

• To select all the objects on one slide, choose Edit ➤ Select All or press Ctrl+A.

Grouping Objects

You can also group objects together so that you can format them as if they were one object. To group objects, select them as described in the previous section, then choose Draw ➤ Group. PowerPoint will display handles around the grouped objects rather than around each individual object; you can then move and format the group as if it were one object.

> **NOTE**   You cannot group placeholder objects.

To ungroup grouped objects, select the group and choose Draw ➤ Ungroup. To regroup grouped objects, select one of the objects and choose Draw ➤ Regroup.

Animating an Object

PowerPoint offers a wide array of animation settings that you can use to choose the order in which objects in a slide are revealed, how they are revealed (with visual effects and sound effects as necessary), and whether they remain displayed or disappear as the presentation moves on to the next object on the slide. You can set different animation effects for each object on a slide.

> **WARNING**   Animation can backfire on the presenter: Use animation well, and you can greatly increase the audience's focus on the current piece of information; but use it badly, and you can distract them thoroughly from what you're trying to convey.

To animate the selected object in Slide view:

1. Right-click the object and choose Animation Settings from the shortcut menu (or choose Tools ➤ Animation settings) to display the Animation Settings dialog box (see Figure 20.10). This dialog box offers different options for different items; in this section, we'll look at the options for graphics.
2. In the Build Options drop-down list, choose Build to build the graphic. This enables other options in the dialog box.
3. In the Effects group box, choose the build effect you want in the first drop-down list, then choose any sound you want in the third drop-down list.

FIGURE 20.10:
Choose animation effects for the selected object in the Animation Settings dialog box.

4. In the Build/Play Object drop-down list, choose when to build the selected object relative to the other objects you're building in the current slide. (For the first build object on the current slide, the only choice available will be First.)

5. In the After Build Step drop-down list, choose whether to change the object to a different color after building it. (If you don't want to change it, leave Don't Dim selected.) Select Hide if you want the object to disappear as soon as you move on to the next object.

6. Select the Start When Previous Build Ends check box if you want the object to build automatically when PowerPoint finishes building the previous object (as opposed to building when you click on the slide).

7. Click OK to close the Animation Settings dialog box and apply your choices to the object.

Chapter 21

GIVING THE PRESENTATION

FEATURING

- **Rehearsing your presentation**
- **Setting timings and transitions**
- **Creating build slides and hidden slides**
- **Printing audience handouts and speaker notes**
- **Giving the presentation**
- **Taking a presentation on the road**
- **Creating your own template**

You've researched like never before, you've cudgeled your brains, you've worn your fingers to the bone typing... all right, actually you've *borrowed* some promising work from your peers, decorated it with statistics gleaned from the Web, quotes from Bartholomew's, and clip art of dubious provenance, and arranged it with surprising ease into a fluent and convincing series of slides with a flurry of mouse-clicks in PowerPoint. But now it's time to give the presentation, and your mouth is starting to get a little dry.

In this chapter, we'll look at how you can rehearse your presentation in PowerPoint, setting automatic transitions and timings so you can leave it to run itself. We'll also look at how you can create *build slides*—slides that you reveal one part at a time, so that your audience can't get to the punchline ahead of you—and hidden slides. Then we'll look at how to print audience handouts and speaker's notes, and how to give the presentation. Finally, we'll discuss how you can take a presentation on the road without taking your computer along, and how you can create templates for quickly putting together a number of similar presentations.

Finalizing the Presentation

In this section, we'll look at the tools PowerPoint provides for finalizing a presentation—smoothing the rough edges, assigning transition effects between slides, and rehearsing to set the correct timing for automatically advancing slides. First, though, before giving your presentation, run the Spelling checker as described in Chapter 3; this can prevent any amount of embarrassment.

Assigning Transitions and Timings

Instead of simply having each slide replace its predecessor on screen when you click the mouse on the slide or press N, you can assign transitions and timings to slides. *Transitions* are visual effects that animate the changeover from one slide to the next; you can accompany them with sounds, and you can run many of them at varying speeds. You can also assign timings to slides so that PowerPoint advances the presentation to the next slide automatically after the selected number of seconds, leaving you free to roam the room and give your accompanying speech.

To assign transitions and timings to your slides:

1. Switch to Slide Sorter view by clicking the Slide Sorter View button.
2. Right-click the slide you want to affect and choose Slide Transition from the shortcut menu to display the Slide Transition dialog box (see Figure 21.1).
3. Choose a transition effect from the Effects drop-down list. The Preview box will demonstrate the effect.
   - To preview a number of effects, click on the drop-down list button and then use ↓ and ↑ to move through the effects one by one.
   - To see a transition again, click the preview picture.
   - The last choice, Random Transition, can be entertaining if you're feeling too jaded to make a choice.

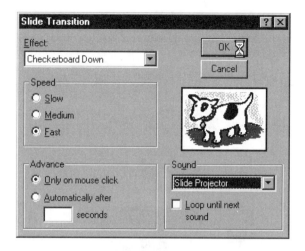

FIGURE 21.1:
In the slide Transition dialog box, set the transition effects and timing for the current slide.

4. In the Speed group box, choose Slow, Medium, or Fast if the choices are available (they are not available for some effects, such as Cut Through Black).
5. If you want this slide to advance automatically to the next slide, click in the Seconds box and enter the number of seconds that the slide should be displayed.
6. To have a sound play during the transition, choose it from the Sound drop-down list. To cause the sound to play repeatedly, select the Loop Until Next Sound check box. Make sure there is a next sound if you use this, or set (Stop Previous Sound) for the next slide—otherwise it will play until you stop it.
7. Click OK to close the Slide Transition dialog box.

WARNING Slide transitions tend to be more amusing to the person putting together the slide show than to the audience. Be careful not to overuse them just because PowerPoint makes it easy to do so.

Creating Build Slides

Build slides are slides that you reveal one bullet point at a time to keep your audience in suspense until the proper moment. To create a build slide from the current slide in Slide view, choose Tools ➤ Build Slide Text and choose the method of unveiling the text from the submenu:

Off turns slide-building off, so all the slide appears at once.

Fly From Left causes the text to fly in from the left of the screen.

Fly From Bottom causes the text to fly up from the bottom of the screen.

Wipe Right writes the text from left to right ("wiping" it onto the slide).

Dissolve materializes the text gradually in place.

Split Vertical Out writes each bullet point out from the middle of the line in both direction at once.

No Animation Effect simply displays the text.

Other displays the Animation Settings dialog box (discussed in Chapter 20).

In Slide Sorter view, PowerPoint displays a Build Slide icon below each build slide, as shown in Figure 21.2.

FIGURE 21.2: PowerPoint displays a Build Slide icon below each build slide in Slide Sorter view.

Creating Hidden Slides

For manually timed presentations where you need to have extra information up your sleeve should the need for it arise, you can create hidden slides that will not appear unless you choose specifically to display them.

To create one or more hidden slides, select the slides in Slide Sorter view (or select the slide in Slide view) and choose Tools ➢ Hide Slide. (To unhide selected slides, choose Tools ➢ Hide Slide again; PowerPoint will remove the check mark from the Hide Slide menu item.)

When you're running a presentation, PowerPoint gives no indication on-screen that a hidden slide is available. To display a hidden slide, press **H** from the slide before it, or right-click and choose Go To ➤ Hidden Slide.

Setting Slide Timings when Rehearsing

The best way to set precise timings for the slides in a slide show is to rehearse giving the slide show and have PowerPoint assign the appropriate amount of time for each slide. Here's how to do that:

1. Choose View ➤ Slide Show to display the Slide Show dialog box.
2. In the Advance group box, select Rehearse New Timings.

3. Click Show to close the Slide Show dialog box and start the slide show. PowerPoint will switch to full-screen view (no title or status bars, no menus) and will display the Rehearsal dialog box in the lower-right corner of the screen. (If it's in the way, grab it by the scruff of its title bar and drag it to somewhere more appropriate.) The Rehearsal dialog box shows two clocks; the left one displays total presentation time elapsed, while the right shows the time for the current slide.
4. Rehearse your presentation. Press N or the spacebar to move to the next slide. PowerPoint will record the time you spend on each slide. If you fluff your lines and need to start again for a slide, click the Repeat button.

5. When you finish your presentation, PowerPoint will display a message box giving you the total time for the slide show and asking if you want to record the new slide timings. Choose Yes to apply the new timings to your slides.

Printing Parts of a Presentation

You can easily print out any parts of a presentation that you need to have on paper. For a computer-based presentation, this will typically mean audience handouts for your victims and speaker's notes for yourself. For an overhead transparency– or paper–based presentation, you will want to print out the slides as well, and possibly the outline.

Before you print out the parts of your presentation, you need to set up the slides for printing. You may also want to modify the layout of the Slide Master and Notes Master as discussed in Chapter 20, or the layout of the Handout Master and the Title Master, which we'll look at in the sections coming up right after the next one.

Setting Up Your Slides for Printing

1. Choose File ➤ Slide Setup to display the Slide Setup dialog box (see Figure 21.3).
2. In the Slides Sized For drop-down list, choose how to output your slides:
    - Choose On-screen Show for computer-based presentations.
    - Choose a paper size—e.g., Letter Paper (8.5x11 in)—for printing to paper. For special-sized paper, choose Custom and enter the measurements in the Width and Height text boxes.
    - Choose 35mm Slides if you want to print your slides to a slide printer.

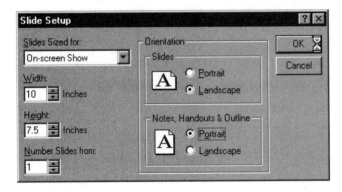

FIGURE 21.3: Before printing your presentation, choose the appropriate options in the Slide Setup dialog box.

3. To start numbering slides from a number other than 1 (for example, for a handout comprising slides from multiple presentations), set the number in the Number Slides From text box.
4. Choose an orientation for slides in the Slides group box.
5. Choose an orientation for notes, handouts, and the outline in the Notes, Handouts & Outline group box.
6. Click OK to close the Slide Setup dialog box and apply your choices to your presentation. PowerPoint will automatically reformat your slides if you changed their orientation.

Modifying the Handout Master

Before you print out your handouts, you will probably want to modify the Handout Master, which controls the elements other than slides that appear on each page of the audience handout. For example, you might want to add to each handout page your name, your company's name, the title of the presentation, the date, or a blank Notes box to encourage your audience to take diligent notes.

To modify the Handout Master:

1. Choose View ➤ Master ➤ Handout Master to display the Handout Master (see Figure 21.4). This contains placeholders for either two slides (top and bottom) or one or two columns of three slides. You set the number of slides per page when you print; if you choose to print three slides per page, the left column of placeholders are used.

2. Add text, clip art, or other visual objects to the Handout Master as described in the previous three chapters. Make sure that none of the items you add will be obscured by the slide boxes you use when you print the handout.

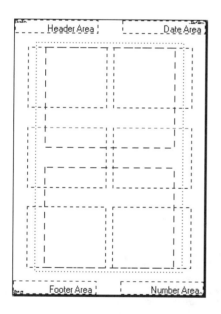

FIGURE 21.4:
To modify the Handout Master, open it by choosing View ➤ Master ➤ Handout Master, then edit it.

3. Add header and footer information as necessary:
    *   Either click in the relevant area, zoom the view as necessary, and edit in the box
    *   Or choose View ➤ Header and Footer and enter the information in the Header and Footer boxes of the Header and Footer dialog box (see Figure 21.5), then click Apply to All.

4. Close the Handout Master by clicking the Slide View button or one of the other view buttons.

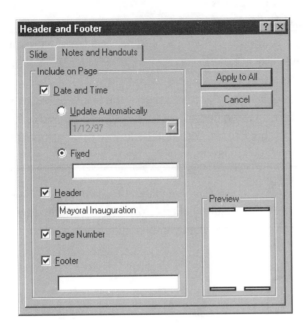

FIGURE 21.5:
Enter header and footer information in the Header and Footer dialog box.

Modifying the Title Master

The Title Master is the slide template for the initial title slide of the presentation (and any subsequent title slides). Here's how to modify it:

1. Choose View ➤ Master ➤ Title Master to display the Title Master (see Figure 21.6).

FIGURE 21.6:
Modify the Title Master for your template by choosing View ➤ Master ➤ Title Master and customizing the Title Master.

2. Customize the Title Master as discussed in *Modifying the Slide Master* earlier in this chapter:
   - Edit the Master title style in the Title Area for AutoLayouts and the Master subtitle style in the Subtitle Area for AutoLayouts.
   - Make changes in the Date Area, Footer Area, and Number Area as needed.
   - Add extra text or objects to the Title Master as necessary.
3. Reposition any objects on the Title Master as necessary. Remove any unneeded objects from the Title Master: Click in the object to select it, click its border to select the whole object, then press Delete.
4. Add any objects you want the Title Master to contain (for example, your name, your company's name, and a logo).
5. Close the Handout Master by clicking the Slide View button or one of the other view buttons.

Printing Presentation Items

To print parts of your presentation:

1. Choose File ➤ Print (or press Ctrl+P) to display the Print dialog box (see Figure 21.7).

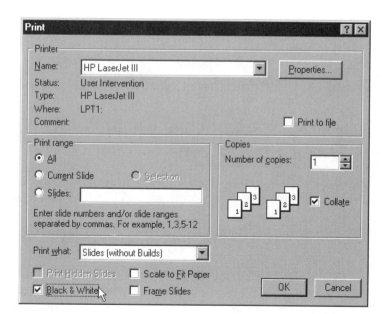

FIGURE 21.7:
In the Print dialog box, choose which parts of your presentation to print, and how to print them.

2. In the Printer group box, choose the printer to use from the Name drop-down list.

3. From the Print What drop-down list, choose what you want to print: slides, handouts (with two, three, or six slides per page), notes pages, or outline view.

4. In the Print Range group box, choose whether to print all the slides, the current slides, the current selection of slides, or a range of slides by clicking one of the option buttons. To print a range of slides, click in the Slides text box and enter the numbers of the starting and finishing slides separated by a hyphen. (To print from a given slide to the end of the presentation, enter just the number of the starting slide and a hyphen.) To print multiple slides, enter the slide numbers separated by commas.

5. To print multiple copies, enter the number in the Number of Copies text box in the Copies group box.

6. Choose further printing options if necessary:
   - Select the Print to File check box in the Printer group box to create a print file you can send to a service bureau for processing into physical slides.
   - Select the Print Hidden Slides check box if you want to print any hidden slides in your presentation. (If the presentation contains no printed slides, this check box will be dimmed.)
   - Select the Black & White check box if you want to print slide colors in black and white for clarity.
   - Select the Frame Slides check box to have PowerPoint print a thin black frame around each slide.
   - Select the Scale to Fit Paper check box to have PowerPoint rescale the slides to fit the paper size you selected in the Slide Setup dialog box.

7. Click OK to close the Print dialog box and print the items.

Giving the Presentation

When you've finished finalizing the details of your slide show, and have rehearsed it to the split second, running it will seem a mere formality:

1. Choose View ➤ Slide Show to display the Slide Show dialog box (see Figure 21.8).

2. In the Slides group box, choose whether to include all the slides in the presentation. To include only a range of slides, click in the From box and enter the starting number. Enter the ending number in the To box if necessary (leave the To box blank to include slides from the starting number to the end of the presentation).

FIGURE 21.8:
In the Slide Show dialog box, choose how to run your slide show.

3. In the Advance group box, choose Manual Advance if you want to change slides at your convenience; choose Use Slide Timings to use the automatic timings that you've assigned.

4. To have the slide show loop at the end and repeat itself ad nauseam (as you might at a trade show), select the Loop Continuously Until 'Esc' check box. (You'll press Esc to stop the looping slide show.)

5. Choose a pen color from the Pen Color drop-down list.

6. Click the Show button to start the slide show.

7. Press **n** or the spacebar to move to the next slide; press **p** to move to the previous slide; and press Esc to abort the presentation.

Using the Slide Navigator

When running the slide show, you can navigate easily by using the Slide Navigator feature. Right-click and choose Go To ➤ Slide Navigator from the shortcut menu to display the Slide Navigator dialog box (see Figure 21.9), then choose the slide in the Slides list box and click the Go To button.

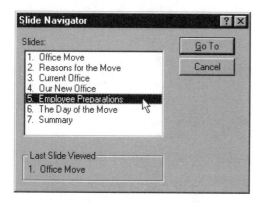

FIGURE 21.9:
Use the Slide Navigator dialog box to move quickly to a slide by name.

Using the Meeting Minder

A successful presentation is likely to provoke discussion and questions as well as roars of approval from the audience, and PowerPoint provides the Meeting Minder for you to keep track of suggestions, to add to your notes pages, and to take minutes. You can also export any or all of these to Microsoft Word at any point.

Keeping Track of Suggestions

To keep track of suggestions during a presentation, use the Meeting Minder's Action Items feature:

1. Right-click on a slide and choose Meeting Minder from the shortcut menu to display the Meeting Minder dialog box (see Figure 21.10).

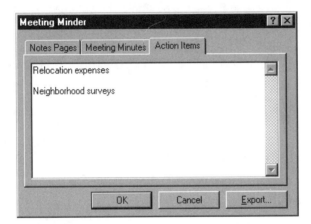

FIGURE 21.10:
Use the Action Items tab in the Meeting Minder dialog box to track action items during a presentation.

2. Click the Action Items tab to bring it to the front.
3. Enter the text of each action item. PowerPoint keeps all the action items for each presentation together, so when you add action items from subsequent slides, you'll see the action items you added before. Enter your new action items in the order in which you want to see them later.
4. Click OK to close the Meeting Minder dialog box.

PowerPoint will create a new slide containing these action items and will display it as the last slide of your presentation.

Viewing and Adding to Your Notes Pages

You can also view your notes pages on-screen during a presentation, and add to them as necessary.

1. Right-click on a slide and choose Meeting Minder from the shortcut menu to display the Meeting Minder dialog box.
2. Click on the Notes Pages tab to display the text for the notes page for the current slide.
3. Edit or add to the text as necessary.
4. Click OK to close the Meeting Minder dialog box.

Taking Minutes

You can take minutes for each slide during a presentation:
1. Right-click on a slide and choose Meeting Minder from the shortcut menu to display the Meeting Minder dialog box.
2. Click on the Meeting Minutes tab.
3. Enter your minutes for the current slide in the text box.
4. Click OK to close the Meeting Minder dialog box.

Exporting Information from the Meeting Minder

You can export information from the Meeting Minder to Word at any point—even in the middle of a presentation. Usually, though, you will probably want to wait until you've finished the presentation before exporting.

To export information during a presentation:
1. Right-click on a slide and choose Meeting Minder from the shortcut menu to display the Meeting Minder dialog box.
2. Click the tab from which you want to export information.
3. Click the Export button to display the Meeting Minder export dialog box (see Figure 21.11).

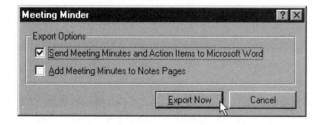

FIGURE 21.11:
In the Meeting Minder export dialog box, choose export options for the information you're exporting.

4. Select the Send Meeting Minutes and Action Items to Microsoft Word check box to export the data to Word. If you want to add the meeting minutes you've taken to your notes pages, select the Add Meeting Minutes to Notes Pages check box as well.

5. Click the Export Now button to export the data. PowerPoint will start Word if it's not running, start a new document, and insert the data in it.

Alternatively, you can export all the slides and notes in the current presentation to a Word table by using PowerPoint's Write-Up tool:

1. Choose Tools ➢ Write-Up to display the Write-Up dialog box.
2. In the Page Layout in Microsoft Word group box, choose the layout you want.
3. In the Add Slides to Microsoft Word Document group box, choose whether to paste the slides in (which will make the Word file bigger but will leave it independent from the PowerPoint presentation) or to paste-link the slides (which will link the Word document to the PowerPoint presentation, with dire results for the document if you move the presentation).

NOTE	Refer back to Chapter 4 for more detail on linking.

4. Click OK to close the Write-Up dialog box and export the presentation to Word. PowerPoint will open Word (unless Word is already running), create a new document, and enter the information as specified.
5. Edit the Word document as necessary, and save it and print it as you want.
6. Choose File ➢ Exit to close Word and return to PowerPoint (or use Alt+Tab or the Taskbar button to return to PowerPoint and leave Word open).

Taking Your Presentation on the Road

Chances are that you will often need to be able to travel with your presentations. If you've got a multimedia laptop, you're all set; if not, PowerPoint's Pack and Go Wizard is a handy tool for preparing your presentations for a road trip. You can even choose to install the PowerPoint Viewer on a floppy disk for use on a computer that does not have PowerPoint installed on it, which is a great way of preventing those "but you *said* you had the software" blues.

Packing Up a Presentation

To pack up one or more presentations:

1. Choose File ➢ Pack And Go to start the Pack and Go Wizard.

2. In the first Pack and Go Wizard dialog box, click Next.

3. In the second Pack and Go Wizard dialog box, choose which presentation to pack up, then click Next.

   - By default, PowerPoint offers the current presentation; to pack other presentations instead, select the Other Presentations option button, then click the Browse button, select the presentation or presentations in the Select a Presentation to Package dialog box, then click the Select button to return to the second Pack and Go Wizard dialog box. The option button will now bear the name of the presentation you selected.

   - You can Shift+click and Ctrl+click to select multiple presentations in the Select a Presentation to Package dialog box. When you click Select and return to the second Pack and Go Wizard dialog box, the option button will be named *Multiple Presentations*.

4. In the third Pack and Go Wizard dialog box, choose the destination for your packed presentation, then click Next.

   By default, PowerPoint suggests the floppy drive on your computer (usually drive A:). To select another drive, click the Choose Destination option button and click the Browse button to display the Specify Directory dialog box. Choose the destination drive and folder, then click Select to return to the third Pack and Go Wizard dialog box. The Choose Destination option button will change to the name and path of the folder you selected.

5. In the fourth Pack and Go Wizard dialog box, select the Include Linked Files check box if your presentation includes linked files (such as sounds or video clips). Select the Embed TrueType Fonts if you want to make sure that TrueType fonts appear correctly on the computer you end up using to give the presentation. Click Next.

6. In the fifth Pack and Go Wizard dialog box, select the Include PowerPoint Viewer check box if you want to be able to give your presentation using a computer that does not have PowerPoint installed. Click Next.

7. In the sixth and final Pack and Go Wizard dialog box, click the Finish button.

   - If you chose to package the presentation on a floppy, make sure there's one in the drive and that it has plenty of free space. (If PowerPoint needs more disk space, it will prompt you to insert further disks one by one.)

   - PowerPoint will save the compressed file with a short filename in the 8.3 format so that you can use it on Windows versions older than Windows 95.

Unpacking a Presentation

At your destination, you will need to unpack the compressed presentation file before you can run it:

1. In Windows 95, choose Start ➤ Run to display the Run dialog box. Enter **A:\PNGSETUP** and click OK to display the Pack and Go Setup dialog box (see Figure 21.12). Alternatively, open an Explorer or My Computer window, navigate to the drive and folder containing the compressed presentation files, and double-click PNGSETUP.EXE.

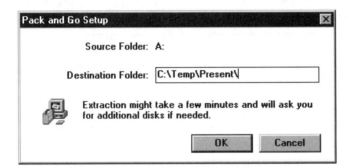

FIGURE 21.12:
In the Pack and Go Setup dialog box, enter the destination folder and click OK.

2. Enter the destination folder in the Destination Folder text box, then click OK to decompress and install the presentation.
   - If the destination folder you specified does not exist, Pack and Go Setup will ask if you want to create it. Choose OK.
   - Pack and Go Setup will prompt you for further disks of compressed presentation files as necessary.

3. When Pack and Go Setup has finished decompressing and installing the presentation or presentations, it will display a message box.
   - If you want to run the slide show now, ignore the missing article and click Yes.
   - If you want to run your slide show later, click No. To run the slide show, navigate to the folder to which you installed the presentation and double-click PPTVIEW.EXE to display the Microsoft PowerPoint Viewer dialog box, then choose the presentation to run in the File Name list box. Select the Loop Continuously Until 'Esc' and Use Automatic Timings check boxes as need be, then click the Show button to start the presentation running.

NOTE If you didn't include the PowerPoint Viewer in the compressed file, run PowerPoint and open the presentation file as usual.

Creating a Template for Future Use

If you need to create a number of homogeneous presentations and you find that none of the templates that PowerPoint provides quite matches your needs, you can create your own template, either from scratch or by adapting one of the existing templates. For example, if you need to produce a dozen human resources presentations for the different departments and locations of your company, you can save time by creating a template that contains your company's name and logo, your scintillating design and layout, and the basic structure of the information you want to use, rather than having to type it in anew each time you create a presentation.

To create a template:

1. Choose File ➤ New to display the New Presentation dialog box.
2. Select the Presentation Designs tab to bring it to the front of the dialog box (unless it's already there).
3. Choose the design most suited to the presentation design you want to create. (If you loathe all of them, click on the General tab and select the Blank Presentation icon.)
4. Click OK to start a new presentation based on that template (or on Blank Presentation if you chose that).
5. If PowerPoint displays the New Slide dialog box, click Cancel to dismiss it.
6. You should now be seeing blank presentation with a slide outline urging you to *Click to add first slide*. Resist the temptation to obey; instead, set up the Title Master as described in *Modifying the Title Master* in Chapter 20.
7. When you've finished setting up the Title Master, choose View ➤ Master ➤ Slide Master to display the Slide Master, then set it up as described in *Modifying a Slide Master* in Chapter 20.
8. Next, choose View ➤ Master ➤ Notes Master to display the Notes Master, then set it up as described in *Modifying the Notes Master* earlier in this chapter.
9. Choose View ➤ Master ➤ Handout Master to display the Handout Master, and set it up as described in *Modifying the Handout Master* earlier in this chapter.
10. Save your presentation template:
    - Choose File ➤ Save to display the File Save dialog box.
    - Enter the name for the presentation template in the File Name box.
    - In the Save as Type drop-down list, choose Presentation Templates (*.pot). PowerPoint will change to the Templates folder; choose a subfolder if you want.

- Click the Save button to save the presentation template.
- Enter properties in the Properties dialog box. Make sure the Save Preview Picture check box is selected so PowerPoint can display a preview of the presentation template in the New Presentation dialog box.

11. Choose File ➢ Close to close the presentation template.

You can now create a new presentation based on the presentation template by choosing File ➢ New and choosing the template in the New Presentation dialog box.

Part 5

Schedule+

Chapter 22

SCHEDULES, PROJECTS, AND TASKS

FEATURING

- **Creating a schedule**
- **Viewing your calendar, to-do list, and contact database**
- **Scheduling meetings and appointments**
- **Working with projects and tasks**

Schedule+ is Microsoft Office's application for keeping you in charge of your calendar, contacts, and projects. Schedule+ comprises a calendar that you can switch among Daily, Weekly, and Monthly views; a to-do list broken up into projects, each of which consists of a number of tasks; and a complete contact database for keeping your contact list up to date and in an easily accessible format.

Among the organizational benefits that Schedule+ offers is that you can use it in group-enabled mode to schedule appointments with colleagues who also use Schedule+, avoiding tedious back-and-forth phone tag and e-mail tag.

Creating a Schedule

Before you can get anything done in Schedule+, you need to create a schedule file. Start Schedule+ by choosing Start ➢ Programs ➢ Schedule+ or by double-clicking any shortcut you've created for it.

If your computer is part of a network (i.e., actually attached to a network or identified to Windows 95 as part of a network though not currently attached), Schedule+ will display the Group Enabling dialog box (see Figure 22.1).

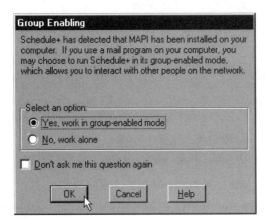

FIGURE 22.1:
In the Group Enabling dialog box, choose whether to work in group-enabled mode or alone.

In the Select an Option group box, choose Yes, Work in Group-Enabled Mode if you want to work with other people's calendars (for example, to arrange meetings) or No, Work Alone. If you'll always be working either in group-enabled mode or alone and you prefer that Schedule+ not bug you about this in future, select the Don't Ask Me This Question Again check box. Click OK to close the Group Enabling dialog box.

If Schedule+ cannot find your schedule file, it will then display the Microsoft Schedule+ dialog box (see Figure 22.2). To create a new schedule, choose the *I want to create a new schedule file* option; to locate an existing schedule file (for example, on the network), choose *I want to use an existing schedule file*. Click OK to close the Microsoft Schedule+ dialog box.

Schedule+ will display the Select Local Schedule dialog box (see Figure 22.3). If you're creating a new schedule, enter the name in the File Name text box, then choose Save.

Schedule+ will create a new schedule and save it under the name you chose. (If you're opening an existing schedule, navigate to it using standard Windows 95 navigation techniques, select it, and choose Open.)

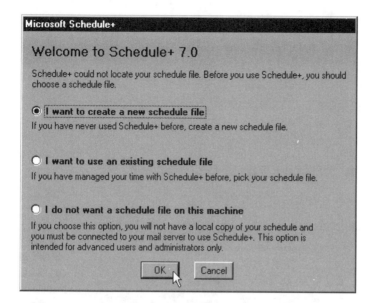

FIGURE 22.2:
In the Microsoft Schedule+ dialog box, choose whether to create a new Schedule+ file or to open an existing one.

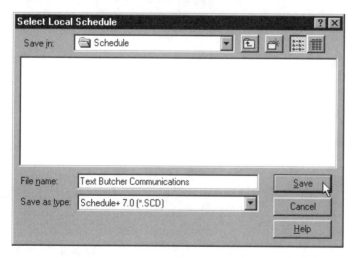

FIGURE 22.3:
To create a new schedule, enter the name for it in the Select Local Schedule dialog box, then choose Save. (To open an existing schedule, select it, then choose Open.)

In the next section, we'll look at the different views you can use of the Schedule+ screen.

Using Views in Schedule+

Schedule+ offers four views for scrutinizing your appointments—Daily view, Weekly view, Monthly view, and Planner view—as well as a To Do view for your to-do list and a

Contacts View for working with your contact database. To change between views, click the appropriate tab at the left side of the Schedule+ window.

Daily View

Daily view (see Figure 22.4) gives you the best view of your appointments for any given day. (We'll look at scheduling appointments later in the chapter.)

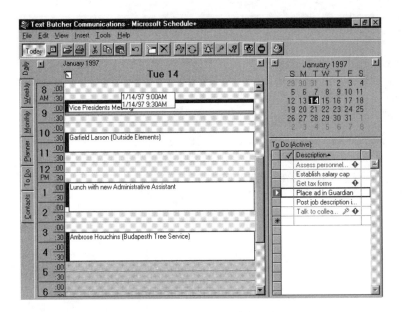

FIGURE 22.4: Use Daily view for scheduling your appointments and checking your schedule for any given day.

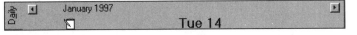

By default, Daily view shows you the current date, but you can scroll back and forth through the dates by clicking the little arrow buttons on the Daily tab as shown here. To move to a different month, click the arro but-

tons on either side of the monthly calendar as shown here. You can also click the Go To Date button on the toolbar and choose the day from the drop-down calendar. (To change the month, click the arrow buttons on either side of the drop-down calendar.)

Click the Today button on the toolbar to move quickly back to today's date. To view more than one day's worth of appointments, choose View ➢ Number of Days and specify between 2 and 7. Schedule+ will display that number of days, starting from the date that was already selected.

Weekly View

Weekly view (see Figure 22.5) is good for getting an overview of the next week, which Schedule+ defines as five days but which you can change by choosing View ➢ Number of Days and specifying between 1 and 7. (Choosing 1 here will show you Daily view.)

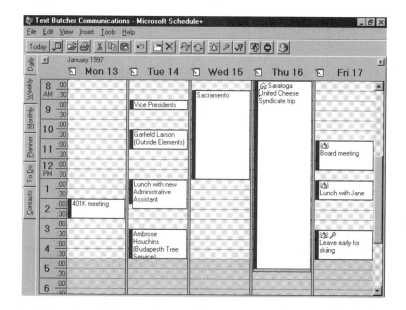

FIGURE 22.5:
Weekly view gives you an overview of a number of days.

Monthly View

Monthly view (see Figure 22.6) lets you see a whole month of appointments at once. Use the arrow buttons to change the month displayed.

Planner View

Planner view (see Figure 22.7) displays multiple weeks at once, starting with the current week. It includes both the monthly calendar and a list of attendees for the meetings you're due to attend. Adjust the dates displayed by clicking the arrow buttons or by clicking the monthly calendar.

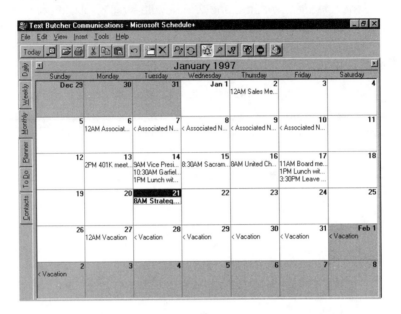

FIGURE 22.6:
Use Monthly view to get an overview of your commitments for a particular month.

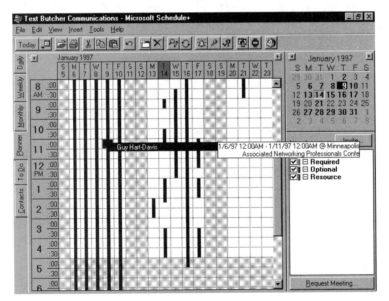

FIGURE 22.7:
Use Planner view to plan out your schedule for the coming weeks.

To Do View

To Do view (see Figure 22.8) displays your projects, together with your choice of the tasks they contain—you can choose to display all tasks, upcoming tasks, not yet completed tasks, and so on. We'll look at working with projects and tasks in To Do view later in this chapter.

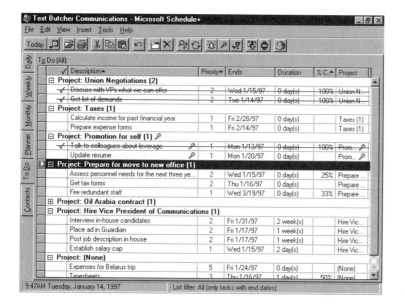

FIGURE 22.8:
Use To Do view to work with your projects and tasks.

Contacts View

Contacts view (see Figure 22.9) is a two-pane view that shows your contacts database in the left pane and the details for the currently selected contact in the right pane. We'll look at working in the contact database later in this chapter.

Managing Tabs with the Tab Gallery

In case the six tabs it provides are not enough for your needs, Schedule+ provides the Tab Gallery to let you adjust which tabs are displayed.

To adjust the tabs displayed:

1. Choose View ➤ Tab Gallery to display the Tab Gallery dialog box (see Figure 22.10).
2. Add, remove, rename, and reorder tabs as you wish:
    *   To add a tab, select it in the Available Tabs list box and click the Add button.

FIGURE 22.9:
Use Contacts view to enter and look through your contacts.

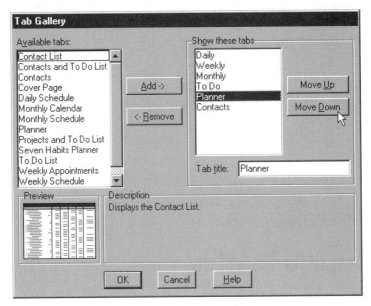

FIGURE 22.10:
The Tab Gallery dialog box lets you adjust which tabs appear in Schedule+.

- To remove a tab, select it in the Show These Tabs list box and click the Remove button.
- To rename a tab, select it in the Show These Tabs list box, then click in the Tab Title text box and enter a new title for it. Click another entry in the Show These Tabs list box to make the change.

- To reorder the tabs in the Show These Tabs list box, click the tab you want to move and then use the Move Up or Move Down button to move it to where you want it.

3. When you've finished making changes, choose OK to close the Tab Gallery dialog box.

Scheduling Appointments

As its name implies, one of Schedule+'s prime purposes in life is to schedule appointments and remind you of them. You can set up one-off appointments or recurring appointments; you can use alarms to remind you of impending appointments; and (if you're working in group-enabled mode) you can use Schedule+ to schedule meetings by manipulating other people's schedules.

Creating an Appointment

To create a one-off appointment:

1. If you're not already in Daily view, switch to it by clicking on the Daily tab. (This isn't compulsory, but Daily view makes it far easier to see what you're doing.)

2. Click in the time slot for the appointment. If your appointment is for more than 30 minutes, drag through the time slots it will occupy.

3. Right-click in the time slot or time slots you selected and choose New Appointment from the shortcut menu to display the Appointment dialog box with the General tab displayed (see Figure 22.11). Alternatively, choose Insert ➢ Appointment.

4. Type a cogent description for the appointment in the Description box. (This is what you'll see in the schedule.)

5. If you want, enter the location for the meeting in the Where box.

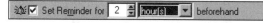

6. To have Schedule+ remind you of the appointment, select the Set Reminder box. Two more boxes will appear to the right of "Set Reminder"; use these to specify the length of time (in hours, days, weeks, or months) before the appointment that the reminder should occur.

7. If you're working in group-enabled mode, you can mark items as private by selecting the Private check box. (Other people looking at your schedule will see that you are busy for the given time, but they will not be able to see the details of your appointment.)

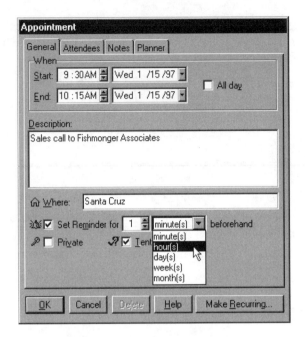

FIGURE 22.11:
Set up the details
for your appoint-
ment on the
general tab in
the Appointment
dialog box.

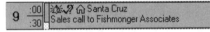

8.   You can mark an appointment as tentative by selecting the Tentative check box.
Schedule+ will display the appointment with a gray background so you can see
it's tentative.

9.   Enter further details for the appointment on the Attendees, Notes, and Planner
tabs of the Appointment dialog box. (We'll touch on this in *Scheduling a
Meeting* later in the chapter.)

10.   Choose OK when you've finished setting up your appointment. Schedule+ will
close the Appointment dialog box and enter the details of the applications in
your schedule.

Creating a Recurring Appointment

If only all appointments were one-off, life would be eternally entertaining—but no,
recurring appointments are a fact of life. Schedule+ can help you deal with those weekly
(or biweekly) progress reports, the monthly strategy meetings, and even those biannual
visits to the dentist.

To create a recurring appointment:

1.   Create a regular appointment as described in the previous section, but don't
choose OK in step 10.

2. Click the Make Recurring button in the lower-right corner of any of the tabs in the Appointment dialog box. Schedule+ will display the Appointment Series dialog box with the When tab displayed (see Figure 22.12) with the data you have already entered for your appointment.

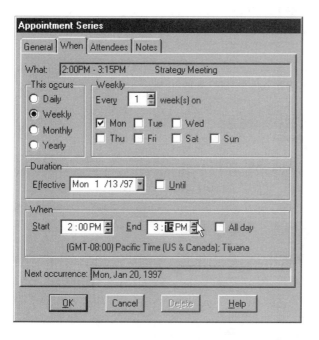

FIGURE 22.12: Set up your recurring appointments in the Appointment Series dialog box.

TIP

You can also go directly to the General tab of the Appointment Series dialog box by choosing Insert ➢ Recurring Appointment.

3. To change the time or description displayed in the What text box, click the General tab and make the changes there.

4. In the This Occurs group box, choose whether the appointment occurs Daily, Weekly, Monthly, or Yearly. (Weekly is the default.) The Weekly group box to the right of the This Occurs group box will change to Daily, Monthly, or Yearly to reflect your choice; these group boxes have different options as necessary.

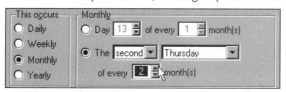

5. In the Daily, Weekly, Monthly, or Yearly group box, choose the frequency of the appointment. For example, with a monthly appointment, you can choose options such as Day 30 of every 1 month or the second Thursday of every 2 months, as shown on the previous page.

6. In the Duration group box, specify the duration for the recurring appointments (unless you want the appointments to go on from the first one you set until eternity, or until you stop them manually). Select the Until check box and a text box will appear to its right; enter the end date in that box. (If need be, change the starting date in the Effective drop-down list box as well.)

7. Choose OK to enter the recurring appointment in your schedule. It will appear at every instance of the interval you set, marked by a circular-arrow icon, as shown here.

Deleting an Appointment

Deleting an appointment is straightforward and painless in any of Schedule+'s views: Right-click in the appointment and choose Delete Item from the shortcut menu. Alternatively, double-click in the item to display the Appointment dialog box and choose the

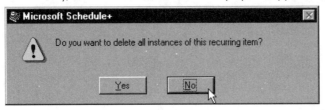

Delete button in it. When you delete a recurring appointment, Schedule+ will display a message box asking if you want to delete all in-stances of the recur-

ring item; choose Yes or No.

Moving an Appointment

To change the time or date of an appointment:

1. Right-click anywhere in the appointment and choose Move Appt. from the shortcut menu to display the Move Appointment dialog box.

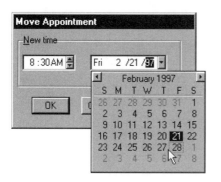

2. Adjust the time using the spinner arrows, or adjust the date by clicking the drop-down calendar button and choosing the new date, as shown here.

3. Choose OK to close the Move Appointment dialog box.

> **TIP** In Daily view and Weekly view, you can move an appointment by clicking in it so that a heavy border appears around it, then clicking in the border and dragging the appointment to its new time or date.

Scheduling a Meeting

By working with Planner view in group-enabled mode, you can see open time slots in not only your own calendar but also in those of your colleagues, which enables you to easily schedule meetings.

> **TIP** If the procedure described in this section leaves you cold, choose Tools ➢ Make Meeting to run the Meeting Wizard, which will give you a more interactive run-through of scheduling a meeting.

To schedule a meeting:

1. If you're not already in Planner view, click the Planner tab.

2. Select the date and time by clicking (and dragging if necessary) on the planner sheet.

3. Click the Invite button below the calendar box to display the Select Attendees dialog box (see Figure 22.13).

4. In the Type Name or Select from List list box, choose the first person you want to invite. Then click Required (if the person must attend the meeting) or

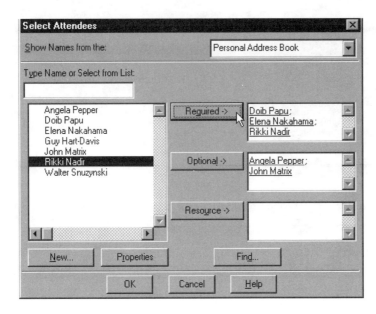

FIGURE 22.13:
In the Select Attendees dialog box, invite the people you want (or need) to attend the meeting.

Optional (if their presence isn't vital); for resources (such as meeting rooms or presentation equipment), click the Resource button. Schedule+ will place the name in the appropriate box.

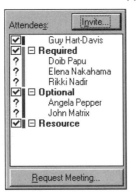

5. When you've finished adding people and resources to the list, choose OK to close the Select Attendees dialog box and return to Planner view. Schedule+ will list the attendees in the Attendees box in the designated categories.

6. Click the Request Meeting button at the bottom of the Attendees box to display the Meeting Request window (see Figure 22.14).

7. Compose your message to the putative attendees, then send it by clicking the Send button or by choosing File ➤ Send.

8. Schedule+ will then add the meeting to your schedule.

Projects and Tasks

Appointments aside, Schedule+ really comes into its own for coordinating your projects and tasks on the To Do tab. Not only can you add any number of projects, each of which can contain any number of tasks, and track the status of those projects and tasks,

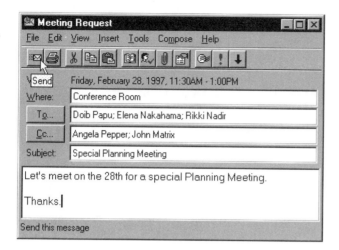

FIGURE 22.14:
In the Meeting Request window, compose a message inviting the attendees to the meeting, then choose File ➤ Send (or click the Send button) to send it.

but you can sort projects into the order that suits you best and filter their tasks so Schedule+ displays only the tasks you need to see.

What Are Projects and Tasks?

Schedule+ understands a project to consist of a number of tasks, each of which can have a deadline, billing information, and notes attached to it. You can set alarms and reminders for tasks; for example, you could set a reminder that would alert you three days before a task was due to be completed.

> **NOTE**   When you've set alarms or reminders, leave Schedule+ running so it can display them. Minimize Schedule+ to an icon on the Taskbar to get it out of the way.

Schedule+ starts you off with a project named (None) for assorted tasks that do not fit formally into any project you create. For other tasks, you start by creating the project to which they will belong.

Adding a Project

To add a project to the To Do list:

1. Click the To Do tab to display it (if it isn't already displayed).

2. Right-click in the To Do window and choose New Project from the shortcut menu to display the Project dialog box (see Figure 22.15). Alternatively, choose Insert ➤ Project.

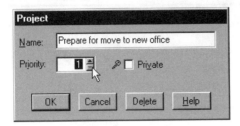

FIGURE 22.15:
In the Project dialog box, enter a name for the project, choose its priority, and decide whether to keep it private or not.

3. Enter a name for the project in the Name text box.
4. Choose a priority for the project in the Priority box. Schedule+ suggests a default priority of 3 for each new project (you can change this default priority if you want). Schedule+ will display the priority in parentheses after the project's name in the To Do window.
5. If you want to keep the project private (so that those who share your schedule cannot see it), select the Private check box.
6. Choose OK to close the Project dialog box. Schedule+ will enter the project in the To Do window.

Adding a Task

Once you've created a project, you're ready to add a task to it:

1. Click the To Do tab to display it (if it isn't already displayed).
2. Right-click in the project to which you want to add the task and choose New Task from the shortcut menu to display the Task dialog box (see Figure 22.16). Alternatively, click in the project and choose Insert ➤ Task.
3. Enter a description for the task in the Description box. This is what you will see in your To Do list.
4. In the Project drop-down list, make sure the task is assigned to the appropriate project. If it's not, change it.
5. Adjust the priority for the new task in the Priority box as necessary.
6. Select the Private check box if you want to keep the project private from those who share your schedule.
7. If the task has a specific due date, select the Ends check box in the Active Range group box:
   - Specify the ending date in the Ends drop-down list.
   - Specify on the second line how many days, weeks, or months before the end date the active range for the task should start.

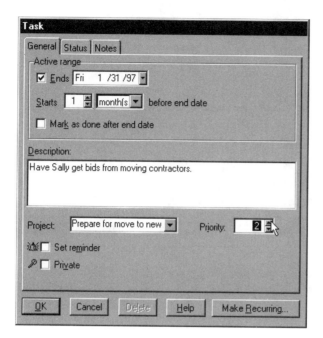

FIGURE 22.16:
Enter the details of the new task in the Task dialog box.

- Select the Mark as Done after End Date check box if you want the task to be automatically marked as done once the due date has arrived (whether you've done it or not).
8. Click the OK button to enter the task in the project you chose.

Tracking the Status of a Task

You can adjust the status of each task to reflect your progress on it:

1. In the To Do window, right-click in the appropriate task and choose Edit Item from the shortcut menu to display the Task dialog box.
2. Click the Status tab to display it (see Figure 22.17).
3. In the Status group box, enter the status of the task:
   - In the Percentage Complete box, enter the percentage of the task accomplished so far.
   - In the Actual Effort boxes, record how much time you've spent on the task.
   - In the Estimated Effort box, enter or alter the time you estimate the whole project will take you.
   - The Date Completed box will become available when the Percentage Completed reaches 100% and will reflect that date. Adjust this date if necessary (for example, if you completed the task a day or two before updating the status).

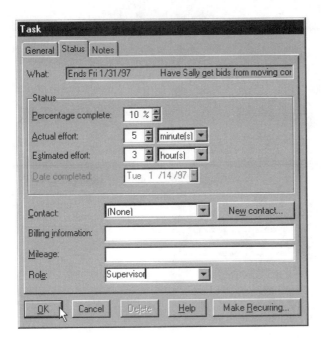

FIGURE 22.17:
On the Status tab of the Task dialog box, track the status of the task, your contact and billing information, and more.

4. Choose your contact for the project from the Contact drop-down list. To add a new contact to your list, click the New Contact button. (We'll look at Schedule+'s contact-management capabilities in *Contacts* in Chapter 23.)

5. Enter billing information, mileage, and the role you're playing in this task as appropriate.

6. Choose OK to close the Task dialog box and record the changes you made to the task's status.

TIP

You can also change a project's status by clicking in the boxes displayed in the To Do window and editing the contents as appropriate. The boxes display drop-down lists or spinner boxes as appropriate; for example, the % Complete box displays a spinner box, while the Project box displays a drop-down list of the projects available.

Marking a Task as Completed

You can mark a task as completed in two ways:

- Click in the Completed column (the leftmost column, headed with the check mark) for the task.
- By changing the percentage completed to 100%.

Completed tasks are marked with a checkmark in the Completed column and are shown in strikethrough text, as shown here.

To mark a task as incomplete again, click once more in the Completed column for the task or set the percentage completed to less than 100%.

Adding a Recurring Task

Schedule+ provides for recurring tasks, such as employee appraisals or monthly time-cards. To add a recurring task to your schedule:

1. In the To Do window, right-click in the project to which you want to add the recurring task and choose Recurring Task to display the Task Series dialog box with the General tab displayed.
   - To turn an existing task into a recurring task, right-click in it and choose Make Recurring from the shortcut menu to display the Task Series dialog box with the existing information entered on the General tab and the When tab displayed. Go directly to step 4.
   - Alternatively, click the Make Recurring button in the Task dialog box while adding or editing a task.
2. Enter the details of the task on the General tab. In the Default Series properties group box, enter the details for the recurring task, as described in *Adding a Task* earlier in the chapter.
3. Click the When tab to display it.
4. Enter the timeframe for the recurring task:
   - In the This Occurs group box, choose Daily, Weekly, Monthly, or Yearly.
   - In the group box alongside the This Occurs group box (which will be named Daily, Weekly, Monthly, or Yearly to match your selection in the This Occurs

 group box), enter the details for the recurring task. For example, choose On November 30 for a yearly task, as shown here.

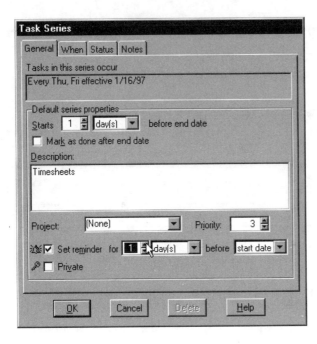

FIGURE 22.18:
Adding a recurring
task to one's
schedule in
the Task Series
dialog box

- In the Duration group box, specify the start date for the recurring task in the Effective drop-down list. If the recurring task has a definite ending date, select the Until check box and enter the ending date in the drop-down list that appears to its right.

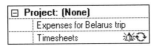

5. Click the OK button to close the Task Series dialog box and record the recurring task. The recurring task will appear in the To Do window marked with a circular-arrows icon, as shown here.

Deleting a Task

To delete a task, right-click in it and choose Delete Item from the shortcut menu. If the task is a recurring task, Schedule+ will ask if you want to delete all instances of it; choose Yes or No.

Deleting a Project

To delete a project, right-click in it and choose Delete Item from the shortcut menu. Schedule+ will display a message box warning you that all tasks associated with the project will be deleted; click Yes if you're sure you want to delete the project and its associated tasks.

Assigning a Task to Another Project

You can quickly change a task's assignation from one project to another in either of two ways:

- Click in the task and drag it from its current project to the project you want it to be part of.
- Right-click in the task, choose Edit Item from the shortcut menu to display the Task dialog box, select the project in the Project drop-down list, and click OK.

Collapsing and Expanding the View

⊞ **Project: Oil Arabia contract [1]**		
⊟ **Project: Prepare for move to new office [1]**		
Assess personnel needs for ...	2	Wed 1/15/97
Get tax forms	2	Thu 1/16/97

You can collapse and expand the view of your projects and tasks by clicking the box to the left of the word **Project:** in each project's name. When the box displays a minus sign, click the box to collapse the tasks contained in the project so that only the project name is displayed; the box will then display a plus sign that you can click to expand the project to show all its tasks again.

Filtering Tasks

If you use Schedule+ seriously as project-tracking software, many of your projects will soon accumulate enough tasks, completed or otherwise, to make for a list far too long to display fully in the To Do window, even if you assiduously collapse all other projects to hide their tasks. By using Schedule+'s filtering capabilities, you can display only the projects you need to see.

To adjust filtering of your projects, choose View ➤ Filter and choose an option from the resulting submenu:

> **All** shows you all tasks (with no filtering).
>
> **Upcoming** shows tasks due to start after the current date but does not show you currently active tasks.

NOTE The start date of a task is the Ends date specified on the General tab of the Task dialog box minus the Starts Before End Date active range. For example, if you set an Ends date of Thu 1/16/97 and specify Starts 3 days Before End Date, the start date for the task will be Monday, January 13, 1997.

Active shows tasks with a start date before and an end date after the current date. It also shows overdue tasks.

Not Yet Completed displays tasks that have not been checked as completed.

Completed shows tasks that have been checked as completed. This filter is useful for viewing what you've done so far on a project.

Overdue Tasks shows only tasks that are not checked as completed and whose due date has passed.

Include Tasks with No End Date is a toggle that does what it says. Choose it once to turn it on, so that Schedule+ displays a check mark next to it on the menu; choose it again to turn it off and remove the check mark.

List filter: Not yet completed (only tasks with end dates) To check which filter you're currently using, look at the right side of the status bar. If Include Tasks with No End Date is off, the status bar will display **(only tasks with end dates)**, as it does in the example here.

Grouping Tasks

As we saw in the previous section, Schedule+ lets you filter tasks so that it displays only those you need to see. You can also group tasks by one, two, or three categories so you can assess their relative importance and devote your resources accordingly. By default, Schedule+ groups tasks by project and sorts projects alphabetically with the (None) project first, which makes for a project-centric view but can obscure which tasks you should be giving the highest priority.

To change the grouping of tasks:

1. Right-click in the To Do window column headings and choose Group By from the shortcut menu (or choose View ➢ Group By) to display the Group By dialog box.
2. In the Group Tasks By group box, choose the first category from the drop-down list and specify Ascending or Descending order. For example, you might choose % Complete and Descending order to see which tasks are nearest completion.
3. In the first Then By group box, choose the second category and specify Ascending or Descending.
4. In the second Then By group box, choose the third category and specify Ascending or Descending.

```
⊟  Priority: 1
     ⊞  Project: Hire Vice President of Communications (1)
     ⊟  Project: Oil Arabia contract (1)
          ⊞  % Complete: (None)
     ⊟  Project: Prepare for move to new office (1)
          ⊟  % Complete: 33%
               Fire redundant staff              1    Wed 3/19/97
```

under the first category. Use the + and - signs to collapse these subcategories and sub-subcategories.

TIP To remove grouping, choose **(None)** in the appropriate drop-down list in the Group By dialog box.

---

5. Click OK to close the Group By dialog box and apply your choices.

Schedule+ displays the second and third sort categories indented

Sorting Tasks

You can sort tasks in Schedule+ by one to three criteria:

1. Choose View ➤ Sort to display the Sort dialog box.
2. In the Sort Tasks By group box, choose the first property to sort by in the drop-down list, then choose Ascending or Descending.
3. In the first Then By group box, choose the second property to sort by in the drop-down list, then choose Ascending or Descending.
4. In the second Then By group box, choose the third property to sort by in the drop-down list, then choose Ascending or Descending.

```
Last name▲    First name▲    Company▼
```

5. Click OK to close the Sort dialog box and perform the sort according to the

criteria you chose. The column headings display up- and down-arrows to display ascending and de-scending order sorts, respectively.

NOTE You can quickly sort your tasks by any of the displayed columns in ascending order by clicking on the column header button, or in descending order by Ctrl+clicking on the column header button.

Chapter 23

CONTACTS AND INTEGRATION

- **Working with contact information**
- **Printing out Schedule+ information**
- **Importing and exporting data**
- **Using the backup and restore features**

Apart from scheduling appointments, projects, and tasks, Schedule+ offers a powerful contact-management database that you can integrate with the other Office applications. In this chapter, we'll also look at how you can print out information from Schedule+, import into Schedule+ information from other personal information management applications, and how you can protect your Schedule+ data by backing it up—and lastly, how you can restore it from backup when things go badly wrong.

Contacts

Depending on your business, you may find Schedule+'s contact-management features even more useful than its scheduling capabilities. To work with the contacts database, enter Contacts View by clicking the Contacts tab to display the Contacts window (shown in Figure 22.9 in the previous chapter), then follow the instructions in the following sections for adding contacts and working with the contact information.

Adding a Person to Your Contact List

To add a person to your list of contacts:

1. Right-click in the Contacts window and choose New Contact from the shortcut menu to display the Contact dialog box with the Business tab displayed (see Figure 23.1).

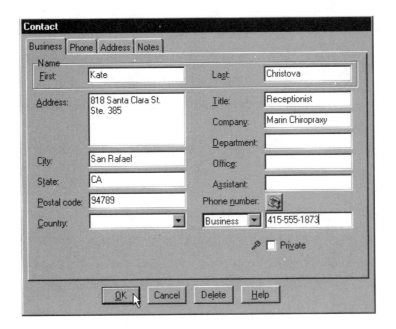

FIGURE 23.1:
Enter all the details you know for your contact in the Contact dialog box.

2. Enter the person's first and last name in the First and Last text boxes in the Name group box. When you press the spacebar to enter a space after the first name, Schedule+ will automatically move the insertion point to the Last text box.

> **NOTE** First name and last name are the information that Schedule+ really craves; if you click OK in the Contact dialog box without filling these text boxes in, it'll check to make sure you didn't choose OK by mistake. Beyond first name and last name, it'll accept any amount of information for each person...

3. Enter further information about the person on the four tabs of the Contact dialog box:
   - The Business tab provides fields for the person's title, company's address, assistant, etc.
   - The Phone tab provides fields for two business numbers, two home numbers, a fax number, an assistant's number, a mobile number, and a pager. (If your contacts have more numbers than this, store them in the extra fields on the Notes tab.)
   - The Address tab provides fields for the person's home address, spouse, birthday, anniversary, and phone number.

> **NOTE** Schedule+ will automatically add your contacts' birthdays and anniversary dates to your schedule as appointments so you can deliver timely congratulations or commiserations.

   - The Notes tab provides four fields for information of your own choosing (i.e., anything that won't fit anywhere else) and a Notes text box for sundry notes. This text box will expand and grow a scroll bar once you overstep its initial bounds.
4. When you've finished entering the details for your contact, click the OK button to close the Contact dialog box and enter the details in your contact database.

Using Your Contact Information

Schedule+ makes using your contact information especially easy. As mentioned in the previous section, Schedule+ automatically enters your contacts' birthdays and anniversaries in your schedule so you'll remember them. You can also get a full list of annual events by choosing Edit ➤ Edit List Of ➤ Annual Events to display the Annual Events dialog box (see Figure 23.2).

Double-click an event to display it in the Annual Event dialog box (see Figure 23.3). Here you can change the date of the event (in the Annual Event On drop-down list) or the

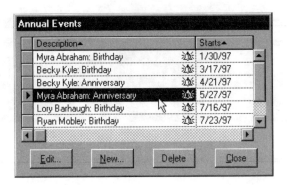

FIGURE 23.2:
In the Annual
Events dialog box,
double-click an
entry to display it
in the Annual Event
dialog box.

description (in the Description box); you can also set a reminder or mark the event as private. Choose OK to close the Annual Event dialog box and return to the Annual Events dialog box.

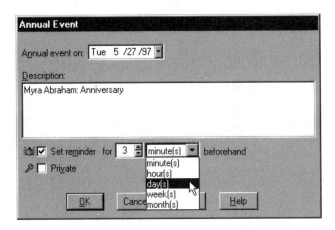

FIGURE 23.3:
You can set
reminders for an
annual event in
the Annual Event
dialog box.

To delete an annual event, click in it and click the Delete button.

To create a new annual event, click the New button and enter the details for the new event in the Annual Event dialog box. Click the OK button when you've finished.

Displaying the Contact Columns

By default, Schedule+ displays several categories of contact information in the Contacts list box on the left side of the Contacts window, together with details for the currently selected contact on the right side of the window.

You can change the width of the Contacts list box by clicking and dragging the border between the Contacts list box and the details panel.

You can also customize the columns displayed in the Contacts list box so you see the fields most advantageous to you displayed in the clearest order. To customize the columns:

1. Right-click in one of the column headings and choose Columns ➤ Custom from the shortcut menu to display the Columns dialog box (see Figure 23.4). For a quick change of the columns displayed, choose Columns ➤ Few, Columns ➤ Typical, or Columns ➤ All from the shortcut menu. Few displays Last Name, First Name, and Business Phone only; Typical adds Company, Title, and Home Phone to the display.

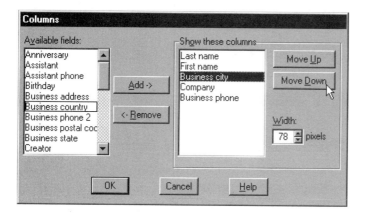

FIGURE 23.4:
In the Columns dialog box, choose which columns you want Schedule+ to display and which order you want them displayed in.

2. Build a list of the columns you want to see in the Show These Columns list box:
    *   To add a field to the Show These Columns list box, select it in the Available Fields list box and click the Add button.
    *   To remove a field, select it in the Show These Columns list box and click the Remove button.
3. Rearrange the fields in the Show These Columns list box as necessary by using the Move Up and Move Down buttons.
4. Adjust the width of any column if necessary by selecting it in the Show These Columns list box and setting the width in pixels in the Width box.

TIP

It's often easier to adjust column width in the Contacts window by dragging the divisions between columns. (You can also change the width of the Contacts area of the Contacts window by dragging the border between it and the contact form to the left or right.)

5. When you've finished adjusting the columns, click the OK button to close the Columns dialog box.

Grouping and Sorting

As with your tasks, Schedule+ lets you order your contacts in two ways—by grouping them (arranging them into groups) and by sorting them.

Grouping Your Contacts by Columns

To group your contact data by a column:

1. Right-click in any column heading and choose Group By (or choose View ➤ Group By) to display the Group By dialog box (see Figure 23.5).

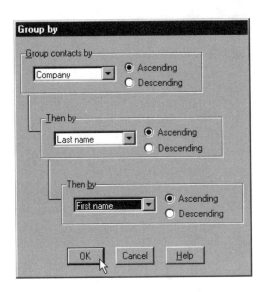

FIGURE 23.5:
In the Group By dialog box, choose how to sort your contact list.

2. In the Group Contacts By drop-down list, select the column by which to group the contacts, then choose Ascending order (A to Z, 1 to 10) or Descending order (the opposite).
   - The obvious choice here is Company, though you might also want to group by a column such as Home State or Office,
   - Schedule+ will group further entries in your contact list by the column you choose here.
3. In the first Then By drop-down list, choose a secondary grouping if you want to. Again, choose Ascending order or Descending order.

4. In the second Then By drop-down list, choose a tertiary grouping if you want to. Choose Ascending order or Descending order.

5. Choose OK to close the Group By dialog box and group your contacts by the columns you indicated.

Sorting Your Contacts

To sort your contacts quickly in the Contacts window, click the heading for the column by which to sort. For example, to sort your contacts by last name, click the Last Name column heading.

To sort by more than one column:

1. Right-click in any column heading and choose Sort from the shortcut menu (or choose View ➤ Sort) to display the Sort dialog box (see Figure 23.6).

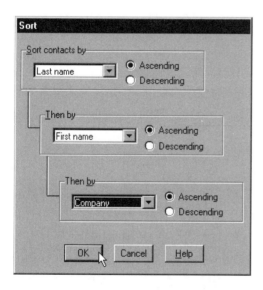

FIGURE 23.6:
In the Sort dialog box, choose two or three columns by which to sort your contacts.

2. In the Sort Contacts By drop-down list, select the column by which to sort the contacts, then choose Ascending order or Descending order.

3. In the first Then By drop-down list, choose a second column by which to sort. Again, specify Ascending or Descending order.

4. In the second Then By drop-down list, choose a tertiary column by which to sort, and specify Ascending or Descending order.

5. Choose OK to close the Sort dialog box and sort your contacts by the columns you chose.

Arranging an Appointment or Task with a Contact

To quickly arrange an appointment or a task from the Contacts window:

1. Right-click in the contact's row and choose Appt. from Contact or Task from Contact from the shortcut menu to display the Appointment or Task dialog box with your contact's details in the Description box.

2. Fill in the details of the appointment or task as described in Chapter 22 in *Creating an Appointment* and *Adding a Task*.

3. Click the OK button to enter the appointment or task in your schedule.

Printing Out Schedule+ Items

Portable though computers are these days, you can't always have one with you. Schedule+ lets you print out your schedule, to-do list, or contact list to take with you—and lets you print on various size of paper, including Filofax size.

1. If you want to print a schedule, display the day, week, or month you want.

2. Choose File ➤ Print (or press Ctrl+P) to display the Print dialog box (see Figure 23.7).

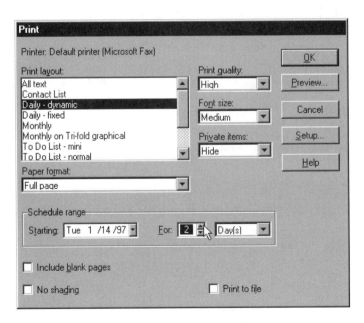

FIGURE 23.7:
In the Print dialog box, choose the item to print, the type of paper to print it on, and a plethora of other options.

3. In the Print Layout list box, choose the item to print. Most of the choices are self-explanatory (for example, Contact List), but some need a word or two of explanation:

All Text prints your schedule in text-only format.

Daily–Dynamic prints your schedule for the day.

Daily–Fixed prints your schedule, the to-do list, and appointments outside work hours.

Monthly on Tri-Fold Graphical prints a tripartite schedule consisting of your daily appointments, the year's calendar, and your to-do list.

> **TIP** For a closer idea of what the items contain, click the Preview button in the Print dialog box.

4. In the Paper Format drop-down list, choose the type of paper to use. Schedule+ offers Full Page, Filofax #106, and a variety of Avery paper types.
5. In the Schedule Range group box, choose how long a schedule you want to print: Specify the starting date in the Starting drop-down list (Schedule+ will suggest the active date) and the length of time in the For boxes.
6. Change the Print Quality and Font Size settings if necessary.
7. Adjust the setting in the Private Items box if necessary:
   - Show will include in the schedule appointments marked as Private.
   - Hide will prevent appointments marked as Private from appearing in the schedule.
   - Hide Text will display **(Private)** for times that appointments marked as Private are scheduled but will not display what they are.
8. Click the Print button to print your schedule.

Using Schedule+ with Other Office Applications

You can use Schedule+ together with the other Microsoft Office applications, which can save time and prevent errors when transferring data from one application to another. For example, you can quickly and easily insert an address from Schedule+ into a Word document, or you can use Schedule+ as a data source for mail merge in Word.

Inserting an Address from Schedule+

You can quickly insert an address from your Schedule+ contacts list into a Word document—for example, to quickly add an address to a letter or to produce a list of the names and addresses of some of your contacts.

To insert an address in the open Word document:

1. Click the Insert Address button to display the Select Name dialog box (see Figure 23.8).

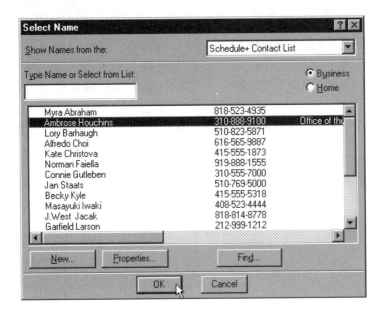

FIGURE 23.8: In the Select Name dialog box, display the names from your Schedule+ Contact List, choose the name, and click OK to insert the name and address in your document.

2. Make sure that Schedule+ Contact List is selected in the Show Names drop-down list.
3. Double-click the name you want to insert, or click on the name and then click the OK button. Word will retrieve the name and address and insert it in your document at the insertion point.

Using Schedule+ as a Mail-Merge Data Source

You can also use Schedule+ as a data source for mail merges. For more details, see *Using Schedule+ as a Data Source* in Chapter 10. As usual with merges, you can limit the merge to a selection of records either by specifying record numbers or by specifying criteria and a sort order for the records.

Importing Data into Schedule+

You can import data into Schedule+ either from one of the other Microsoft Office applications or from just about any contact-management application. The main requirement is that the other application must be able to save the data as a text file in comma-delimited format.

First, run the other application and save the data in comma-delimited format. For example, in Excel, you would choose File ➤ Save As to display the Save As dialog box and choose CSV (Comma delimited) (*.csv) in the Save As Type drop-down list; in Sidekick (as an example of a non-Microsoft personal information manager you might be using), you would choose Tools ➤ Export Cardfile to display the Export Cardfile dialog box, then choose the Comma Delimited (*.csv) format.

Then import the data into Schedule+:

1. Choose File ➤ Import ➤ Text to start the Text Import Wizard.
2. In the first Text Import Wizard dialog box, specify the file to import in the File Name box: Either type it in or click the Browse button to open the Import Schedule+ Interchange dialog box, find the file, and click the Open button. Click the Next button when you've selected the file.

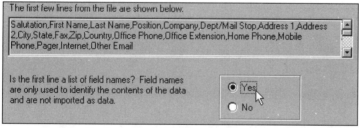

3. In the second Text Import Wizard dialog box, Schedule+ will display the first few lines

of the file and ask if the first line is a list of field names:
    *   If the first line is a list of field names, choose Yes and click the Next button.
    *   If the first line does not contain field names, choose No and click the Next button.
4. Schedule+ will display another Text Import Wizard dialog box to allow you to select the character used to separate the fields (comma, space, semicolon, or tab) and the character used to surround text fields (", ', or None). Make your selections and click the Next button.
5. In the next Text Import Wizard dialog box, select whether the data in the file contains appointments, a to-do list, events, or a contact list. Click the Next button.
6. In the final Text Import Wizard dialog box, Schedule+ asks you to match the fields in your data file with the field names that Schedule+ provides (see Figure 23.9). If it cannot directly match a field's name, Schedule+ suggests Ignore

This Field. Change this by clicking in the second column and choosing the Schedule+ field to which you want to map the imported text field from the drop-down list that appears.

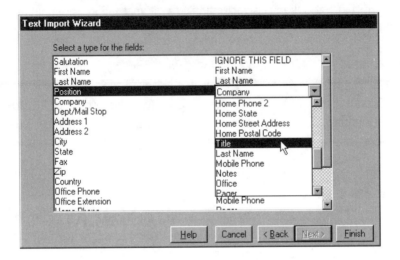

FIGURE 23.9:
In the final Text Import Wizard dialog box, tell Schedule+ the Schedule+ fields that match the fields you're importing in your data file.

7. Click the Finish button to import your data into Schedule+.

> **TIP**
>
> To import data created in an earlier version of Schedule+, choose File ➤ Import ➤ Schedule+ Interchange, choose the file in the Import Schedule+ Interchange dialog box, and click the Open button.

Exporting Data from Schedule+

Schedule+ provides full capabilities for exporting data as well as importing it. You can export data either to another version of Schedule+ (or another installation of Schedule+), to a comma-delimited text file, to a Timex Data Link watch. To export data from Schedule+, choose File ➤ Export to display the export submenu, then choose the destination and follow the instructions that Schedule+ provides.

Backing Up Your Schedule+ Data

To keep your Schedule+ data safe, back it up regularly using Schedule+'s built-in backup feature:

1. Choose File ➤ Backup to display the Select Backup File dialog box.
2. In the File Name box, enter the name for the new backup file. Schedule+ backup files have the .SCD extension. You can choose to overwrite an existing backup file by selecting it in the Select Backup File dialog box.
3. Click the Save button. Schedule+ will display a status message box as it backs up the data, then will return you to the application. If you're overwriting an existing file, Schedule+ will display a Select Backup File message box asking if you want to replace the existing file. Choose Yes.

Restoring Your Data from Backup

To restore your data from backup:

1. Choose File ➤ Restore to display the Restore Backup File dialog box.
2. Choose the backup file.
3. Click the Open button. Schedule+ will display a message box warning you that

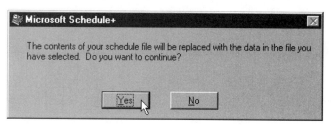

the contents of your schedule file will be replaced with the data in the file you selected.

4. Choose Yes to have Schedule+ restore the backup, replacing your current data.

Appendix

INSTALLING MICROSOFT OFFICE

FEATURES

- **System requirements for Office**
- **Installing Office**
- **Installing extra components**

In this Appendix, we'll look at installing Office on your PC—both installing from scratch and installing components that whoever first installed it neglected to include.

System Requirements

You can install and run Office 95 on any computer capable of running Windows 95 or Windows NT Workstation 3.51 or higher. That means, in practice, a 486 or higher Intel processor (Pentium, Pentium Pro) or equivalent (AMD 486, Cyrix 5X86 or 6X86, etc.) with 8MB or more of RAM for Windows 95 or 12MB or more of RAM for Windows NT Workstation.

NOTE Technically, you can run Windows 95 and Office on a 386DX with 6MB of RAM. In practice, this will be horribly slow.

You'll need approximately 28MB of disk space for a basic installation, 55MB for what Microsoft considers a typical installation, and 89MB for a full custom installation.

Installing Office

To install Office from the distribution diskettes or CD-ROM:

1. Choose Start ➢ Settings ➢ Control Panel to display the Control Panel window. If you're installing on NT Workstation 3.51, choose File ➢ Run to display the Run dialog box. In the Command Line text box, enter **cd:\setup.exe**, where **cd** is the drive letter assigned to your CD-ROM drive (or, for diskettes, your floppy drive), and click OK. Go directly to step 6 (do not pass Go, do not collect $200...).

Add/Remove Programs

2. Double-click the Add/Remove Programs icon to display the Add/Remove Programs Properties dialog box.

3. Click the Install button to display the Install Program from Floppy Disk or CD-ROM dialog box.

4. Insert the first installation diskette in your floppy drive or the CD-ROM in your CD-ROM drive, then click the Next button. Windows will display the Run Installation Program dialog box and will suggest the installation program to run (SETUP.EXE on the drive containing the diskette or CD-ROM).

5. If this is the correct installation program, click the Finish button. (If by some mischance Windows 95 has selected an installation program on an inappropriate disk—for example, if you have multiple diskette drives or CD-ROM drives

containing installation programs—correct the choice and then click Finish.) Setup will display the Microsoft Office for Windows 95 Setup dialog box warning you to close any open applications and reminding you that you can install each copy of Office on only a single computer.

6. Click the Continue button to continue with Setup. You'll see the Name and Organization Information dialog box.

7. Enter your name and organization information and click OK. Confirm these in the Confirm Name and Organization Information dialog box, then record the Product ID number that Office gives you in the next dialog box (you'll need this if you call for technical support).

> **NOTE** If you're installing from a CD-ROM, you'll need to enter your Product ID number or CD Key number in a dialog box after the Confirm Name and Organization Information dialog box. You should find this number either on the Certificate of Authenticity in the CD-ROM's sleeve or on a sticker on the CD-ROM's jewel case. Type the ID number into the boxes and click OK.

8. If you're upgrading to Office, the Setup program will check for a qualifying product for the upgrade.
   - You'll find a full list of qualifying products on the Office box. These include almost every major word processor, spreadsheet, and presentation graphics program ever used during living memory, not to mention the major office suites.
   - If you've uninstalled the qualifying product, Office will ask you to insert the product's setup disk, which it will then quiz and approve.

9. Next, Setup will suggest a destination folder for the installation of Office (e.g., **C:\MSOffice**). Accept this by clicking OK, or first click Change Folder and pick a more appropriate folder in the Change Folder dialog box. (If the folder doesn't exist, Setup will invite you to create it. Choose Yes.)

10. In the next Setup dialog box (see Figure A.1), choose between Typical, Compact, Custom, or Run from CD-ROM setup options.

NOTE

Run from CD-ROM places approximately 30MB of files on your hard disk and leaves the others on the CD-ROM. You'll save disk space, but the applications will run much more slowly (and you won't be able to play BTO as you work).

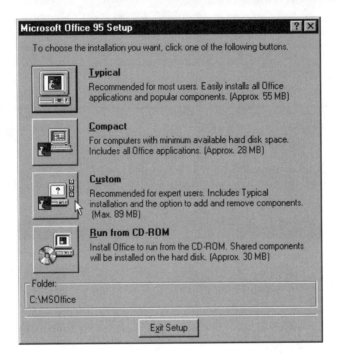

Microsoft Office 95 Setup

To choose the installation you want, click one of the following buttons.

Typical
Recommended for most users. Easily installs all Office applications and popular components. (Approx. 55 MB)

Compact
For computers with minimum available hard disk space. Includes all Office applications. (Approx. 28 MB)

Custom
Recommended for expert users. Includes Typical installation and the option to add and remove components. (Max. 89 MB)

Run from CD-ROM
Install Office to run from the CD-ROM. Shared components will be installed on the hard disk. (Approx. 30 MB)

Folder:
C:\MSOffice

E_xit Setup

FIGURE A.1:
Choose the type of setup you want—Typical, Compact, Custom, or Run from CD-ROM.

11. If you choose Typical, Compact, or Run from CD-ROM for Office, Setup will go ahead and install those Office options for you. If you choose Custom, Setup will display the Microsoft Office 95 - Custom dialog box (see Figure A.2), in which you get to choose which options to install. Options whose check boxes have been selected will be installed wholesale; options whose check boxes have been selected but grayed out will be installed with the selected options; and options whose check boxes have been cleared will not be installed.

- To select all the options (for a full installation), click Select All.
- To reach the options for one of the applications listed, select the application in the Options box, then click Change Option.
- To change one of the options, select it. To select options for an option (yes, this gets deep), click Change Option to view a list of the options after first

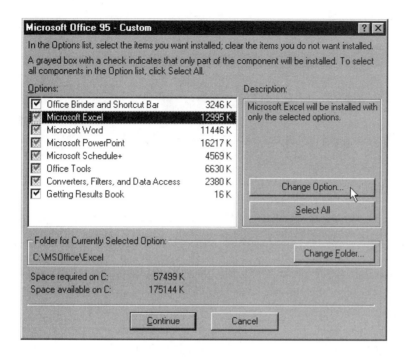

FIGURE A.2:
In the Microsoft Office 95 - Custom dialog box, choose the parts of Office you want to install.

selecting the "main" option. Again, select the check boxes for the options you want to install, and then click OK. (You may need to drill down to a further layer of options for some options.)

- When you've selected all the options you want, click Continue to install them.

12. Setup will install the options you chose. If you're using diskettes, you'll need to swap infinite numbers of diskettes in and out as Setup prompts you. (If you're using a CD-ROM, you can now go out and get some coffee and let Setup do the hard work.)

13. Once installation is complete, Setup will offer to walk you through Online Registration, which is handled via the Microsoft Network. If you have a modem up and running, this saves you the cost of a stamp.

Installing and Uninstalling Items

Depending on how you (or whoever) originally installed Office on your computer, you may need to install extra items:

- If you need to work with text or graphics files created in another application, you may need to install extra text or graphics converter files. Office uses these files when opening text or graphics files created in another application (or another format) and when saving Office documents in other formats for use with other applications.

> **TIP**
>
> **If you have plenty of disk space, go ahead and install all the converter files. Besides exercising squatters' rights on part of your hard disk, they won't do you any damage, and you'll be equipped to deal with many different types of files.**

- You may need to install extra templates or Wizards.
- You may need to install specific Help files (e.g., the WordBasic Help files).
- You may want to uninstall items you never use to save disk space.

To install or uninstall Office items:

1. Choose Start ➤ Settings ➤ Control Panel to display the Control Panel window.
2. Double-click the Start/Remove Programs icon to display the Add/Remove Programs Properties dialog box.
3. In the list box, select Microsoft Office and click Add/Remove. Setup will prompt you to insert your Office CD or first floppy (depending on which you originally installed from).
4. Insert the Office CD or floppy and click OK. Setup will check your computer to see which Office items are already installed and then will display the Microsoft Office 95 Setup dialog box.
5. Click Add/Remove to display the Microsoft Office 95 - Maintenance dialog box, which is a thinly disguised version of the Microsoft Office 95 - Custom dialog box shown in Figure A.2. The dialog box shows which Office components you currently have installed.
6. Choose which components to install and which to uninstall:
   - To install components, select their check boxes as described in step 11 of the list in the previous section.
   - To uninstall components, clear their check boxes.
7. Click Continue to continue with the installation. (If you chose to uninstall components, Setup will display the Confirm Component Removal dialog box. Click OK to proceed.) When Setup is complete, you'll see a message box informing you of this. Click OK to return to the Add/Remove Programs Properties dialog box and click OK to close it.

WARNING This dialog box is somewhat counterintuitive: Think of it not as a list of what you want to install, but what you want to have installed at the end of the installation. For example, if you already have Word and PowerPoint installed and you want to install Excel, select the check box for Excel *and leave the Word and PowerPoint check boxes selected.* If you clear the Word and PowerPoint check boxes and select only the Excel check box, Setup will install Excel and will uninstall Word and PowerPoint.

Index

Note to the Reader: Throughout this index main entries are highlighted in boldface. **Boldfaced** page numbers indicate primary discussions of a topic. Italicized page numbers indicate illustrations.